Didn't See That Coming

Didn't See That Coming

*True stories of a geologist's
adventures, challenges, friendships
and self-discovery
from far afield*

Roger James Kuhns

Leaning
Rock
Press
Gales Ferry, CT

Leaning Rock Press, LLC
Gales Ferry, CT 06335
www.leaningrockpress.com
leaningrockpress@gmail.com

www.rogerjameskuhns.com

All the monologues have been performed in public.

Cover Design, Maps and Illustrations by Roger Kuhns
Author Photo by Julia Minchew
Edited by Siobhan Drummond

978-1-950323-07-4 Didn't See That Coming, Hardcover
978-1-950323-08-1 Didn't See That Coming, Softcover
978-1-950323-09-8 Didn't See That Coming, eBook

Contact the author for information and performance monologue bookings:
rogerjameskuhns@gmail.com and www.rogerjameskuhns.com

Publisher's Cataloging-In-Publication Data
(Prepared by The Donohue Group, Inc.)

Names: Kuhns, Roger James, author.
Title: Didn't see that coming : true stories of a geologist-
    writer's adventures, challenges, friendships and self discovery
    from far afield / Roger James Kuhns.
Description: Second edition. | Gales Ferry, CT : Leaning Rock
    Press, [2019] | Previously published: Mystic, CT : musicTOears
    Press, [2014]. | Includes index.
Identifiers: ISBN 9781950323074 (hardcover) | ISBN 9781950323081
    (softcover) | ISBN 9781950323098 (ebook)
Subjects: LCSH: Kuhns, Roger James--Travel. | Adventure and
    adventurers--United States--Biography. | Geologists--United
    States--Biography. | Civilization--Anecdotes. | Geology--
    Anecdotes. | Natural resources--Anecdotes. | LCGFT:
    Autobiographies. | Travel writing.
Classification: LCC CT9971.K84 A3 2019 (print) | LCC CT9971.K84
    (ebook) | DDC 910.92--dc23

Library of Congress Control Number:2019909510

Printed and bound in the United States of America second edition

This collected works volume of performance monologues is dedicated to my father, William R. Kuhns, and my mother, Joanne G. Kuhns, for their love and insights and for encouraging me to wander off and explore beginning at a young age, and to my son, Matthew, and daughter, Madeleine, who have explored the world with me.

As Spaulding Gray once told me,
"Tell it like you see it, and that is the truth."

And upon the advice of my dear friend Oliver Warin,
"Write your stories, Roger, think of all you've seen!"

Contents

JUNGLE GOLD

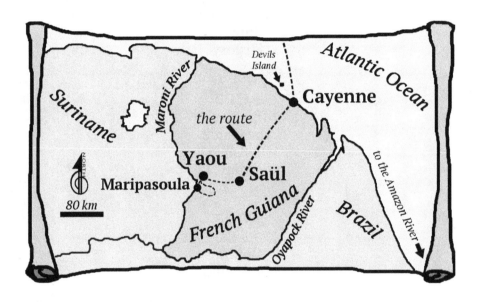

ACT 1
In Country
Yaou Camp
Jungle
History

ACT 2
The River
The Guide
Invisible
Inini

ACT 3
Aloike
Wedding
Outbound

ACT 1

In Country

I am standing perfectly still by an ancient white-barked tree that towers 120 feet. Green and brown lizards the size of small cats scurry nervously around me. The sudden sharp calls of monkeys fill the humid atmosphere. Sunlight streams down like golden vines through the high jungle canopy. Blade-like leaves of the palms offer spectral images that shimmer in gentle breezes.

Yesterday: the jet is on approach to the Rochambeau airport in Cayenne, the morning flight from Martinique. As we fly toward the French Guiana coast, just a bit north of the equator, the Atlantic takes on a coffee brown color—and I realize it's sediment from the Amazon River as it spreads out along the South American coast. It is all jungle southward to the horizon. The company I work for—called BIG C—is a partner in a venture, and I am here to assist with the evaluation of a gold deposit. Our partners, the French Bureau de Recherches Géologiques et Minières aka BRGM, the French Bureau of Geology and Mines, have found gold deep in this jungle.

To get there I fly south to a small river town called Maripasoula. The Air Guyane plane is a twin-engine Series 300 Otter—the same kind I'd so often used for exploration in Canada. Reliable. Cramped. Noisy. Smells like a hockey team.

Signs of civilization are drifting away from me as we progress farther across the jungled terrain.

The jungle is a palette of every shade of green. Brownish-gray glistening rivers meander through it like giant pythons. After a time we're banking over the Maroni River and back around to the concrete landing strip at Maripasoula. Faded pastel-colored buildings crowd the dirt streets. To me the town looks like a collection of blocks strewn carelessly along the river.

Roland Wagner, a forty-year-old prospector with a round young face, and Pascal, the rotund cook, are here to meet me. Roland has a barely visible scar that runs above his lip and along his left cheek and another on the right side of his neck below his jaw.

As we're off-loading supplies, Pascal nods toward Roland, and whispers to me in his thick French accented English, "Hey, ex-paratrooper in French army."

I say, "Ahhh—I see, yes, I see." I'm babbling away in my Americanized pseudo-French accent, not speaking French just speaking with a bad French accent. And I don't understand what Pascal is talking about.

"He runs away," Pascal whispers.

"From France?"

"No! No! From life, mon ami, from life!"

"Ah, oui, oui—from life. Ah ha ha ho ho, from life! But of course!"

I realize I'm speaking in my *Franglish* Jacques Cousteau-in-the-mini-sub accent . . . I can't help it, too many of those *National Geographic* shows as a kid—in them, Jacques would say something like:

"*. . . and we find ourselves in the emerald jungle with these strange men who have survived here. They are our friends . . .*"

I had better stop doing this or these guys will think I'm mocking them . . . who knows what Roland would do.

We load supplies from the Twin Otter into a woebegone white Toyota pickup.

Pascal is touching the boxes: FOOD! He opens one and hands me a beer.

Everything here is warm.

Roland leans toward me and says, "Cuire, il et cuire!"

"Ahhhh, oui," I say.

"Be good to our friend the cook or you cook yourself!" Roland says. When Roland Wagner looks at me he looks deep into my eyes.

I can tell right away that Pascal is fun, but Roland, I don't know. He's a little bit scary.

Well, we must pick up more things while in Maripasoula before going out to the gold camp. So we finish loading the supplies into the truck—and then it's just a minute or two drive into town.

The first stop is the post office: Pascal drops off letters to France, there is one that has arrived from his family—he holds it with both hands, like it is sacred, and opens it—reading it as we drive on through town.

The second stop is along the road: Roland chats with a deeply tanned woman carrying some groceries from the market. She's pretty, he's looking at his feet and kicking at something on the dirt road, he can't quite make eye contact. She's looking directly at him trying to get a peek at his eyes. Her smile is coy, alluring; I think she wants him. I think he's thinking so too. He wants her. They both glance at me . . . three's a crowd. We're standing in the middle of the road under a hot sun, and I decide I'm suddenly interested in a flowering tree nearby . . .

"Meet you there!" Roland says pointing to a shack at the end of the dirt street.

I wander off. Pascal catnaps in the truck—I think he's used to waiting on Roland's courtships. I'm pretty sure I'm witnessing what Roland likes to do best—wooing the women of Maripasoula.

As I walk on down the road I realize I could live here. This is a poor man's paradise. I always think about the livability of a place when I'm in-country.

I have to make a decision over the next couple of months: GO or NO GO on this project. I'm jazzed about working on gold in the jungle; what a kick to build a gold mine here. It's my call. There is power in this decision, and it could profoundly affect people's lives. We could build a school or a hospital, give people jobs.

The third stop is the market, where I meet up with Pascal and—from what I can tell—an unsatisfied Roland. I guess the roadside encounter didn't progress to a level he'd hoped for. Well, it's market time. The building is just a tired two-story wooden thing at the end of the street. An elderly African woman welcomes us as we duck through the low door. She blends into the shadows of the weathered dark wood. Sun streams through holes in the walls and illuminates the dusty atmosphere; the mixed aromas are heavy with ginger, cinnamon, soap, motor oil, vinegar, coconut, human sweat, citrus candles, French perfume, and dirt—lots of dirt. The shelves behind chicken wire hold all manner of goods: batteries, Sugar Smacks, wire cutters, Ovaltine, spark plugs, music tapes, Q-tips, a Barbie doll, dried garlic, shaving cream, toothpaste, small amber bottles of French perfume, chocolates, condoms, baby food. You point . . . the old woman fetches.

Roland picks out shaving cream . . . I guess he's not at the chocolate or condom phase of the roadside relationship. And then hands me a *warm* Heineken!

Next stop: the hotel. Ah, it's the only one in town and it has a bar. We park ourselves at the bar in one fluid masculine motion—through the door, across the room, onto the stool, elbows on the bar.

The barmaid approaches: she is slender, older, weathered, and her smile shows a couple of brown, corroded teeth. I ask her: "Mademoiselle, je voudrais du pan ah ah et fromage, s'il vous plait." She fetches a plate of bread and cheese, slides it along the counter and stops in front of me. She uncaps a bottle of warm beer for Pascal, Roland, and me—there's no refrigeration in the hotel.

Roland to the woman: "Hmmmm, ça va, chérie . . . how are you?"

Woman to Roland: "Comme ci comme ça . . . so so."

Woman to me: she leans forward toward me, the top of her shirt falls open, she pouts her lips and tilts her head, and says, "Et tu . . . and you, American?"

Me to the woman: "Oh, me? I'm good . . . bon."

Roland looks at me and growls—and I don't know why he's jealous.

Chérie slaps Roland on the arm and feigns disgust like this is an old game the two of them play; and she folds her arms over her small sagging breasts which swell beneath thin fabric.

She winks at me just to bug Roland.

Oh, he's after this one too, and I'm a new unwelcome variable in his jungle courtship equation.

The barmaid is not as pretty as the other woman so Roland has more confidence. Her smile puts me off, though . . . I think, jeez, you gotta fix those teeth! I wonder: Is this why Mona Lisa didn't smile?

Tacked to the barroom wall is a map of French Guiana. There's a reddish brown clay smudge on the map over Maripasoula.

I imagine years of beer drinking clients hammering the location with their dirty fingers and saying,

"There—that's where we are!"

"We're past the end of the road."

"We're far, far, far up the river!"

I'm not sorry to leave the woman with the bad teeth, but the jarring ride out to the BRGM camp with a belly full of warm beer . . . well . . . I should have known better.

Yaou Camp

Soon we turn onto a narrow road that winds its way up a hill through quiet jungle, and at its crest is a cluster of small buildings.

The gold camp, called Yaou Camp, is nestled deep in the interior of this womb-like jungle. Heat and humidity are on tap. The BRGM has hewn the camp out of the rain forest. Every board and plank sawn from the trees cleared on the ground of this hill.

Over to one side are a couple dozen small shack-like one- to two-room buildings; that's where we sleep. And over on the other side—Pascal's open-air kitchen. And in the middle of the camp is a one-room geology office. I'll do my map making and store my rocks here.

In this primitive settlement I meet Ikelou for the first time; he will be my field assistant. The camp also has about twenty other workers, mostly local men like Ikelou. Well, the next day Ikelou and I set out to look at rocks.

Weathered outcroppings of rock are along the rough roads cut with a bulldozer to access sites for drilling. Trenches have been dug between the towering trees to see if gold is hiding amongst the roots. I find small patches of rock in the overgrown creeks and valleys.

Ikelou is a young Wayana man rich in curiosity. He goes through my notebook after I've written or drawn something and studies the sketches, now and then nodding when he can see that I'm drawing a particular geologic shape or feature that he recognizes.

Sometimes Ikelou looks over my shoulder to watch me work, like when I use my compass. The needle points north, and he looks up in that direction, and then at me: *What's out there? Why is that direction so important?*

Ikelou speaks French and Taki Taki and his native Wayana.

I combine my broken French with mime-like gestures and sketches—that is our language. Lots of head nodding, rubbing of chins, and looking about.

The field workers go out each day into the jungle and collect silt and soil samples. This is reconnaissance geochemistry. The silt and soil are put in small bags and sent off to an analytical laboratory in France to see if there is gold in them. Wayana, the Boni, the French, and a few Brazilians comprise our field crews: a ragtag lot who venture into the bush with their machetes, augers, and shotguns, all under the commanding leadership of ex-French paratrooper Roland Wagner.

Roland Wagner is a conundrum, a cross-cultural enigma. The jungle has affected him; he has morphed from perhaps a realist, maybe like Jean-François Millet, that great Normandy artist—seeing people and trees as they are—to perhaps more of an impressionist. I have seen him just standing there watching the trees; maybe he's noticing what I notice—the effect of light on the jungle. Is this how Alfred Sisley saw the forests and Claude Monet the water lilies? Roland, though, is in his own world here.

Pascal said to me one day in a very serious voice, "Roland can never be part of society, how can he be—with his paratrooper life."

I say, "What do you mean? What happened?"

"In the paratroopers he was taught to kill men." Pascal frowns to express his dislike of such an education.

<<<>>>

Later, back at the makeshift office, I get a fax from my boss in the head office in San Francisco. It reads:

FAX
How's the work coming? We hope you can confirm our belief that we will be building a gold mine out of this project. We await your report.

As I read the fax I am watching the field crews ready for departure. It is the day-to-day life here that is so foreign to the soul of this multinational corporation I work for. The field crews are always foraging when they're out working. They'll come back to camp with a hundred-pound pack full of rock and soil samples and with a hundred pounds of food—whether it be a bird, or deer, or monkey, or some kind of plant. This is an odd concocted blend of a hunter-gatherer culture with that of the corporate money-making machine.

But Roland hunts on his own on Sundays. In camouflage gear and with a gun under his arm he silently leaves camp. There will be one shot. He always comes home with a kill, usually a *biche*, which is a small deer, that's draped over his shoulders.

Now, on the other hand we have our fun-loving Pascal. He also professes to hunt. "I go into the wild! I go into the jungle! Ha ha!" And off he goes once a week in Burmuda shorts, a flowery shirt, knee-high gumboots, and a rusty old rifle. We hear gunshots now and then, sometimes a lot of them . . . like he's taken on an army of rebels in the jungle. I don't think he's hunting; I think he's got a little garden project in the jungle. I picture him sitting on a log, getting high and firing off his rifle to let us know he's *really* hunting. Pascal returns from these hunts always very happy and always empty-handed.

Today the field crews have caught two big *Aras*—those majestic green-blue-red parrots. One is still alive and squawking loudly. That's dinner, and I'm told *Ara* tastes like chicken.

I say to Ikelou, "How can you guys kill this bird that looks like a rainbow in the jungle?"

He looks at me, puzzled, "We hungry!"

Jungle

At night the jungle sleeps only restlessly, if at all. The nocturnes come out to play! I remember my first night there: I'm lying in bed, listening to the occasional birdcall. THEN a gruff almost hooting sound that slowly builds with pulsing breaths and then rises to a crescendo before trailing off as if in despair . . . *huh huh huh huh huff huff aaaAAAOOOOOOOaaaahhhh huh huh oooo.*

"Jesus! What the hell was that?" I'm sitting up in bed, thinking, *That thing is CLOSE!*

In the morning over breakfast I ask Pascal, "What was that huffing, roaring, screaming sound that I heard last night?"

Pascal looks up from his cooking and says nonchalantly, "Oh that, ah—it is our friends the howler monkeys. We wonder—are they hungry? Are they looking for love, maybe? Are they making love? We do not know."

And I just can't get that sound out of my mind, I mean—wow—you'd call the cops if you heard that in the city.

Later that day I'm back in the field, and I'm thinking about these howler monkeys. How big are they? How aggressive? They sound aggressive. Should I be worried about being mauled by monkeys? Monkey *maulings* . . . not a pleasant way to go.

Well, if I'm going to be hanging around with all these monkeys, I had better get into the swing of things. There's a vine that's hanging about 100 feet down from a tree. And I've just got to swing on it—and I do the Tarzan yodel. I just had to do that!

But there's no Jane to rescue. I realize it's been a long time since I've seen my wife and family. It's been a long time since love was on the evening menu. Even though I send letters home, I never get replies. And I wonder why—maybe I'm just gone too much, maybe her dreams and my dreams are different now. Over a pizza in San Francisco one time she told me she didn't want any surprises in life, no challenges, no peaks and valleys. I didn't know what to say—you see, I live for that. I live for the challenges, I live for the peaks, I live for the valleys. And now I throw myself into my work so I don't have to admit what's really happening.

There are a vast variety of vines in this jungle: they cover all the bases—creepers, climbers, and danglers. Vines are pretty much like people: creepers are like lawyers or regulations, and danglers are like undecided teenagers.

But the most notorious of all is, what the French call the climber, the *figuier etrangleur* aka the fig strangler (*Ficus aurea*). It uses the host tree as a superstructure for its future self. Theft and murder in the forest, naturally. This is kind of like an end-running corporate climber; my company is full of them. You gotta watch out for these guys! The tendrils drop down to the ground to root—like an ominous memo coming down from headquarters. Then vines envelope the host tree: *the seemingly innocent takeover has begun.* Soon, though, some tree trunks bulge out between the coiled vines like an arm in a tourniquet—slow-motion death. Sometimes I feel like the company is doing that to me. In time the dead host tree rots away, leaving a hollow form of itself—the network of vines remain in the shape of the host trunk and fuse together to make one continuous trunk by filling the hollow interior—the vine has stolen the tree's soul.

In from the field—sweaty, muddy, bug-bit, sore-muscled from my sixty-pound backpack full of rocks. I strip down in the wooden shower room. The water is hot, and I step into the shower stall. But something in the corner catches my attention. It's big and brown and crawling. Just what I needed. The spider is big—big as a salad plate, and with each splash of water it moves closer to my naked, exposed toes.

Sometimes the best strategy is a bold retreat—which I do immediately.

Evening in camp finds all of us in our ritualistic dinner schedule. Pascal proudly brings the food to the table.

Even here the long arm of the French government seeks to control every aspect of our lives—including dinner! They allow only so much wine per evening meal—they limit our French wine intake. So, we drink water with the meal after the wine allotment is consumed.

But you can't take the water for granted. Do you know what could be in there? In camp the water is drawn through charcoal filters to keep the microbes out of our intestines. Pascal keeps the water in Dillon rum bottles—Dillon is a distillery on Martinique. From a distance it looks like we're drinking vast quantities of rum. Well, we had to empty the rum bottles so we'd have something to put the water in, after all—we didn't have enough empty wine bottles . . . thanks to the government control. Of course the French government never said anything about limiting our rum supplies.

The French are very polite while dining—always offering someone else the first serving. Mealtime is slow and measured and savored; after an appetizer of soup or salad or cold meats there's the main course, then cheese, then a dessert. We do not lose weight here.

Some of the local workers prefer their own food or are simply not invited to join the French for dinner. This is somewhat of a class society the French have brought here. But people who are colonized never really welcome their conquerers or controllers—and Ikelou's tendency to keep a polite distance from the French is proof of this. So tonight Ikelou and his compatriots are eating *Ara* parrot again, the other one.

After dinner the work crews crank up their tape decks, and we get a blend of musical presentations deep in the jungle:

✓ Beatle's *Yellow Submarine* is the Monday selection.
✓ Tuesday: Bob Marley and the Wailers.
✓ Wednesday the Bee Gees' *Saturday Night Fever*.
✓ Thursday is country night—Hank Williams in the jungle, kind of weird.
✓ Scott Joplin's *The Entertainer* on Friday.
✓ Followed by a weekend of Mozart's Requiem Mass
 . . . and that really gets the howler monkeys going!

Deadly snakes in the toilet this morning! One of the men had seen some kind of snake the night before in the shower. Deadly snakes in the toilet are not good.

Just imagine: "Ahhh I've been bit in the ass by a poisonous snake! Quick, suck out the poison! Anybody? Anybody? SOMEBODY!!!"

"Right . . . you're gonna die, man!"

Speaking of snake bites, later, back in the makeshift office, I get another fax from the head office. It reads:

FAX
Yes, work harder, faster, better, bigger, cheaper . . .
yeah, yeah, yeah, go team!

I've got a command and control boss. He doesn't hear most of what I report because he knows everything. You know—this company isn't going to build a school or a hospital.

I recall Clayton Christensen's wisdom in his book *The Innovator's Dilemma*. He says that one of the five laws of disruptive technology is: "an organization's capabilities define its disabilities."

I am wondering if the head office knows it's looking through rose-colored glasses, or any glasses at all? They don't always help. They don't always come to the rescue. It doesn't always suck the poison from the wound. The Big C just wants to make money, and is it at any cost?

History

Analogies abound in the jungle. For instance, I see the ants that live their lives in the *salir rouge*—red soil. They collect leaves and flower petals from the jungle floor, each clutching a piece of leaf in their pincers as they march toward their hill. The leaves are carried deep into the ant mound—sometimes down twenty feet or more. One of the drill roads has cut through a mound, exposing the maze of tubelike tunnels. They use the leaves as a substratum to grow mushrooms underground. This is food for the colony: these ants are so well organized that they're practicing agriculture; I can't even do that.

What brought the French here four hundred years ago? The greed for *gold* of course: this is called the Gold Coast. The Dutch and British and Brazilians and Portuguese also grabbed it at various times—for gold and diamonds. The Treaty of Paris sorted much of it out in 1814, and by 1915 all the border disputes with European powers seemed to be resolved. French Guiana gained its French overseas department status in 1946. But everyone forgot to ask the indigenous people what they wanted to do.

The BRGM was brought in with the aim of developing natural resources to encourage self-sufficiency here, and everyone believes *gold* is the answer. But the Wayana people have gotten along fine without gold since before history.

What color are those glasses we've been looking through?

ACT 2

The River

In Maripasoula the local black children are being given baths on this late Sunday afternoon. The women are doing laundry—knee-deep in the muddy water and bent over scrubbing the clothes. I'm not sure how this water can clean anything.

We came to the village to pick up Pascal; he's been on leave. We're also getting supplies for the coming week.

Pascal has been fishing for piranha.

And he tells me, "But only for petit poisson, no danger for people."

That's not what I've heard.

I'm looking at the African women wading hip-deep in the muddy water doing laundry . . . "careful! We don't really know what's in that murky river!"

I look down the river, and Pascal follows my gaze to a sentinel tree along the shore. It towers 150 feet. "Ah, that is a sacred tree. It is the *fomage* (fo-ma-jay), sacred to the Boni African people here."

"Why?"

"It has, how you say, spirits in it, and you are bad to disturb them. Do not cut that tree."

There is simplicity in beliefs here, and I sense it is well grounded, being born of the jungle.

The river is crowded today, lots of activity. Along the banks are the river canoes called pirogues, and these are made by the Boni. The Boni are direct descendants of the Burkinabé West Africans brought to the Caribbean as slaves who escaped from the ship once they were in port. They made their way up the river and met the indigenous tribes, who around Maripasoula are the Wayana. They did not war upon each other, but rather a sort of truce was agreed upon. The

Boni would have the river and some shore land for farming, but the Wayana would keep the jungle—for you see they had always been a jungle people.

Pascal says, "If it is the river you want, go with the Boni, but if the jungle is what you seek, then go with the Wayana."

On the up-turned flat ends of the pirogues the Boni paint intricate, symmetrical patterns and colorful designs. These are unique to the Boni, for they have not adapted the tradition from any South American tribe, nor do they claim to have brought it with them from Africa. Some designs resemble intertwined serpents, others interlocked chains, and yet others are just wandering lines that suggest circular patterns. Maybe they represent the trials, bondage, and arduous journeys of their ancestors—I don't know.

Back in camp that night we discover that the work crews have captured a tortoise from the jungle. A big one. It's for their dinner, and yes, you've probably guessed it—they tell me it tastes like chicken.

The following day Ikelou explains to me that too many fish in the river Maroni are being killed. The Wayana have a traditional method of catching fish. When the water is low and the fish are forced into isolated pools, they cut up and crush a certain type of vine and put it into the water. The vine has a narcotic effect and essentially stuns the fish, which then float to the surface. In this way the Wayana can catch many fish relatively quickly.

The problem, says Ikelou, is that too many Wayana are using this method to catch fish. The old tribe practiced intuitive ecology gained from hundreds or thousands of years of experience in the jungle. But the new generation does not do this. They're doing as they please. Now they have boats with motors. Now they use modern fishing nets instead of woven vines. Now they catch all the fish.

I'm wondering what a gold mine here would do to the jungle if a simple modern net and outboard motor are having such an impact?

Roger James Kuhns

The Guide

Roland and I are sitting in the open-air kitchen today. Not talking. He's mostly in his own world, and not good in crowds, and rather withdrawn when there aren't any pretty girls around to get his blood moving. He's reading one of those spy assassination novels— like *The Day of the Jackal* or something.

I'm paging through a brochure I found in camp—"Tourism in French Guiana." It has all the pretty sites you can get to within an hour or two of Cayenne.

Looking over at the tourist brochure Roland says to me, "Do you know one of the values we French saw here? We saw it as prison: Devil's Island."

I remember this—it's that island off the coast of this country; it was made famous in the book *Papillon*, by Henri Charrière, and that movie with Steve McQueen as Charrière and Dustin Hoffman as his suffering companion. You know, they kept trying to escape. They ate bugs to survive; they were brutally beaten for even the simplest infraction and dumped into solitary confinement—just a pit in the ground. It was a real hellhole. The brochure states: "The prison closed in 1937 after 85 years of service to France."

Roland says, "Over seventy thousand men were imprisoned on that island—and now . . . you go there as a tourist."

"Hey, and now prison is a paradise!" I say, and he nods.

"Why make paradise a prison?" Roland asks me.

"Oh, why make paradise a gold mine?" I ask him.

Roland looks at me with that penetrating stare. The scar on his cheek is pulsing pink against his tanned skin. "Look—you know what we got here?"

I think Roland feels like his government could have put him in a cell on Devil's Island—maybe because of something that happened in the paratroopers—and now he's feeling perhaps threatened by his government's plans to build a gold mine here, which would take away this refuge he has found.

Roland is getting kind of mad, and I try to make peace and say, "Well, at least you've got a good job here in a beautiful jungle away from those powers that be in Paris."

But Roland is stressed—he's intense and glaring at me even harder, and he says, "You just don't understand what's going on here!"

Then I realize Roland has his own lifestyle to protect here. And there's his conflict—he gets his paycheck from the very government he now despises.

That night under my mosquito netting I'm reading my book on Buddhism, trying to get better at this life thing, you know. And I'm thinking maybe Roland Wagner has come to the jungle to liberate his mind from anguish. This place is like his own private retreat! I can see it in him, with the pulsing scar and all—there are just too many ghosts for Roland back in France.

So now, here in this camp, I realize that maybe Roland is on the Buddhist path—or some path! I'm starting to see this in me, too! I think I'm feeling some of the jungle karma, or maybe it's my own karma. Who is the cause and who is the effect? Are my past actions affecting me? I'm seeking dharma . . . that insight thing now. The jungle is opening my eyes; it's acting like my own spiritual guide.

And then another fax comes in from headquarters. This one reads:

FAX
Your last report was not as positive as we had hoped. Do you need help on the project? Are you sure you're working hard?

God, I hate these things.

The work crews came in today with a couple of red monkeys. They're for dinner. Look—I don't want to see my dinner staring up at me from one rung down on the evolutionary ladder.

The music selection tonight will be the Bee Gees. The work crews are down there eating monkey and listening to *ha ha ha ha stayin' alive, stayin' alive.* I'm eating chicken—not the monkey.

That night as the howler monkeys scream and bellow and howl in possible protest over the evening's dinner another drama is taking place . . . under my bed.

I'm thinking about karma again . . . howler-karma. What you eat you are . . . what goes around comes around . . . I'm thinking of all the old adages and metaphors!

In the inky night I'm laying under my mosquito netting listening to the noises of the jungle and trying to get some sleep. Suddenly I hear this odd rustling in my room. I'm trying to figure out the sounds, it's dark, and the flashlight is on the table beyond reach—smart. The animal sounds like it's moderate in size, like a cat or small dog, and now it's snooping about under my bed. Then I hear the squeaking of the rusty hinges on my door. Something else has followed the first animal into my room. There's this sudden scurrying of larger clawed feet. I'm lying perfectly still in my bed. Now I've made another quick decision—I will not be putting my bare feet on the floor and going to fetch my flashlight. I'm not moving. Suddenly there's a pouncing sound. Then a thud and then a tangled fight; more thumping and squealing. It is a struggle to the death.

The fight ends with a pathetic fatal gasp—I presume from the lesser critter; then there's the distinct sound of something being dragged out of my room.

In the unsettled silence, I dare to step over to the table and get the flashlight. There are a few blood droplets on the floor.

I think it's time for me to read up a little more on Buddhism.

I realize . . . the workers go into the jungle and catch dinner and bring it into camp. The jungle comes into my room to catch dinner and take it out of camp. I'm living in a frigging restaurant! And everything tastes like chicken!

Invisible

Morning arrives without further incident, and I head off into the jungle to map.

Geologic mapping is a lot of fun. It is essentially a task of solving a jigsaw puzzle as one methodically finds the right pieces and puts them in place. Sometimes you don't know what the picture is until the puzzle is complete, whereas other times you see early inklings of the solution. I spend the next couple of days mapping the rocks in deep trenches dug by a bulldozer.

In the trenches I measure the direction of quartz veins and fault zones. The veins, like white lines on a wall, project up through the weathered rock—rock that has all but turned to red clay from millions of years of weathering but still looks like rock. The veins are important because they, along with pyrite, indicate the likelihood of gold. We know there's gold here, but we don't know which way to go to find more. That's what I've got to figure out.

But something else is happening. I'm getting a little worried here. Working in this place is like going to a masquerade ball; nothing is what it seems. Behind every leaf: a new animal. In every root: a new cure. In every pattern: a mystery.

Back in San Francisco the company wants a report with facts and figures on mining gold. But how do I quantify the intangible?

And then this comes in on the fax machine:

FAX
Work harder, faster, we need a positive GO decision!
Can these people be trained to drive mining trucks?

In the field today I just watch the jungle, I don't map any geology at all. I just watch. I notice. I absorb. I become invisible.

There's a big macaw perched just above me. The bird has a red head and breast, a green stripe on its wings, and blue from there on down. The macaw has the same colors as the forest profile—except upside down. The red head being the soil, the green stripe the forest, and the blue is the sky. It is a mirror to what it flies over.

What's going on here—these coincidences, symmetries, and patterns? Is this what the Boni try to carve into the bows of their boats?

Yesterday at dinner Roland said to me, "Are the lights going on?"

He just drops these things in my lap . . . our camp paratrooper spiritual jungle recluse wants to know where my head is at... How am I doing on my Buddhist thing? . . . and there's Cousteau in my ear: *Are the lights going on?*

Sure, that's enlightenment—I think I'm getting my priorities in order, I'm getting out of that samsara thing of recurring delusion. Am I so deluded? Hey, I just came here to make a gold mine!

There's this very large toad in the shower tonight, I mean almost rabbit size, really big. It puffs up when I stomp my foot to chase it away. But then it just hops around to face me—me, the naked human threat. I'm getting used to having things watch me take showers.

Inini

The next morning: I still need more information to understand the bigger picture in more ways than one, so a trip up one of the smaller rivers is in order.

The Inini River runs just southeast of Yaou Camp. I make the journey with Ikelou and his friend Casidy, who carries an old Italian rifle. Departure is at first light. To get to the river we take a shadowy, winding game path through solid jungle.

As we leave camp Pascal, who is cleaning up after breakfast in the open-air kitchen, yells out, "Ah, now you go to the river of no return!"

"Save me some chicken, Pascal! I shall return!"

"One never knows . . . one never knows!" Pascal said and wagged his finger.

Roland is sitting at one of the tables. He smiles thinly at me, then orders, "Take good notes!" I can tell he'd rather be going up the river than doing some paperwork in camp today.

Just as I leave camp I look out over the expanse of humid wilderness from on top of our hill. Four great *Aras* are flying two by two in the mist and appear through breaks in the jungle. They look for all the world like *Archaeopteryx*—the long-extinct Jurassic link between dinosaur and bird. The parrots' long tails and great wingspans rival an eagle's. The normally brilliant red, green, and blue plumage is muted pastels in the mist.

There is no time here—yet there is nothing but time.

A few steps into the jungle, and the camp vanishes—it's all too thick to see very far. The jungle canopy towers above us as we walk into this dark world; diffuse light filters down.

We take a narrow trail that meanders up and over steep hills and through swampy lowlands. The singing and screaming and squawking of birds keeps us company—all the sounds drifting down from the canopy overhead. It is hard to spot birds when they are hidden in the green so far above.

Still, I glimpse a toucan, a white-breasted black bird with an orange bill. The toucan rudely squawks down at me—*eh eh eh ow ow ow!*

I'm anthropomorphizing all the time now: that toucan just said *ow ow ow* like it's yelling at me not to hurt the jungle!

I learn about the trees from Ikelou. I pick up a small flower with four green petals that open to reveal a riot of red and yellow stamens. It's from the *wapa* tree. Ikelou points to the tree with his machete and hacks a chip out of the bark. The wood is hard with fine tight grain and a light orange-red color behind moderately shaggy bark. The roots grow up like fins of a rocket—a buttress to support the tree. The shallow roots interlock with neighboring trees, just as the branches in the canopy are all offering support to another—it's collaboration on an enormous scale! They fall over when their neighbors are taken down, like in storms, or areas clear-cut for timber or farming, or when you build a gold mine.

I look up and see the silhouette of a monkey leaping from one branch to the next—no net.

Casidy leads the way with his old Italian rifle over his shoulder and machete in hand. His worn brown cotton flannel shirt has both sleeves ripped off at the shoulders, revealing leathery brown skin over sinewy muscle. I cannot guess his age, I think he's ten thousand years old. Sometimes when I look down the path where he's supposed to be, he's just not there. Then he is; it's weird. Casidy has an underbite that gives him an expression of constant disapproval—although he seldom speaks to me.

He stops and plucks a palm leaf stem and rubs it on the blade of his machete like he's playing an instrument, creating a deep squeaking sound. The jungle explodes in a riot of song and squawk from all the birds we can't see. He looks back at me and grins an underbite grin. He seems to say: *Are you paying attention?*

Ikelou is dressed in his usual—a black T-shirt, worn French designer blue jeans, gumboots, and a baseball cap.

His shirt says: *I may not be perfect, but parts of me are terrific.*

The jungle is multileveled: life upon life—here a lichen or moss grows on a bromeliad that sprouts upon a small tree that is rooted on a larger tree. It is a symbiotic micro-habitat city.

Simple complexity; complex simplicity; fractal symmetry!

Bromeliads grow all over on tree limbs and fallen trees. These odd plants, of which the wild pineapple is a member, have swordlike leaves that gather water at their center forming micro-ponds, and offer sustenance and protection for other life forms. Frogs, salamanders, and insects use these micro-ponds as their home. Falling leaves and other debris collect in the plant, creating a faux firmament. In such soil one finds insects and microbes unique to that specific environment. It's all one big hanging-garden effect. It's where the orchids blossom.

Everything is inside out here: spiders eating birds, poisonous frogs hopping around, formic acid–excreting ants in your pants, gardens up in the treetops, if this isn't chaos, then I don't know what is!

Suddenly the trees thin out, and we squint into the brilliant sun. We're standing on the muddy banks of the Inini River. There across the chocolate water is the small village of Winiwe. Ikelou calls out, "Hey bateau! Hey boat!"—and someone pushes one across—the pirogue is torpedo-shaped and so light that it shoots across the river so fast the current can't carry it away. We paddle across.

Winiwe is just a few palm-thatched roof and pole-grass huts without the walls. Several have hammocks strung across them—bedrooms. There's an open hearth for cooking. On the rocks around the habitat are fish and mammal bones, all the refuse of many meals. One of the men lounging in a hammock is wearing a T-shirt that reads: *Poison—WORLD TOUR, 1989*. Everyone speaks Wyana, not much French.

These people don't seem to have any particular opinion of me going up the river to look for gold. I'm just one more odd change in their lives. Ikelou just accepts me. I don't know if it's a friendly or practical trust or what; I get the feeling I'm more like a project or something, like Jane Goodall studying her chimps—Ikelou is studying me. Watching what I eat, how I write, where I go. I never go hunting, I just come back from the jungle with a bag full of rocks.

Ikelou says, "Why you do that?"

"Collect rocks?"

"Oui. Pourquoi?"

"To see if there's gold in them."

Ikelou looks closely at the rock sample, he studies it in detail. He says, "But there is NO gold here!" He points to the rock. "See—*où est l'or?* Where is gold?"

I explain to him that sometimes the gold is too fine to see. It's called micron gold and can be recovered by modern mining methods. But he only frowns and gives me a grin that seems to say I've confirmed what he's always thought . . . that we geologists are all crazy. At one point I did find visible gold. It was a small sun-yellow nugget in the white quartz veins. When I showed that to Ikelou, he smiled and nodded. But then a look fell across his face, more contemplative, maybe a little sad, as if he was now realizing what this might mean.

Soon we're in the twenty-foot pirogue. Ikelou's young nephew is joining us. It's a Boni boat; there are spiral and zigzag patterns on the bow—intricate, indecipherable. I'm putting this all down as trying to understand chaos. These carvings are familiar to me, yet I can't quite place them. But they're affecting me, like that feeling of trying to remember the taste of a favorite food you haven't had in years.

In the boat Ikelou is at the stern, revving the Johnson ten-horsepower outboard, and Casidy is in the bow with a river pole, looking for rocks, submerged logs, and sandbars.

Jagged-rock rapids are common on the river. We shoot through them like a spawning salmon. The river exposes the great dolerite dikes: black, massive, fine-grained mafic rocks intruded the terrain 200 million years ago, back when the supercontinent of Pangea existed. This was at the so-called Permian-Triassic boundary, when massive vulcanism occurred worldwide—especially in what is now Siberia. This time in geologic history not only formed one of the largest copper-nickel-platinum deposits in the world, known in Siberia as Noril'sk, but it also ushered in one of the most extreme mass extinction event in the Earth's history. Right here I am standing on igneous rocks that were part of the cause of that horrific event. The supercontinent had been in existence for over seventy million years, but now it began to break up—first from a rift that would ultimately separate South America from Africa, thus creating the Atlantic Ocean.

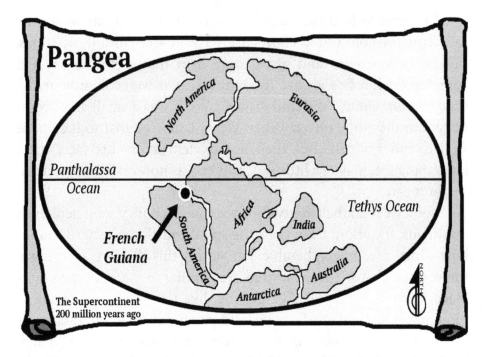

The two modern continents of Africa and South America share this common Pangean heritage. The rocks on the shoulder of South America are the same as those in West Africa. The so-called African Birimian rocks are collectively referred to as the West African Shield, and the South American counterpart is the Guiana Shield. And not surprising, the many gold deposits on these two shield areas of the modern continents have a same geologic history as well. Understanding one helps us find the other. If the two continents were still joined, then Cayenne would face Freetown in Sierra Leone, and the Amazon River would flood into the Ghana. Rio de Janeiro would be opposite Benguela in Angola.

Ikelou steers the boat to a large rounded island of coarse-grained granite. He cuts the engine as we glide into a cleaved inlet. I hop off to look around, to do some mapping. Ikelou's nephew runs off to explore. After a time the kid notices a tree with numerous swallow nests—they hang from the branches like balls in nets—but now they're infested with wasps, and what's the kid do? He throws a rock at the cluster of nests—scores a direct hit.

Suddenly he's yelling and running back to the boat. Just as I turn, wasps attack me. I run, too, pulling them off my arms and face and crushing them between my fingers; they're tough buggers, and they seem to come in stinger first as they land on me. They hang on, and I keep them away from my eyes. I just keep grabbing handfuls of the wasps and crushing as many as I can. I dive into the boat as Ikelou rams the motor in reverse, and we roar away from the swarms rising off the infested outcrop. And I've still got my rock samples!

I've been stung dozens of times. The kid doesn't have a single sting; he ran right past me, and guess who the wasps saw! Smart kid. Anyway, we pull up along the shore, and Ikelou digs out the surprisingly long, double-pronged stingers with his knife. The welts hurt and itch, but I don't have an adverse reaction to them.

By late afternoon I find one of the large fault zones that could host gold that I'd been looking for. With this new information and rock samples we turn the boat around and head toward Maripasoula. But I keep looking up river, it's like it won't let me go. I want to know its source.

What did Roland say? "Pay attention!" Okay, okay, I'm paying attention.

Suddenly Ikelou cuts the motor and motions to Casidy to hand him his rifle. "Iguana!" he whispers.

I can't see it. Neither can Casidy.

"La haut, sur la branche!"

We still can't see it. I'm looking for a green lizard in a green tree against a green backdrop.

Ikelou fires the rifle. The loud crack shatters the quiet afternoon: birds squawk and lead flies through the air impacting an insouciant lizard sunning itself on a branch. There are frenzied movements in the tree. Ikelou has wounded the reptile and quickly fires another round. The iguana falls through the greenery and lands on the muddy bank with a dull thud. It's about three feet long, dark green on top, light green on the bottom, and speckled like a trout in between.

Casidy retrieves the lizard, dips it in the river to clean off the blood. He tosses it in the bottom of the boat. That's dinner.

Ikelou looks as me. "It tastes like chicken."

"Have you guys ever tasted chicken?" I say.

"Yeah, here have some!" Casidy says and holds up the iguana.

ACT 3

Aloike

We come around a bend and merge with the main river. The Maroni looks like a great long brown lake compared to the Inini. Ikelou stops at his village, Aloike, which sits on a bluff overlooking the Maroni.

In Aloike each family has an area, complete with their own fruit trees and huts, which is separated from the other families by a few hundred feet. I help carry water up from the river while Ikelou presents the iguana to his family. He introduces me to his sister, a short attractive Wayana wearing just a wristwatch and a rather minimal washcloth-on-a-string kind of thing around her waist.

She smiles, "Bonjour." And stares at me: the unusual visitor.

Ikelou's uncle—tan and fit, lounging in a hammock—waves hello.

The huts are like those at Winiwe. Dogs wander freely and scrounge food scraps. Fish bones are strewn everywhere. Under the thatch roofs is a conglomeration of stone-aged and space-aged stuff and everything in between.

Fishing spears, called *pamtas*, with a trident of barbed metal points, lean against a post.

There's an old Singer sewing machine—a treadle, you know, the kind with the foot pedal that you pump.

There's a wooden bow.

A bucket of handpicked cotton sits next to a Sony cassette player and one Nike tennis shoe.

A woven vine backpack called a *katali* leans against a tree.

Ikelou shows me one of his prize possessions. It's a television!

I am momentarily stunned. I haven't thought about TV in months—it's like I'm looking at some new invention. Ikelou is smiling—showing off this trophy!

"Do you have power for this?" I ask.

"Apres!" he says—later, he'll get power later. Next he lifts up a towel on top of the television and proudly reveals a videocassette recorder. He hands me a bundle of cables and points to the TV and VCR. "You do."

I make the appropriate connections, but still no power. "Apres!"

With such optimism he should be a geologist.

Next Ikelou opens a metal cabinet and hands me a videocassette box. He even has a tape for the VCR. This is planning! The video is *Le Loup-Garou de Londres (The Werewolf of London)*. "Is American, is good," he says.

Here's stuff from the forest and stuff from France. He does not resist these trappings of civilization, he embraces these things, and I can only wonder at the wisdom wanting these goods of consumption! But I also realize he is adaptable, just as the jungle has always expected of him.

I sit down with Ikelou and his family by a cooking hearth, and we all eat some iguana. The dogs beg for scraps, prowling around us nervously like any begging thing. The gentle breeze is nice and the view exquisite, and I'm having dinner at this archaeological stone-age-like place that is Ikelou's village.

I feel like I'm momentarily lost somewhere along the fringes of the future.

I am this close to going AWOL and asking Ikelou if I can rent a hammock for the rest of my life. Almost all I do is work . . . for the Big C. They don't care about me, really. I have companions and friends in the business, but if I don't make their gold mine and increase the all-important SHAREHOLDER VALUE . . . well, I'm like so much mud down the river. Maybe I should just fade into this jungle?

Isn't that what Roland is doing?

Casidy is complaining about a pain in his foot. Ikelou wipes the iguana from his hands and kneels down to have a look. Doc Ikelou recognizes the problem right away; just below a leishmaniasis scar is a hard, long lump. He starts probing this with his knife as Casidy grits his teeth.

30

The problem is cutaneous myiasis; it's a skin irritation caused by the infestation of botfly larvae. Dermatobia hominis is the clinical name for the insect, but basically some damn little fly lays an egg in you and it grows into a larvae—oh, this gets good. Next it generates lesions while it eats its way out of you. This itches and hurts like hell, and soon there's an oozing, bloody, purulent discharge from your skin.

Great stuff. Deadly snakes in the toilet, poisonous frogs and giant spiders in the shower, mean old wasps and formic acid ants at every turn, piranhas in the river and bug eggs in your flesh . . . *paradise with a twist.*

Doc Ikelou pops the larvae out with his knife. Casidy inspects the little white nasty before squashing it.

As it turns out I, too, had been bitten by a botfly. It laid an egg under the skin above the upper left cheekbone in my face. A month later in Martinique I just couldn't stand it anymore. The infestation had grown into a noticeable lump that moved around when I pushed on it. It felt pretty weird. So—I went to the minibar and drank most of those small bottles of whisky, rum, vodka—you know, the complete medical anesthetic selection in your average hotel. I saved one bottle of brandy for use as an antiseptic. Then, using Ikelou's technique, I made a short cut while looking in the mirror. There was more blood than I thought there would be, and I poured the brandy over the incision. Wow did that sting. With a squeeze, the larva popped out. I squished it. The scar is a reminder of one of the transformative days in my life.

Well, after Casidy's surgical event, Ikelou's uncle hands me a warm Kronenbourg beer, and we raise them in toast to something in Taki Taki.

Ikelou downs his beer and gives me a satisfied look . . . *hey, this is the life, hey, we got warm beer, and we're not infested with anything.* He pitches his empty beer bottle into the river when he's done.

The river is everything—transportation, source of food, water for drinking and bathing, a place to do laundry, a sewer for refuse, and a toilet. To me the river seems timeless, and to some it also seems limitless.

Before dark Ikelou and I make our way down the river and back to camp.

Back in camp Roland Wagner asks me about the trip. He looks at the wasp stings and nods slowly. I can tell he's been through all of this. He listens intently, asks about the landscape, the color of the river, the type of trees, and how the rocks force the river to turn and flow. It's like a mental painting. He nods and smiles at me. I can tell he's wondering what my decision will be. I'm still wondering too! We haven't talked much about it; he doesn't want his world to change, for his own personal reasons, yet he is content to live off the French government. Wasn't it the French who said something about having your cake and eating it too? That's what he wants.

Late that night it rains again—great torrents rattling and drumming on the sheet metal roofs of our shacks. I couldn't even hear the howler monkeys. Although the wasp stings throb, I sleep like a log.

Wedding

The plastic cup I've been drinking from for the past four hours has seen far too much rum punch. The air is moist but comfortable, the stars are out, and we're all standing in the small yard of a house in Maripasoula. It's a wedding reception for a friend of Pascal's—all very casual.

The bride is wearing a light-colored short dress, and the groom is in jeans, a long-sleeved shirt, cowboy boots, and a bolo tie with a silver and turquoise steer's head. The stereo plays Tom Waits, something I don't usually associate with weddings, but the English words in the songs are almost all I understand amid rapid-fire, rum-soaked French conversations.

The simple house is made of unpainted, roughly hewn weathered boards that are decorated with half coconut shells planted with orchids.

There is a board with Boni designs on it, and I ask Pascal, "What do they mean?"

Through a veil of cigarette smoke Pascal says, "No one knows. No one can know." He looks in my eyes, deep; there is distance there. Jungle distance.

Roland is tracing the patterns with his finger. He's into them, almost trancelike, like he's connected with something. He looks straight up at the stars, as if there is an answer there.

When he looks at me, I shake my head no—the answer is here, and I pound my hand over my heart.

There's much rum and wine and punch. And the place is crowded and full of life. We're toasting friends and happiness. Someone has put on rhumba music; we liven up and sip our rum and toast them again in the heart of paradise—no darkness here.

There is gold on the bride's finger, the same metal I came here to find.

Wait, wait, wait . . . this is messing me up! I'm struggling with the paradox. These Frenchmen go to the jungle to get away from CIVILIZATION . . . They find the girl they love . . . put gold on her finger, marry her . . . then get a job digging up gold in the jungle . . . then the jungle is gone! You have to go back to CIVILIZATION . . . you have to go back to FRANCE!!! What's the sense of that?

A yellow sliver of moon hangs in the sky like a Cheshire grin. I point my face toward Pleiades—that small cluster of stars in the night—and offer a toast to my family: *I love you, do you know where I am and that I'm alive?* I have been months in the jungle; there were letters and crackly phone calls. No replies.

What of these wandering careers some of us have. The impact is heavy on our families. And sometimes these families fail; someone comes home to an empty house, or is replaced, or simply forgotten. When the time came for that to happen to me I would not be ready for it.

Certainly the job can be fun and exciting, and at the same time hard and demanding. The price is high to experience the world. Home is so distant.

Life isn't fair, I decided, *c'est dommage, c'est dommage* . . . so I had some more rum.

A man with Einstein hair and buckteeth tends to the sheep roasting over glowing coals. The sheep is being basted with a rag on a long stick. The Einstein hair guy dips it into a bucket and slaps the juice-soaked rag on the sizzling meat. Wonderful cooking smells waft up from the flames.

A couple on the porch is being very friendly with each other; now and then his hand wanders over her breasts, causing her to giggle. Her loose top is revealing, and her form is silhouetted by the fire. I notice I am not the only man watching the sensuous interlude.

Next to me is our bulldozer operator, Maurice; he's there with his Brazilian wife, who possesses a severe beauty. She is a foot shorter than he but always looks down on him. Now she elbows him out of his gawking, and he grunts, smiles, and laughs. The smile reveals brown teeth stained from the tobacco he is never without. He loves it here—you can see it.

The town doctor is wandering through the crowd looking very healthy and holding an infant he had delivered several days earlier. The doctor is a tall handsome man with a de Gaulle nose and an infectious smile, and he coos at the baby. The women crowd around him; he recognizes every single one of them. They place their hands on his arm.

There is a lot of electricity here . . . oh, these French. Maybe Ikelou can harness some of this for his TV.

In the crowd is an attractive—hmmm, very attractive—Boni woman named Nichelle. She speaks to me in a soft British English accent on top of her French Guyana accent.

"Oh, you're the American?" she asks me.

"Hmm-ya," I say, and she tells me she studied in Britain for two years but now teaches here in Maripasoula.

"I came home after Europe. I wanted to teach, be in my home again."

"But it's different, isn't it, coming home?"

"Yes, sometimes I am the stranger in my own country."

We understand that in each other; it's not something you plan, it's something that happens.

The evening wanders along in two-four time. We eat the sheep after hours of cooking. The bride and groom dance to reggae and rumba; there's a lot of dancing, heartbeat stuff, heart against heart.

Nichelle finds me in the crowd and grabs my hand, pulling me into the dancing bodies. "I will now teach you the rumba!" she says. She pushes her body into mine, and her lithe form is like melted chocolate all over me. I'm drunk and suddenly can dance perfectly. One of her legs is between mine, and she's pushing into me as we sway and swing to the rumba. Wow. Motion, heat, sweat, rum—no wonder these people live here! More dancing and more rum—I decide I really like to rumba.

The stars spin lazily in the night. There are champagne toasts all around and then Tom Waits is singing "Closing Time."

I'm standing in the back of the truck for a ride back to Yaou Camp, hanging on to a roll bar and enjoying the air and the unusual clarity of my mind. The stars are muted now by the humidity, and the air is rich and full of oxygen—that balminess you get only from the breathing jungle. Just breathe the jungle.

Suddenly there's a medium-sized cat on the road. It looks up in the headlights, stunned, like any animal in the light, like people dazed by progress! The cat's eyes reflect like small mirrors. Mirrors in the jungle making me look at myself. I can see its gray and brown spotted markings ending in a ringed tail. It's a margay, and as it runs down the road the boys in the truck yell, "Tiger, tiger, tiger!" before it veers off into the dark forest.

Outbound

It is two weeks since the wedding, and it is time for me to leave.

I have collected my information. I have completed my report. I board the Twin Otter to retrace the route back to Pepper Town: Cayenne.

All the farewells in camp were sincere, and final. Roland went into the jungle the day I left.

Pascal said, "He's no good at farewells."

I saw him look back once. Did he smile? I think he did, and then he vanished in the dark green shadows.

I shook hands with Ikelou. "Au revoir," I said.

He smiled and nodded. "Thank you for teaching rocks," he said.

"Thank you for teaching me," I said.

Then Ikelou returned to work.

They know I will not recommend we mine here. I have written the report to explain how the economics limit this project. I have not tried to call upon the emotional side of the argument with management.

But it is not gold that brought these people here in the first place. From the air the jungle remains a serene and mottled verdant sea—but now that I have been under the canopy, beneath the waves of green, I sense more of its heart.

Through a break in the clouds I see cultivated fields scalloped into the forest like a cancer. A paved black road with a neat dashed white center line comes into view. It's like a great zipper that opens the forest—the road gives access, and access brings people, and people clear forests. A gold mine would do the same.

How do we deal with this? How do we develop a fractional part without damaging the whole? Mining would give needed jobs to people, but we're destroying almost 50,000 square miles of jungle every year.

One man in the BRGM scolded me, "You can't tell us not to mine this gold, just look at what you did in your country. That's why America is rich. You mined it!"

In Cayenne the streets are narrow and lined with two-story apartments and businesses. The air is heavy and humid and smelling of exhaust. It's a view of balconies and windows with shutters. Motor scooters weave in and out of the chaotic and congested traffic.

A wedding procession slowly drives by—flowers on cars and impatient horns blaring—none of the joy and uniqueness of a Maripasoula wedding.

Shops display their souvenirs—butterflies in framed boxes, giant spiders and beetles encapsulated in clear plastic paperweights, and lacquered piranhas.

On a corner they have flown in small, cut pine trees from France for Christmas for the people who can't simply accept the jungle.

In my mind I see Roland tracing the Boni carvings on the bow of a boat. My finger becomes his; I trace the pattern. I make a decision I did not expect to make. I am invisible in the jungle. I breathe the jungle.

I realize now that I finally understand what the Boni are saying.

JESUS IN SUMBAWANGA

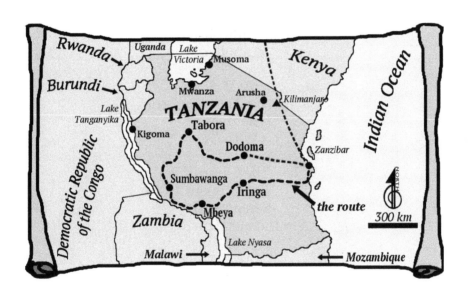

ACT 1

Kilimanjaro
The President
Fool's Gold
"Fools Gold" song
Dar es Salaam
Safari
Serengeti I
Olduvai
Annulled

ACT 2
"Clouds Are Gathering" song
Refugee
Witness
Attack
The Camps
"Roots" poem
Serengeti II
Independence

ACT 3
Lions
"Can't Ever Go Home Again" song
Sumbawanga
Jesus
"Jesus in Sumbawanga" song

ACT 1

Kilimanjaro

Habari gani.
[Hello to a local in Swahili]

Jambo.
[Hello to a foreigner]

Kilimanjaro lounges on its lava blanket like a large, white-haired woman showing off a sprawling dress. Uhuru—the old woman of a mountain's snowy crest offers a stark contrast to the dry savannah that spreads out from her volcanic apron. She's the tallest freestanding mountain in the world (19,340 feet)—the grand dame of Africa, about a million years old. But she is younger than our ancestors.

I am flying back to Dar es Salaam, and the stratovolcano is a poignant reminder of the harsh contrasts that exist between nature and humans, time and relationships, in this cradle of humankind—Tanzania, East Africa.

This volcano and her many kin manifest the Great Rift Valley—that maw splitting East Africa apart. In places the rift looks like great gentle lowland. Elsewhere it is like an axe wound in the earth's crust, festering with volcanic caldrons. It is restlessness in slow motion upon which nomadic and agrarian tribes live, where the refugees of Africa try to find a home.

But I have just received some mail that has finally caught up with me: a letter from a bishop in Wisconsin.

The President

A day earlier—before my flight over the big mountain—I had a meeting with Tanzanian president Benjamin Mkapa in the town of

Arusha. My traveling companion is Ferdinand Koffi from Côte d'Ivoire; he is very anxious to meet the president. Ferdinand helps run the company's Tanzanian exploration office with an Australian named Geoff Woad.

Ferdinand says to me, "If I can't meet Bill Clinton, then I will meet President Mkapa!"

President Mkapa is a round, sturdy man with thinning hair and a smile that turns down at the edges; seriousness and satisfaction are at play here. His black skin is shiny with sweat in the heat of the day as we sit in a meeting room in our suits and ties. President Mkapa holds his glasses in his right hand and gestures with them when he speaks:

"You see what I mean? You understand what I am saying? I want to bring people together, preserve the African family. And how do we do that?"

I look at the president and realize this is a rhetorical question. "You have a plan Mr. President? I would very much like to hear it."

"Yes, it is a vision of prosperity for Tanzania. It is a bringing together of the Tanzanian workers and the big foreign companies, such as yours. So I want to investigate that—how we can work together."

You see, I am working for a huge Australian resource company, and I say to the president, "We are working on gold and nickel projects in Tanzania. But it is early days, and going slow."

"And you have hired many Tanzanian workers?" the president asks.

"Many. We have dozens on the nickel site, and several helping with fieldwork on the gold site," I say.

"And what about tanzanite?" the president asks.

Tanzanite is a gem mineral that is only found in the rocks near Arusha in northern Tanzania at a place called Merelani. It is a gray to colorless mineral called zoisite that when heat-treated transforms into a beautiful blue to purple-blue gem.

"That one I am not so sure about, Mr. President. The mining areas are so very crowded, and it is difficult to mine safely," I say.

"But," the president says, and points with his glasses, "we need a company such as yours to teach them safety and good mine methods. You have seen these deep shafts in the ground dug by hand? It is into these death traps that boys and young men climb to work all day. You know of the downpour last year—many died when the workings flooded."

"Yes, it is a tragedy this happened," I say.

"Tragedy. Yes. But we mine this only to sell to make shillings and dollars, and the gems go to your Fifth Avenue New York. So it is important to us that we use our resources wisely. The families must benefit."

The miners that the president is speaking about only earn a few dollars for every gemstone that will sell for thousands on the market.

"We must," Mkapa is saying, "behave as if we are all part of this local community. That is why I invited you here today; your international firm can partner with these unskilled miners struggling through life working in dangerous jobs. There are 600,000 miners in Tanzania. You know this? Mining is an engine for the future," Mkapa says. "We are up to the challenge of mining and making repairs to our economy and to the environment. It's like a marriage!"

Uh oh . . . I get the geology, the mining, the ecology, even the culture and economics, but I don't think I'm too good at things like marriage. Absentmindedly I touch the Wisconsin bishop's letter in my pocket.

I must have paused too long. President Mkapa laughs. "You will find a way! I will find a way! We are all in the same boat." He pauses, and then looks up at us, and smiles. He says, "Now, please excuse me, for I have many meetings. But, you are invited to dinner with me tonight. I will see you then."

And with that he stands up, shakes hands with Ferdinand Koffi and me. Then a photographer enters the room, and we pose with the president for a photo. The meeting is over for now.

Fool's Gold

Dinner is with the president and his entourage. Ferdinand Koffi and I sit at the president's table.

Next to me is the president's personal assistant Ombeni Sefu. "I understand you are the gold man?" Ombeni says.

"I'm a fool for it, maybe, but yes, we're looking for gold, as well as copper and nickel."

"I don't like the countryside too much. It's dangerous. Lions, you know. And unfriendly people."

Ombeni is right, it can be. Only a couple of years ago one of our field camps was attacked by terrorists with mortars and guns. Then there are the lions; there are always the lions.

Across the table from me is the Tanzanian high commissioner to South Africa, Ami Mpungwe.

Mpungwe finds out that I live in Cape Town—"Ah, a South African!"

"I'm an American living there. But I feel very welcome," I say.

"Of course . . . and your family; how do they like the Cape?"

"I'm between families," I say.

"Ah, I have that on my resume too—the price of being in the diplomatic corps," Mpungwe says. "Now, though, I have a mixed marriage—never do that, take my advice."

"What do you mean?"

"Well," he begins, and sighs heavily, "my wife is Christian, and I am of course Muslim. That is an argument without saying, hey? So, when we got married we made a deal. She was to only make small decisions and I the big decisions! Ha, ha, ha, ha!"

"How's that going?" I ask.

"Hmm. Not too well," Mpungwe says. "But how about you—you being between things?"

"Me? I'm just looking for gold, and maybe some sanity along the way."

"Don't settle for fool's gold! My friend, that will get you nowhere," Mpungwe says. And that is good advice.

Fool's Gold

D GaddD   A   GaddD   D
People think I'm crazy for digging for gold in your heart,
Been crawling up these hills in back country in the dark.

    Refrain:
    Bm   E   Bm   E   A
    But every miner's got to know the glitter of fool's gold.
    D   GaddD   A GaddD   D
    Hey Hey, Hey Hey, I'm a fool for your love, ya ya ya ya (2x)

So I stopped in for a drink after a long hard day.
I asked around about you, but they said you'd gone away.

    Refrain

        A   G   D
    Bridge: Take for granted this one fool's heart,
        A   D
        You might not see it again.
        Like a tree in a hurricane wind,
        I continue to bend.

So I went down town in the city to have a look around.
But I didn't know the territory; you went underground.

    Refrain

Dar es Salaam

A couple of days after meeting with President Mkapa, I travel south to Dar es Salaam. The Tanzanian city is on the Indian ocean and presents itself as some artistic montage of stranded rusting ships, seaside resorts, aromatic fish markets, fleets of simple fishing dories, and bustling, dusty businesses: magnificent and primordial. The Indian Ocean backdrop reveals a temperamental pallet of shifting blue and green hues. The pungency of raw sewage wafts along the beach. Still, children play in the warm salty water.

One aging hotel stands like an archaeological monument, colonial in antiquity. Its five stars have fallen like a meteor to considerably lesser status. I feel like I'm riding a comet . . . I am of course in a taxi.

"You are here for safari?" asks the taxi driver. The vehicle swerves to the right as he looks back at me over his shoulder.

"No . . . watch out!" The car comes within a camel's hair of another car. Horns blare.

The driver grins back at me. "Not to worry, I'm a good driver!"

"Yes, I'm sure . . . but . . ." I yell and point forward.

The driver looks forward again, "Ahhh-yeeee!" We swerve around two young men running across the street—just missing them. I see a flash of colors and shapes out the window—people, vehicles, people, carts, people, shops, people, animals, people, people, people. Some of my geologic staff drive like this, and now I know where they learned.

I roll the window down so I can climb out if we crash! The air is humid and sweet with vegetative heaviness, pungent with humanity, moist with tropical urgency. Tanzania—ah, perhaps a long time ago it was the Garden of Eden.

I am swimming in life being lived for the moment. This place has handed me an apple—and do I have to take a bite? I know I will. I always do.

Safari

After two days of office work and field preparations, our supplies have been packed into the Land Rovers for an upcoming field excursion.

Audace Ntungicimpaye, my companion of many trips, is a tall Burundian Tutsi. He leads our safari, five of us, including Geoff Woad, the office manager. We leave the warm, green coastal environment of the Indian Ocean in our rearview mirror.

The Land Rovers bounce and jostle along 500 kilometers of dusty terrain in the country's interior (Iringa). The land becomes increasingly dry, rolling, and old. We're all geologists looking for billion-year-old gold and copper in the ancient rocks of Tanzania. This is real Sherlock Holmes detective work.

But the terrain is mantled with dirt and sand and vegetation. It is stippled with wattle-and-daub villages. Huge gray elephants trod upon the land. They rumble their barely audible communications as we pause to study the earth.

Alien-looking baobab trees offer sparse forestlands. The baobab looks like someone yanked the tree out of the ground—roots and all—and then stuck it back in the earth upside down.

Audace says, "They say it is the devil tree."

"This upside down tree?" I ask.

"It is said it is evil, I am just saying," and Audace holds his hands out like he's just repeating a widely known fact, "but I don't know why it is upside down?"

"Sure, why not? From *his* point of view down there it might look pretty good!" I say. "But I guess you have to believe in the devil?"

Audace looks at me and says, "The devil—he has been to Rwanda. He is real."

I'm thinking of the devil. I'm thinking of Jesus. I am thinking of Mohamed. I'm thinking of all the faiths and beliefs ...in this cradle of humanity, this Garden of Eden, this land of conflict.

"Would the devil plant tree to remind people of his presence? Would he expect people to fear this? Audace, think of the contrasts here in these places where people's faith and fear collide."

I find myself mentally rereading the bishop's letter that caught up with me. My ex-wife wants to annul the marriage she has already ended with a divorce. She wants to do this so that it will no longer have ever existed in the eyes of her church. My two children are very confused by this.

At that moment I have no idea there will be a sighting of Jesus in a town called Sumbawanga, but that will not be for a number of days. First we must leave this region of the devil's forest.

Serengeti I

Let me take a moment—it was a year earlier, and I was driving across the Serengeti and the historic Olduvai Gorge, studying the geology and the history of the region.

This was the East African Rift and the land of the Maasai and, as I would soon see, the land of the refugee. Geoff and I and our small team crossed the deep incision from Kilimanjaro to Lake Manyara and Lake Natron. Lake Magadi, one of the soda lakes, teamed with pink flamingos—their hue sourced from the pigment of the brine shrimp they eat.

On that morning we woke to the sounds of roaring lions in Ngorongoro Crater—the mist-filled volcanic throat rimmed by rainforest and teaming with wildlife just east of the Olduvai Gorge. Just off to my left from my vantage point on the crater rim were twelve elephants silhouetted in the early light, walking tail to trunk.

At the Ngorongoro Crater's edge were three Maasai—each standing tall, foot on side of leg in a resting stance, each holding a long, double-ended spear. Women in their bright yellow or red wraps stood near by, and gave the eye prime color contrast to a pastel landscape. The Maasai stared unabashedly at us, and they, upon approaching us, did not hesitate to take up conversation. Their earrings swung dramatically from long, stretched lobes as they launched Swahili questions at our small, unadorned ears.

A Maasai woman approached me; her rich brown eyes conveyed curiosity, and her approach was like a dance—her body swayed like the wind. She came close just to look into my eyes.

God entrusted his cattle to someone; he had to—how could he take care of them all? So he chose the Maasai.

Traditionally the Maasai measure their wealth by the number of cattle they are caring for. A tall, slender, handsome black man leans on his double-ended spear and gazes across the heat waves rising from the dry, grassy Serengeti. He tends to the herd. Time is hard to measure here, but it's done by the coming of new calves, by the brief seasonal enrichment of grasses, and by counting generations. Ancestors, back to the progenitors of the human race, practice the same watchful stance.

The Maasai man's red shuka is a flag in the wind. It is like a signal telling the lions to give way. Lions fear no man, except a Maasai—this protector of God's cattle. This man—in order to become a man—killed a lion by himself with his double-pointed spear.

The Maasai man will return to his kraal by nightfall. He will go through the opening surrounded by a fence of thorn bushes that keep out the lions, hyenas, and jackals. His cattle will follow him into this enclosure, this haven.

He will sleep with his wife in a hut she built from twigs and grass held together with a cement-hard plaster made from clay, cow dung, and urine. The fire pit will be hot, and the meat from a recent kill will be cooking. Dried cow dung and sticks will fuel this fire to cook food, to keep them warm, to add additional protection, to brighten the night.

He will make love to his wife on a bed of woven branches, grasses, and animal skins. He will hope for a son.

Olduvai

But humanity—my God, so many people.

Carved into the Serengeti Plain, Olduvai Gorge exposes the pages of human history. Like a scribe might chisel a barely legible text into stone, Olduvai reveals nearly three million years of geologic, animal, and human stratigraphy . . . animal bones—and those of the great ancestors of you and me, the early hominids.

The first time I walked through Olduvai Gorge, I couldn't believe all the bones. No wonder the famous archaeologist Louis Leakey came here—he couldn't go wrong. There are bones everywhere! I started picking them up—huge mammal bone fragments, teeth, jaws, fingers and toes—incredible. Among the bones and weathered rock were angular stone tools, crudely made by some early, self-aware being.

Olduvai—think of it. Imagine a small person walking westward across a dry lakebed just 27 miles south of here. The sticky volcanic Laetoli mud causes him to sweat. His small feet leave tracks that archaeologist Mary Leakey, wife of Louis Leakey, would find 3.6 million years later (1959). Mary Leakey, a *Homo sapiens*, would recognize the hominid species who made these tracks *Australopithecus afarensis*, one of our ancestors that had been discovered by Donald C. Johanson only five years earlier. Mary Leakey had found a male equivalent of *A. afarensis, Australopithecus (or Paranthropus) boisei*, in younger geologic strata dating 1.75 million years ago. But these foot prints were so much older, and indicated bipedalism in our ancient ancestors.

This *Australopithecus* person carries an animal skin bag with a few crudely made stone tools. Over his shoulder he carries a small gazelle, gutted and feet tied, like a backpack. A lion killed his companion during their hunting trip. Now he holds the spear tightly, trying to understand why his friend was taken—was it in exchange for the gazelle? In his animistic belief—that belief in nature—his reasoning mind tries to find the logic in the events of the day, but there is so much magic and mystery.

He looks about for danger: a lion, a hyena. But there are powers here greater than he can understand.

The earth suddenly rumbles as he approaches the streamside camp where his family is waiting. Ngorongoro is erupting again. It spews fine ash into the air, blotches out the sun. The small man runs—why is the mountain angry again?

As the small *Australopithecus* man reaches his campsite, he can see the ash eruption subsiding. His family runs to greet him. They notice the absence of his companion and understand. There is much talking, some crying, but thankfulness for the meat and the return of the husband and father. The father's youngest son holds his spear for him and looks out at the savanna wilderness, thinking of when he too can go on a hunt. Later, around a campfire, stories will be told of the hunt, of the loss, and of the myth and mystery in nature.

This ancient camp would become Olduvai Gorge: the birth of invention, of language, of faith, of family and a sense of the future. That is why it is important. And years later I would participate in the National Geographic Genome Project. In my DNA is a link to ancient relatives, one being a Neanderthal woman in North Africa and the Mediterranean, another being a Cro-Magnon progenitor in southern Europe. But all of me originated from Africa, and deep in my genetic memory are the links to the most ancient hominids, the early humans, and the interrelations with coexisting species like the Neanderthals. The NGGP also confirmed that, like everyone who came out of Africa, I am related to the root ancestor, the mother of all who migrated north, known as Mitochondrial Eve. Around 180,000 years ago she lived in a small village on the Nile River, now in the vicinity of Bor in South Sudan. Her distant relatives walked north from the Great Rift Valley and Olduvai Gorge and likely sat on the young rim of Ngorongoro, wondering in awe at the eruptions and keeping a keen eye on the game. We are part of the global whole—we are all Africans; we are a global genetic community.

Annulled

But in the here and now I am southwest of the Serengeti and several days into the trek with Audace Ntungicimpaye along the western regions of Tanzania on our way to Sumbawanga.

Seasonal rains pelt the savannah, resulting in mud that can imprison a foot. For hours it grabs at our tires and boots. We continue west across the ancient shield terrain. Another 400 kilometers finds us below one of the rift escarpments in the town of Mbeya, just north of the long lake called Nyasa—Lake Malawi.

Lunch is the usual bread, hard-boiled eggs, plantains, and water. The sound of a train imparts a long, midrange whistle call announcing the arrival of the Tanzam Railway into the new station at Mbeya. It is the line from Tanzania to Zambia. The train is chock-full of passengers and goods. Chickens, goats, cattle, luggage, people; it is like an ark.

By late afternoon low gray rain clouds afford only fleeting views of the towering escarpment wall outside of Mbeya town.

Time to a child passes slowly, time to the mother passes too quickly, and time to the Earth passes as it will.

Rain and time, a marriage of patience and persistence, wear down the rocks. Soil is the result—good stuff for coffee plants. We sample the brew from beans at the Mount Livingstone Hotel, where we hire rooms for the night.

The evening is long, quiet, and heavy. I am six months divorced, after almost two decades of marriage. But I don't feel divorced. She said she would annul the marriage in her church so that I would never have existed in her faith. Erased, forgotten . . . annulled. She said the whole town would forget about me.

My son had asked why this was happening. We talked a long time about too much work, too much travel, growing apart—none of that mattered to him; just the broken home he now lived in. In his Catholic school they had taught him to ask, "What would Jesus do?"

I just don't know!

I sit quietly, motionless in a wooden chair, watching the late-night stars just starting to peek through the diminishing rain clouds.

I find myself actually wondering what Jesus would say about all of this. He was a clever man, by all accounts.

I imagine in my solitary room in the Tanzanian darkness that he and I would have a good laugh about it all, perhaps over some cups of wine, which would never run short, of course, in his presence.

"Another round, barkeep," I'd say.

"No," Jesus would say, holding out his hand to cancel the order, "I've got it covered."

We'd open with small talk. "So what did you do in those years in between?" I ask Jesus.

"Wandered north, wandered west, mostly," he would say. "But everywhere I go people say, 'Don't I know you from the market?' or 'Didn't we graduate together from the temple?' Stuff like that. But you know, fame—eh, it comes, it goes." He would shrug; he would absently scratch his beard. "Fame is nothing one can rely on. It'll get you in the end. Know what I mean?"

"Yeah, I think so." I would sympathetically scratch my beard. "But tell me about this annulment thing. What's that all about?" I would ask.

I imagine I'm on my fourth cup of wine, the cup never seems to empty. It's red wine, of course. It's a *bloody* good wine!

"Oh that. Annulment—go figure. I suppose the powers that be must think marriage is like a television. You just turn it off and then pretend that no one is broadcasting. Don't sweat it; your kids are real, they'll figure it out for you." Then he would look at me with an expression of mild concern. "You okay?"

"Yeah, I suppose. Jesus, I'm tired," I would say.

"Yeah, me too."

ACT 2

Clouds Are Gathering

    D   Gdim A+D Gdim
I want to tell you what I saw
walking through the street last night, I heard a call.
Wasn't from my lover, wasn't from my friend,
but every heart will miss a beat when it's closer to the end.

     Refrain:

    A   G   D
    Clouds are gathering on horizon;
    A   G   D
    I wonder will it rain?
    Another hungry day; sun is rising.
    What you give is what you gain.

Lady said she cannot smile; turns to look away.
Child crying in the dirt, we're all made from this clay.
A tear tracks down her cheek, I brush it away.
In this human condition there's not too much we say.

     Refrain

I can feel the wind blowing all through this town.
I can feel the trembling hearts that will bring it down.
 Dry air underneath the sky, one more out stretched hand.
Another dream lost again. Another grain of sand.

     Refrain

Refugee

Audace Ntungicimpaye had been the deputy mines minister in
Burundi before the Burundi-Rwanda genocide. My company was
able to hire Audace and bring him to Tanzania. This, in his deep,
Swahili-accented English, is what he told me:

I am from Burundi. East Africa [in 1995] is
suffering from the atrocities of the Rwanda-Burundi
genocidal war. It is a terrible time in my home. I fled
Burundi with my family. I am a peaceful man. My
family has already suffered from the violence.

Roger is traveling to the refugee camps, and I
cannot go along, because I am a Tutsi, and many of the
refugees there are Hutu.

All of these horrific events are rooted in colonial
misdeeds. Before German colonialization of East
Africa in the late 1800s the kingdoms of Rwanda (to
the north) and Rundi (to the south) were strong and
well organized. They relied on a monarchy—a king,
whose bloodline was divinely linked. This was the
result of my bloodline of people, the Tutsi coming into
the Tanganyika area. They say through persuasion and
some force my people controlled the region and the
Rundi population. But we both became strong in that
joining. So strong were our people that the combined
Rwandans and Rundians were able to repel Arab slave
traders.

But my grandfather and many others fell under
the powerful guns of the German colonialists.

However, the Germans did not destroy our culture,
they just demanded obedience. But when the Belgians
took over after Germany was defeated in World War I,
well—it was all so different. The Belgians played upon

the Hutu-Tutsi differences. They spread rumors and lies and made flames of hatred.

I was the deputy minister of mines for Burundi. I have a doctorate degree from Paris. There are many well-educated people in Burundi and Rwanda—so I don't understand why we could not find reason and peace. I don't shoot guns. My wife and three sons had to leave. You see I am Tutsi, and my wife is Hutu.

No one knows for sure how it all got out of hand, but many suspected Rwanda president Juvénal Habyarimana. He was assassinated in 1994 and may have plotted the genocide as far back as 1993. But in the three months in 1994, in spring—the devil came to Rwanda and Burundi.

The Hutu militia used a code word—"*Gukora*"— for murder of the minority Tutsis. You could hear it on the radio. You could hear it on the streets. The Hutu retaliated for the Tutsi aggression. But more than a million Tutsis were murdered with machetes and guns and knives and by strangling or drowning when there were no weapons to be had.

Witness

I remember well the day when one of my staff geologists, Joas Kabete, came in from the field to the Dar es Salaam office. He was a wreck; he'd been crying, and he was shaking. I urgently asked him what had happened.

Joas said, "I have been to the Kagera River. I have seen the bodies." He choked up and tears welled up in his eyes. "You don't know what I have seen. I have seen the bodies. Hundreds and hundreds floating down the river. How can they do this? I cannot go on because of what I have seen."

Joas was shaking. "But how can they do this? How can they do this to people—there are men, women, and children in the river."

The bloated bodies fell over the waterfall and down the lake, and hell came down in Africa in 1994.

God could not save them. Is there a better afterlife? If there is, why do so many have to suffer so terribly in this life? Joas and I sat silently for a long time trying to find grounding for our sanity.

"Where is God?" Joas asked.

So now Rwandan prisons are full of Hutus charged with playing some part in the genocide—90,000 of them. The government is in disarray, financially destitute, and lacking even simple supplies. Now there is a tribunal to be set up to try the guilty, especially the higher-ups. Over the next ten years there will be 750,000 court cases filed. It will take decades to sort this out, but a delicate peace would eventually return. And years later my daughter, Madeleine, would visit Rwanda as a young news reporter and graduate student. She remembered my stories, and she told me of the powerful resiliency of people and of how even peace can rise from such ashes.

Attack

I receive a fax one afternoon.

URGENT
TO: Roger Kuhns,
  Africa-Mediterranean Exploration Mgr
FROM: Miles Shaw,
  Administrative Manager Tanzania

Roger—call on the satellite phone immediately. Our Luhuma camp in western Tanzania has been attacked by militia. Mortar fire started late in the afternoon. Everyone got into vehicles and evacuated in the opposite direction. There was gunfire. One of the vehicles was stopped. Two of our workers—they are okay—were told to get out and lay on the ground. The militia fired machine guns into the vehicle, and then all around our people lying on the ground. No one is dead. We are evacuating the area. Please call immediately.

Miles would later tell me that the men pinned down by gunfire were then left to fend for themselves until help could arrive, even as lions prowled the area.

The Camps

Against this backdrop, my team and I mobilized our response teams, and everyone was saved. The local managers—Geoff, Audace, Ferdinand, and Miles—and employees did a remarkable job of dealing with the event.

A month after the attack on our camp, I am invited to join an honored Canadian delegation to fly to Ngara to see the refugee camps.

Mrs. Verona Edelstein, the Canadian high commissioner based in Dar es Salaam, and her entourage of six other career diplomatic people crowd into a small aircraft.

Mrs. Edelstein is a spunky, reddish-blond-haired woman with the measured diplomatic tone in her voice.

"I am pleased you can join us, Dr. Kuhns," the high commissioner says. "We need all the perspectives possible on this refugee business."

"My pleasure, Madame High Commissioner. We've been here a while now, and want our staff to be safe. We have many Tanzanians in our employ. Our work in the area has brought about $9 million into Tanzania in just three years. But one of our camps, our Luhuma Camp, was attacked recently, and I was hoping to talk to one of the regional authorities about that."

"We'll help with making those connections," the high commissioner says. "As you know our interest here is large—Canada is donating $2 million towards the building and improving of roads in central Tanzania, Kagera Region, where your mineral properties are, and the refugees have camped."

Soon we're flying over the refugee camps near the Rwanda border. They are cities! Blue United Nations plastic tarps define the grass and stick huts. The narrow streets between the huts are muddy and crowded. We land on the dirt runway at Ngara—there we find half a dozen new Land Rovers, all with the neat, round blue UNHCR insignia stenciled to the doors.

Jacques Franguin meets us. He is the UNHCR field coordinator, a tall blond Frenchman who seems weighed down by fatigue. He welcomes the high commissioner and the rest of us. We pile into the Land Rovers. I am in with the assistant district commissioner, Mark Bakebula.

Mark Bakebula is a large and imposing man in a green military uniform. He says he is very concerned about the situation here. "These refugees are the Rwanda Hutus who fled from the Tutsi-dominated Rwandan Patriotic Front and aggression in Burundi. But also in the same area are Tutsis fleeing from the Hutu militia. You see them everywhere—here and Uganda and Zaire. Do you know there are three-quarters of a million refugees here now? It is a government in meltdown. That is what you are seeing here.

"Many people here hide guns in the bush outside the refugee camps. Some here are former prisoners who escaped jails during the genocide last year—these are the troublemakers. These Rwandan Hutus have conflict in their blood. I received word of your camp, that it was attacked by mortar fire. It was probably the rogue militia who hide amongst the refugee population."

All around us we can see the refugee camps, which drape the hills like a human carpet. The land around the camps is denuded of forest. There are nearly 720,000 refugees in western Tanzania in 1995.

We arrive at the largest refugee camp, Benaco, with over 211,000 refugees. The mass of humanity here is at once staggering and numbing. The multitude of faces is the first thing that hits me as I walk through the crowds. Thousands of eyes focus upon us. The people reach out and touch me: soft gentle touches. It is like a need to confirm our parallel humanities. They look to the aid workers for miracles, for food, for anything. The UNHCR, CARE, and CONCERN Worldwide workers—some of the thirty-three aid groups here—are clustered on the other side of this massive encampment, dealing with new arrivals. Five hundred people arrive every day—people who are just walking across Tanzania to find safety.

Bakebula says, "This is barely civilization, and this is possible only because of disaster relief money."

Looking into the mass of people it is clear that there is no economy here. There is no leisure time, there is no life planning, no work or education or retirement; it is just a refugee camp. People are waiting. Everything is temporary, yet these people seem to settle in to this improvised, stressed life in these ad hoc new cities of plastic and straw.

I am thinking—how lucky I was to have a home, and I blew it. I have no problem as daunting as these peoples'.

All around the crude huts are crops. The refugees sow even a single maize plant wherever there is room. Pushing each seed into the dry ground with a leathery finger. Maize and beans are the most common food.

Here and there great pots of a white sticky porridge are bubbling away. This is *bugali*, a local maize-derived porridge, kind of like grits in the southern United States. *Rica*, brewed from millet, and *mgorigori*, brewed from maize, are the local "beers" being made.

Along the roads are shallow pits in which garbage is burned. The bodies of the deceased are buried on the outer perimeter of the camp. I see a dead child.

Bakebula says, "These people have no idea how long they'll be here, so they get right to the business of making food. If you don't eat, you die. Africa has plenty experience at that one. But they can't stay here. But where do we tell them to go?" And within a year Tanzania would force these people to go back to Rwanda.

Jacques Franguin, the UNHCR field coordinator, says, "We have built a hospital here. Recently we dealt with a cholera outbreak. There was even a rumor that the dreaded Ebola virus from Zaire had reached here, but I don't think so." Jacques points to large canisters of water. "We get it from the river and a couple local wells. There is only enough for seven liters per person per day. It's all we can do."

"Is the water any good?" I ask.

Jacques shrugs, "Yeah, it's okay." He took me through the refugee processing. "Names and number of family members and their sex and age are recorded. We give benefits—so much per family, so the mothers tell their sons to sign up separately to get more relief benefits. Then they get a little UNHCR plastic card, which is punched each time rations are handed out."

We stand next to a line of people that goes on as far as I can see—hundreds and hundreds of people. I watch as a woman exits the tent and is directed to a huge bucket filled with purple dye.

Jacques says, "You can see after processing that each person dips a hand into a bucket of this purple dye. We have to do this, or else everyone will just turn around and getting back in line for a second ration card. The relief workers know many ways to get around it, but it's the best we can do."

We're helping them set up schools, churches, and markets so they can at least try to call it home. We have all the responsibilities of a big city, but with no infrastructure."

Around the camp are stern men standing in military poses. Their shirts say, "Guardian." Jacques tells me, "Community leaders are not dealing well with increasing crime. The district police and Tanzanian military brief these people you see here. There are also the Songusongu or vigilante militia who came from the Tanzania-Uganda war."

There is a sign describing the United Nations Centre for Human Settlements motto: "A home is not just a physical space where certain activities are performed. It is a value-laden symbol of warmth, security and identity."

Roots

I had thought it a root
washed free from soil's purchase
by sudden rains late in the season.
The twisted, gnarled plant looked so
much like fingers—
reaching in vain towards heaven.
In horror I realized
that root had held a mother's hand,
that root had reached for precious food,
that root had waved farewell to a father,
that root had shielded weeping eyes
from the evil hate behind a machete.
Dizzy and vomiting . . .
Staggering back . . .
Oh why is human life so cheap
in this red earth called
Africa?

Roger James Kuhns

Serengeti II

Just think moving life. A quarter million gazelles, nearly that number of zebra, and topi, buffalo, eland, wildebeest, hartebeest, gemsbok, and giraffe by the tens of thousands each—nearly 300 animals per square mile. Lions, cheetahs, jackals and hyenas, elephants and rhinos. And the birds—countless.

Horns, hooves, paws, teeth, hides, fur, and feathers.

And *Homo sapiens* with big brains.

One evening as a waxing moon rose over the Serengeti and the animals were crowding in their herds for the night, there came a blood-chilling inhuman scream, loud and terrifying—and suddenly cut off.

A lion had taken an animal. It was the sound of the food chain, the agony of the last of a life force, the anonymous death on the Serengeti. The zebra barked, and the wildebeest grunted as the herds shuffled nervously, remembering death is always near but not, for the lucky ones, at that moment. Moving life—transitions.

The Maasai woman is busy her whole life. There are few easy moments, but there are joyful moments. There is family and community.

As I watch the Maasai I feel that there is a greater understanding of partnership than what I think I sometimes see in the fast modern world on other shores. There is a greater sense of tradition and propriety than perhaps remembered when deadlines and bills and traffic and failed dreams surround my world back home in the cities. How can I better understand my sense of priorities when compared to this African template of survival and community?

The Maasai are good teachers. They teach by example; they are windows to the past and doors to the future. But wars and economics are closing in on these unique people.

Fetching water, milking cows, preparing food—the Maasai woman cleans a calabash gourd and prepares a mixture of honey and milk, water and cornmeal and cow blood. Her husband stuck a vein in a cow with an arrow and let the jugular blood flow into the gourd. She knows it will make him strong to drink this mixture.

She wears her beaded earrings and ornate necklaces to please her husband and to show their status and to adorn her dark slender beauty.

The Maasai woman's first son is coming of age, and she helps him prepare a headdress of ostrich and eagle feathers. He will have his head shaved, he will be circumcised and pass into manhood as a *morani*—a young warrior.

In the old tradition the boy would paint his skin red and then hunt a lion and kill it solo with a spear. He would hold the spear up, with one end planted at his foot. As the lion leaps at him, he would direct the point to the lion's heart. In the middle of a leap—in the air—the lion cannot change direction and would fall on the spear.

The boy would then be a man. But lions are not as common now, and the tradition has flexed to allow for this change. The rite of passage is acknowledged, and the young man's grandfather will now organize the celebration. There will be a girl, a young woman, who will want the boy who is *morani*.

Independence

Back in Mbeya, morning arrives with its chorus of barking and howling dogs. I'm pretty sure I don't have malaria, maybe it is just the heat or my workaholic syndrome.

I jot this note in my journal before going downstairs for breakfast:

> *Worlds rushing by one another.*
> *Ghosts to rile the hounds.*
> *Wine with Jesus.*

"Happy Independence Day," Audace says as he greets me at the simple table in the dining room. "December 9th already, and

Tanzania is free! Still!" Audace smiles broadly as the others gather in the room. "And we are still working!" Audace is very glad to have a job.

"Ah, as usual! And I don't feel independent! I live to work." I select two hard boiled eggs from a tin bowl; white bread toast is on the table. I dish up two roasted plantains, and a waiter pours very, very strong coffee. No sign of Jesus this morning; Audace and I break bread alone.

I tell Audace of the bishop's letter and my ex-wife's annulment plans.

"I don't understand," Audace says. "You have two children, how can you erase that?"

I point to a sign in the Mount Nelson Hotel that reads: *By wisdom a house is built, but by understanding it is established. Solomon.*

Audace and I both nod like wise men. Who am I fooling?

"She wants her independence," I say. "The annulment lets her remarry in her church."

"But in doing so, she denies all you had and what conceived your children."

"Yes," I say. "That's what that means."

The geology takes us far afield; it leads us like we're bloodhounds on a scent. There are grand discussions at each outcrop about how these rocks came to be. Once a volcanic island arc of some sort, they were crumpled between ancient continents and squeezed up into mountains and weathered down to the rounded surfaces we see today.

In this contorted mélange of rocks are gold and copper deposits— hidden treasures to a country such as Tanzania. If discovered and developed in an economically and environmentally responsible manner, then the people could greatly benefit.

But the environment is very much a back-burner consideration. Basic survival and low-paying jobs are the chief concerns of the bulk of the population.

Kids crowd around us everywhere we go; they stare at our clothes and pens and touch my white skin. Swahili is the language, and my grasp of it is weak, so Audace acts as interpreter when needed.

"Raja, the kids think your Bic pen looks very nice," Audace says to me.

"I suppose I'll incite a riot if I give one of the kids a pen."

"Likely so," Audace agrees.

One of the kids has a short stick and is writing on imaginary paper in the air in front of me, he smiles broadly at us hoping we will get the hint.

As I turn, I slip the kid the pen, such a smile.

"Asante!" ("Thank you!")

A cheer goes up in the crowd of kids . . . the White Man has given the Boy a Pen!!! Yeah!

Days drift by, my beard grows longer, and the villages become more primitive. We are modern travelers, almost nomadic in our own way. My team in East Africa is from Tanzania and Uganda, Burundi and Kenya, and one from Australia and another from America, and yet another from Mali. We have left families behind to wander these lands; it is a kind of wonderful independence one experiences in the bush, but one that has come at the cost of companionship.

Even with my fellow working companions, I feel very alone.

The kilometers tally up, and we turn the Land Rovers north along an escarpment that forms the edge of Lake Tanganyika. There have been intermittent gully washers, and some of the bridges are out; patches of mud lie in wait to trap unsuspecting vehicles. There is a lot of shoveling, pushing, spinning of wheels, flailing of arms, and flying of mud.

Bananas, mangos, and avocados recharge our energy levels.

We cross many steel-beam bridges as we drive. These are called Bailey bridges, after the British engineer who designed them decades earlier. But sometimes the steel in them has been taken.

"The Maasai take the steel," Audace tells me. "They hammer it down and make spear points out of it."

This makes perfect sense to me. The old Maasai don't drive trucks; they just walk across the low areas. And if you are walking, you'd probably rather have a good long spear to fend off the lions rather than a bridge!

Along the road I encounter a Maasai with two spears. I buy one of them—a six-foot-long, double-tipped spear to fend off lions. I put it in the Land Rover.

Audace says, with his own sense of humor, "Oh good—Raja—we're safe now."

We stop at a hut for dinner. There, in the dark, is a lone lantern and a tin table. A sign reads "Café—Open."

"Do you have any meat?" Audace asks the vendor.

"Of course. What would you like?"

"Do you have beef?"

"No."

"Do you have fish?"

"No."

"Do you have chicken?"

"Yes."

"Then we'll have chicken," Audace says.

Next we see the vendor chasing an old rooster around the yard. A flurry of feathers, twenty minutes, and we have a chicken dinner.

Dinner was fresh. But my God, it was tough.

ACT 3

Lions

I am thinking of lions again. One morning on our earlier trek across the Serengeti, I ran into a couple of lions.

Bones are everywhere—ancient and modern, the work of carnivores.

We had camped near the southern arm of Olduvai Gorge. We parked our two Land Rovers in an L shape and then put the tents in a curve to enclose the space between the trucks.

At night thousands of wildebeests and Thomson's gazelles roam about. We can see predator eyes glowing in the firelight, but their bodies are hidden by darkness. The pairs of eyes move this way and that, sizing us up, looking for an opportunity to do what they do.

I recall that it was a fitful sleep, as we had animals walking past the tents all night.

I was up at first light and rekindled the tired fire. I start walking around the campsite look for spoor—tracks from the animals the night before. Of course nearly everything is overwhelmed by wildebeest tracks, but I soon find sign of hyena and jackal. I walk out from the campsite with Paul, a friend who is also up.

Paul is the son of a Maasai, but he calls himself a "New Maasai" because he's gone to college. Paul is a geologist. His city instincts are stronger than his wilderness ones, and he tells me, "I have never seen a lion in the wild!"

I have my Maasai spear in hand.

Paul did not bring one. He says, "I knew I should have bought one from those guys we saw yesterday."

Those "guys" were Maasai warriors.

The grass of the Serengeti has been chewed to the roots by the immense herds.

But soon I notice we have walked about a kilometer from camp, and that is when we notice the wildebeests behaving peculiarly—they move this way and that and then part as two large lions dart out from the moving herd. Their musculature moves with grace and power as they trot along.

"Are those lions?" Paul asks.

"Yes indeed. And they are coming our way. So we best turn back toward camp. At least I have my spear to protect us!"

I long ago learned you never run from animals—they'll give chase out of instinct. So we walk with purpose toward the camp, and these lions angle toward us. These cats know geometry—they're taking the hypotenuse.

People who see or realize amazing things often "find faith."

So, here I am—facing the lions. Real ones. I'm thinking of this faith versus scientific proof; what do I believe, really? I'm thinking—lions in the Colosseum. And at this moment it really doesn't matter. Luck, faith, proof—law of the jungle, survival of the fittest, what does not kill you makes you stronger . . . all that stuff.

And what did *Australopithecus* think when the lions spotted him? "Oh boy, I'm a biped now; come on feet, make like a tree and leave." Very practical. Or, perhaps: "Yes, I ate some of your energy yesterday, so today you eat my energy." Very fatalistic.

And Einstein's faith? And Stephen Hawkins' faith? And Darwin's faith? And Schmidt's faith? And Hubble's faith? Faith in God? Faith in the scientific method? Faith in nature? Darwinism? As a geologist I think in terms of billions of years. Astronomers think in terms of billions and billions of stars; biologists—billions of cells, and chemists—billions of compounds. Scientists are always peering into the proverbial Eye of God—what do we see?

Well, I am at that point right now. These lions are coming closer . . . and they're not metaphorical. You know how urgency compresses time? How we can shift our realities into slo-mo so we can sometimes have a few extra moments to get things right? Well, that's not happening now.

"Let's see, how did the Maasai do this?" I crouch down and set one end of the spear at my foot and point the other end toward the lions, which are indeed getting closer. "Paul—have you done this?"

Paul says, "No! Besides, what are you going to do with just one spear—there are two lions? Look, the lions are closer, and we must walk faster."

"But if we run, they'll really give chase. I've got a plan," I say.

"Pray tell, what is it?" Paul says breathlessly as we power walk.

"It's a working plan."

"Is there any substance to this working plan?"

"Yes, there's substance, but it's in the works," I say.

But what I'm really thinking about is this—maybe God is just using the laws of physics to make things happen. I mean, if he or she made everything, then there would be a process to his or her methods, and maybe the physicists have stumbled on it. Maybe the molecular biologists and geologists and chemists and doctors have too, maybe also the fortune-tellers! Maybe God's whim is something like string theory.

And I am being annulled. I don't want to be annulled. The divorce is over, finalized—the ink has dried. But that's not enough; she's got to annul me. That means the marriage didn't exist; my kids and I are having a big problem with this. Maybe if I'm annulled, these lions won't see me!

I'm trying to understand what I believe, and why I believe it, what ever it is. Is this too much self-analysis? Am I being self-psychoanalytically Freudianistically weird?

Huh—look at that, the lions are definitely closer.
Paul is picking up rocks to throw at the lions.
What would Jesus do? He wouldn't throw stones—that won't work.

I mean think of it, all these religions, all these beliefs and rules and ways. "The way of the higher truths" or "the right way of living"— the Dharmic religions (from India), you know, Hinduism and the derivatives and relatives of Buddhism, Sikhism, Taoism, and Jainism and the rest—there's a bunch of them. There's a lot of *natural law spirituality* in these things.

And I have my science.

But Hinduism has the fundamental belief in the unity of everything; a totality called Brahman. Wow: unity of everything. String theory?

A Hindu belief is that we must realize we are part of God, and once we have realized this we can leave this plane of existence and rejoin God. There's a catch: it takes a few tries—gotta go through the cycles in nature, known as samsara, the cycles of birth, life, and death. Along the way we measure our progress toward enlightenment and assess our karma—the summation of all of my good and bad deeds does that. Whether or not I need to be reincarnated depends on how they balance. The good deeds mean I could be born at a higher level, and the bad ones—well, I'm coming back as a turtle or something.

Maybe a lion? Maybe a zebra?

But I have my science.

Buddhism seeks the middle way to enlightenment, not the extremes. But my life is extremes. I think that's why I'm *so successful* at marriage . . . strike two . . . too much adventure?

There's this reincarnation thing, going through the cycles of what we go through naturally: birth, life, death; wash, rinse, repeat . . . Presumably after going through this a number of times I'll learn to give up my dependence and attachment to my self and my desires and finally achieve nirvana—is that like heaven?

Maybe this annulment thing is part of a review, like in a company you get your annual performance review from the human resources department—maybe this is the Christian or Hindu or Buddhist or Islamic HR review method:

Let's see—Roger—you did well on production work. Okay as a father. Good marks on the budget stuff. Oooooh—you got annulled. Got to go through all this again. Sorry. Oh—and watch out for those lions—they're not in your career development plan. NEXT!

But what is our purpose for being on this earth? How can we annul someone? The refugees have seen unbelievable death in the face of their personal Muslim or Christian faith. How can this be balanced? How do we preserve sanity?

In the Abrahamic religions, Muhammad the Prophet followed some heavy hitters, such as Abraham, Moses, and Jesus. What did Muhammad do? He added formality and clarity to the Islamic faith. Allah is the just, omnipotent, and merciful creator. You can go to hell if you're bad, don't repent, and don't believe. The Islamic believers consider Jesus to be a prophet, not divine.

Well, that seems to be grounds for serious conflict by some, this we know.

Well, at least I have my science.

"CAN WE PLEASE WALK FASTER?" Paul is saying.

And Christianity—a breakaway sect of Judaism, which is of course the Jewish people's covenant relationship with God. So Islam and Judaism see Jesus as a prophet, but all these Abrahamic and Dharmic faiths have a merciful God. Are they really that different?

But in Christianity—*wow*—Jesus was conceived through the Holy Spirit and born from a virgin.

My son asked me, "Dad, if you're annulled, does that mean mom's a virgin again?"

Jesus was a teller of parables, a miracle worker, a teacher, a conqueror of death. Should I, as he recommends, "turn the other cheek" on this annulment thing? Well, you know what happened to him!

The animists believe in nature; I think the lions believe in that—they're getting really close. Some people believe in the Wizard of Oz. Yes, these lions are getting closer.

And now I have no home. I am annulled. I need a wizard of some sort. But there will be no clicking of heels to get me home from Oz.

The way I'm going on this path to enlightenment certainly means they'll be sending me back for another try to get it right.

Roger James Kuhns

Can't Ever Go Home Again

C   Am
Had a home once and it may show,
F   G
can't tell how the winds will blow.
No telling when a house is going to burn;
play with fire and you will learn.

Sometimes it lasts one's entire life,
to stick it out through the good and strife.
But I am just an ordinary man,
I don't fit into her hometown plans.

   Refrain:

   F   G
And it's all over town, it's me and them.
C   Am   G F
Can't ever go home again.
A big old twister has blown through my heart,
tore everything I had apart.
I need a wizard, I need a sign.
Guess you know I've run out of time.

Give me a candle I'll let both ends burn,
I'll even bet that the world won't turn.
There are corridors that I can't see,
I never thought this would come to be.

Can't see the future, don't understand the past,
I don't know when these dies were cast.
If I could read the very last page,
I don't think I'd walk on the stage.

Refrain

Throw the dice and place your bet.
Let's watch this cat get wet.
Jackals are yelping at the gate;
it's nearly dark—that's my fate.

Clouds obscure the full moon's light.
I look left, then I look right.
A voice is calling, I turn to see,
there's a figure approaching me.

Refrain

Well, as you can guess, my friend and I got back to the Land Rovers before the lions caught up to us—but they got within a few hundred feet.

Our bones would not be added to Olduvai on this day.

Sumbawanga

We arrive in the bustling town of Sumbawanga after a seven-hour spine-cracking drive over muddy potholed roads. The village is a wide spot in the road with buzzing bugs, howling dogs, the rattle of rain on tin roofs, and the acrid smell of poor sanitation.

I love these places.

Audace, the crew, and I are wet, muddy, somewhat bedraggled, and anxious for a meal that is not just fruit based. I need a shave and a haircut—my beard is long and scraggly. We all need food and showers.

In the dark, driving along the muddy streets of Sumbawanga, we find the Upendo View Inn Hotel. We can't seem to find the view, but it is paradise in the roughest sense, the Garden of Eden on $3 a day! We drink it in, along with the Serengeti beer we order in the Sumbawanga Bar. There are two waitresses, one at the bar, and one in the far doorway. The one in the door way is studying me. I lean back on the well-worn wooden bench of the bar and nurse the beer.

Talk is light, and I am suddenly aware that this diminutive woman in the doorway is really focusing on me. She approaches with great reverence, she holds her hand out in offering, her eyes grow wide and wondrous, and she speaks to me in rapid-fire Swahili.

I sit up on my bench and put my beer on the table. This woman's eyes are transfixed on my face. "Audace, what is she saying, what does she want?"

Audace touches the woman's shoulder, and she looks at this gentle giant of a man. Pointing at me she rattles off long Swahili phrases.

"What?" I ask. This woman has caught my attention; you see, I just don't have this kind of effect on women very often.

"Oh, Raja, I cannot tell you what this woman wants."

"Is it what I think it is? Just tell her, well, don't tell her I'm not married because I'm not married anymore, I'm annulled, and—I don't exist—well I do, but I don't—I mean—but, no!" I can't take another reincarnation.

"It is not that!" Audace says with a serious tone. "It is much worse."

"I don't know this woman, does she think she knows me?"

"Yes, she thinks she knows you, but she doesn't know you, well, not that way, it's all too embarrassing. Maybe she'll just go away."

But the woman stands there, and Audace, the field crew, and I just look at her. Some of the crew understand Swahili and start chuckling.

"What?" I ask again. Then the woman squeezes in between Audace and me and slips her arm through my arm and holds on tight. She looks up at me with big brown eyes, her head just reaching my shoulders. "What does she want? Audace you must tell me."

"Oh," moans Audace. "She thinks you are Jesus!"

As my jaw drops open in amazement, I realize I don't know what to do with this woman; she reaches up and strokes my beard. She takes my hand and holds it to her heart. "No! I am not he, tell her, Audace, that I am not he."

I am thinking about my Catholic son who was taught by his teachers to ask: *What would Jesus do?* Well, he'd just be himself, I guess. Jesus this is awkward.

Audace says, "I did, but she won't believe me. She says she has a picture of Jesus, and it looks just like you. She thinks you're Jesus! And she wants to take Jesus home!"

I wonder if the missionaries have a position on this issue?

I cannot help but laugh, and this makes her smile and pull closer to me. This woman thinks she is making Jesus laugh. I look into her uncomprehending face and say, "I can't feed the crowds without my credit card."

I look across the room, which is fortunately mostly empty, and spot a sign above the bar that reads: *Be kind to those around you on your way up, because you'll see them again on your way down.*

I'm thinking of the devil's view of baobab trees and my evening of wine with Jesus. And how the lions didn't get me, but my ex-wife did.

"Oh boy," I say to myself and pat the Tanzanian woman's hand. She stares in wondrous awe at me as I finish my beer. Jesus drinks beer! She then whispers something to me and rests her head on my shoulder.

"What is she saying?" I ask Audace.

"Oh, Raja, she is saying she is loving Jesus. Oh, she wants you home now, and she wants to make you food—cook Jesus dinner. She wants to kiss Jesus." Audace truly looks worried. His Christian sensibilities are being rattled.

"Well, tell her again I'm not Jesus."

Audace speaks to the woman again, but she shakes her head vigorously NO! "She won't believe me, she says you look like the picture."

And I'm thinking—we have evolved from the small family unit that had trekked across the Serengeti some three million years ago.

We have survived dangerous animals and natural upheavals. And here I am in the Sumbawanga Bar being mistaken for Jesus as I drink beer. Just after I've been annulled in His church!

Rinse, wash, repeat: I bet I'm going around again.

Jesus

After another few beers, and with my arm falling asleep from the woman's iron grip, I manage to extricate myself from her grasp. With a sincere nod I urge her to go back to work. But she follows me out into the bustling dirt street.

Across the street is the Love Station Theme Discothèque—no kidding. There's a disco in Sumbawanga, Tanzania. The owners have tried to create the true ambience of a discothèque. From the ceiling they've hung a mud ball with pieces of broken mirror pushed into it. They spin the ball and shine a flashlight on it—instant disco. The waitress wants to take Jesus to the disco.

Does Jesus even dance? I can see ballroom, but disco?

And I am wondering if Jesus would go to the disco. I am wondering if Jesus would somehow make the tough chicken dinner more tempting and tender; would that be with red wine or beer?

I am wondering what Jesus would be doing tonight in Sumbawanga.

And then I hear Jesus in my ear: "*Oh hey, don't worry about it. This kind of thing happens to me all the time.*"

Jesus in Sumbawanga

```
   D                                        G
I was minding my own business in the Sumbawanga bar
      A                    G              D
when a waitress approached me, like she'd seen a star.
```
She was pointing and talking in a different tongue.
She said, "You look like Jesus, God's only son."

Now she sat down beside me, real close.
She looked into my eyes like she'd seen the Holy Ghost.
She took my hand in hers and with trembling lips said,
"I love you Jesus, can I have a kiss?"

Refrain:
```
   A                              D
```
I said I only walk on water when the ice is hard.
I can only feed the crowds with my credit card.
I cannot take you home 'cause I lack a devil's heart.
```
   G                        A          D
```
So we drank another beer in the Sumbawanga bar.

Now she asked, "Would you please do a miracle for me?"
She sat there waiting for the parting of the seas.
In my beard and my jeans I said, "I cannot play this part!"
She didn't believe me, held my hand to her heart.

Refrain

There was music playing but no angels in sight.
There were mosquitoes buzzing in the hot African night.
She flashed me a smile, and I downed my beer.
She gave me a blessing; Oh man I'm outta here.

Refrain

Kwaheri, Tutaonana.
[Goodbye, we'll see you.]

Roger James Kuhns

RED RUSSIAN GIRL

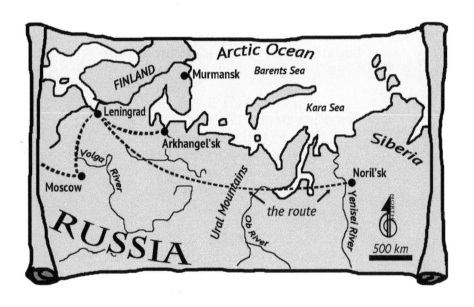

Opening

ACT 1
Attention: Welcome to Leningrad
Enter the Protagonist (1991)
The Street Musician in Leningrad
Noril'sk: Metals and Bones (1996)
Proletariat of All
Oktyabrskiy
Ludmila, the Translator's Point of View

ACT 2
We Visit Dante's Gates of Hell (1996)
The Gulag Survivor
The Red Russian Girl (1991)
Fields of Diamonds
Promoria Town

ACT 3
A Scientist Tries to Understand Life
The Matryoshka Perspective
The Russian Ballet

Opening

My traveling companion Hugo Dummett and I are standing in front of a Siberian hotel waiting for a bus.

"I never want to drink vodka again," I say to Hugo.

"Ha!" he replies. "That's no way to be a Russian!"

Alexi, our Russian friend and contact while in country, is opening a bottle of vodka and filling glasses—big glasses—full of the stuff. It's 7 a.m. He holds out the vodka with chocolate and tomato juice from a can. "Ahhh—this is what it is all about!"

"Vodka, chocolate, and tomato juice?" I say.

"Da!" Alexi says. "You know you are living if you don't fall over! Here. This will cheer you up." And he hands me the vodka.

"To not falling over!" I say, and follow the vodka with chocolate and tomato juice.

"Da!" he says. "You are standing like a Russian."

ACT 1

Attention: Welcome to Leningrad

Crowded airport waiting room.

The night is damp and cold in the dark forest of the living Russian ballet.

The Aeroflot jet that's brought me to Leningrad now sits on the tarmac—looking tired with its sagging wings like weary arms.

Humanity is shoulder-to-shoulder in the terminal. Pungent cigarette smoke defines the atmosphere.

Hugo Dummett stands a head above just about everybody in the terminal. Hugo is South African, with an Australian passport, an American green card . . . and a Russian visa. He's my friend and my boss. Hugo is a diamond expert and the man primarily responsible for discovering the new Canadian diamonds. His easy quick smile offers contrast to the severe faces of the airport clientele. We jostle with the Russians to grab our luggage.

A sign in the airport reads in English:

Attention. Welcome to Leningrad.
If you want to sell some things—welcome to Store Moskovsky.
You will get money immediately.

"Ah," Hugo says, "nothing like the American dollar to get a good Russian going!" He surveys the bustling chaos around us. Hugo's long Dutch South African face defines him as a foreigner—he attracts attention. His addiction to chocolate has helped add to his imposing size. Hugo commands the space he occupies. Me—I blend in.

Hugo pulls out a roll of US dollars. "We gotta get some rubles!"

"Jeez Hugo . . ." Before I can say anything else Russians crowd around Hugo.

One man leans in to Hugo, hand on arm, and whispers coarsely above the din of the room, "I give you much nicer prices than the government. Golden ruble price."

It's like throwing raw meat into a pool of sharks.

"Golden ruble?" Hugo says. "That sounds good."

"Very good," the Russian says.

"Whaddya think?" Hugo says.

KGB-like men dressed in black leather jackets cast their shifting eyes upon us.

"Hugo, you'll lose your visa . . ."

"Oh!" He stuffs the bills in his pocket.

The sharks drift away.

Blend in, blend in, blend in—it is the Soviet way.

But the *Soviet* is dead . . . now what?

<<<>>>

Late May of 1991 is a hungry time in the new Russia. Everybody is scrambling for the dollar, the deutschmark, the pound, and the underground "golden ruble" . . . worth a lot more than the official ruble.

Secretary general of the Communist Party Mikhail Gorbachev is less than three months from the coup d'état that will lead to his resignation. His policies are causing volcanic upheavals in Russia. It has been less than eight months since Gorby made his famous speech to the Politburo of the Central Committee of the Communist Party of the Soviet Union (September 20, 1990). In that speech he sought support for conversion of the USSR to a market economy.

But the men, women, and children in this airport look like they have been beaten down. They are hungry. Blending in isn't working anymore.

The company we work for is trying to be smart—to capitalize on the so-called "New Russia" investments. We want to partner with long-standing Soviet businesses. Hugo has sent some of his geologists to set up shop here. But Hugo and I also spend time looking at other opportunities, just the two of us. Hugo says that the company wants to drink vodka to glasnost and perestroika. But the company is really just a new actor in an old play.

I've heard most newcomers here suffer from a bit of stage fright once they see the script.

Enter the Protagonist
(1991)

Andre Sinitsyn—the New Russian. He oozes confidence—the kind you get from manipulating people or reading too many spy novels . . . or from being a spy.

Andre wears a long black leather jacket—kind of a Siberia meets the O.K. Corral motif. He offers a firm handshake—cold, a little clammy. His stance argues business: no nonsense, no smile wasted, no kidding—every angle an opportunity. Introductions are brief, and then . . .

"We must go to hotel," Andre says, and we push through the crowds and out of the terminal building.

We have been warned that he might be the new Mafia, or the Black Mafia, as it's called here—but we really don't know.

A taxi takes us from the airport to a grand old hotel. The building stands like a masked bourgeois madam posing uncomfortably among the proletariat masses. Inside are great empty spaces that were once— long ago—filled with stately furniture, smoking rooms, reading rooms, and vodka bars. The gift shop has just a few matryoshka dolls—those nested rounded wooden forms with the painted likeness of ladies in traditional costume. Shelf after shelf is barren. A young woman sits at a cash drawer reading a pulp novel. She doesn't look up.

But our attention is drawn to the central lobby. There, standing alone, is a beautiful woman. She wears a knee-length red coat. The coat is open to reveal a simple modest dress of the darkest red hue with a white lace collar over a perfect and enticing figure. She exudes temptation. The woman glances everywhere but at us. Hugo's eyebrows go up, and Andre smiles.

She turns toward us then—as if on cue. Her liquid eyes brighten in recognition. She waits for us to approach her and formally gives Andre a shallow hug.

"Hello, Daddy. Are these the Americans, the diamond experts?"

This vision before us is the dark spy's beautiful daughter!

Andre takes a long drag on his cigarette, pinching it between his thumb and forefinger, like giving his daughter the "okay" sign. He exhales and, as he does so, says, "Yes, allow me," and he gestures toward Hugo. Andre's smile is sanguine, partially concealed by a cloud of cigarette smoke. "Hugo, meet my daughter, Dasha. She will be accompanying us on our trip." Then to me, "And this is Hugo's colleague, Dr. Kuhns."

Dasha is slim, and her hair is braided and rolled in high-class fashion. She immediately zeros in on Hugo, for he is the one with the company signature.

"Ahh! Mister Hugo—the diamond man of world renown," she says.

Hugo breaks into a huge toothy grin.

Andre grins.

Dasha grins.

So much grinning here.

Hugo says, "I look forward to the next few weeks, seeing your beautiful county."

"And I more of you," Dasha says, tips her head slightly, eyes look down in faux submission.

Dasha touches my hand in secondary greeting. "Pleasure to meet you too, Doctor."

"Come," Andre says. "To your rooms to freshen some, then we have a big dinner planned for first night in new Russia!"

We are handed well-worn keys and take a creaking elevator to our floor. The rooms are Spartan. Mine has a TV—black and white, no stations. The room's atmosphere is chilled but stale.

Out of the cold water faucet: cold water. Out of the hot water faucet: cold water. There are several 4 by 6 inch sheets of waxed paper next to the toilet . . . reusable?

Dinner is at Bilesi, a small private restaurant in the heart of Leningrad. The space is warm and decorated in muted earthy colors. The waitresses are young, buoyant, light on their feet; I get the feeling one of them was perhaps a ballerina.

I look out from my front row seat before this human stage. Andre has strategically crowded Dasha on a bench seat next to Hugo. Hugo is center stage, and—from his body language—relaxed, confident.

Dasha is stage left, so as not to impede Hugo's right hand that he'll use to eat dinner. She knows that much. I notice she is using her left hand to eat—keeping the space between them open but close, her right hand free to touch Hugo's shoulder . . . "Tell me, Hugo, tell me about America."

He lets out a jolly laugh. "You would do very well in America!"

Dasha almost blushes. "No, I would need you to guide me."

The collar of Dasha's dark-red dress is loose layers of delicate white fabric that fall open with the slightest breath. Her alabaster neckline is graced with an equally pure white silk scarf, tied high and loose as if to imply modesty, as if to pretend surrender.

Dasha: "You wish to make business in Russia?"

Hugo: "Hmm. If we can find something good."

Andre: "You will like our diamonds."

Roger: "What kind of opportunities will we see?" I spread a spoonful of orange caviar on a slice of dark bread.

Andre: "Good ones. The best the world has not yet seen. Too many to count—like, how do you say it—shooting barrels full of ducks!"

Roger: "Fish in a barrel!"

"That too!" Andre roars in delight. "Have some *bustermei*." And he passes a plate of dried meat to each of us. "Here, please, more vodka."

There is no music in the restaurant Bilesi—excepting the Tiffany melody in Dasha's voice. There is nothing of background diversion, just talking in Russian and accented English, all soaked in lots of vodka.

Andre's eyes wander from Hugo to me and back. Andre uses his cigarette as a mask—holding it between Hugo and himself in a cloud of smoke when thinking, then lowering it—as if it were a saber— when he parries and thrusts to make a point or seek an advantage.

"I looked at your very big company. Very big—very good. That's why I agreed to invest my resources in showing you Russia. You are pleased to be here when you see our diamond mines."

Andre takes a drag on his unfiltered cigarette. "Let me tell you about one of our heroes. Mikhail Lomonosov! Lomonosov is the Michelangelo of the Soviet Union! You see Russia is very high class because of such people. He was a scientist and a poet and an artist. It is all possible here for you!"

Dasha says, "You know Leningrad is called the Venice of the North."

Andre says, "But now look at what we are. We need your investment. Your US dollars investment. I can handle all of that for you."

"Lomonosov—that's the diamond field to the north," I say.

"Precisely. In his honor. We go there soon." Dasha's presence dances amid our discussions. Every movement and pose is choreographed to divert attention. An unfocused mind makes mistakes and leaks information. They wish to gain a share of the foreign money that is entering Russia. They compete against many. There are no rules. And the prize is so valuable.

I think Andre wants to be like an American—what ever that is. He looks us over like a pickpocket . . . *I deserve this!* Or like a small-town tourist gazing at a Hollywood movie star . . . *that should be me?*

Maybe more like an old man lusting after a young girl . . . *I must have you!*

The orchestra in my head strikes up Tchaikovsky as scenes from the 1917 Revolution, the gulags, the Cold War, and Gorbachev's perestroika march before a rising curtain. I am thinking—how do people change a country such as Russia? How do they overcome this Sisyphean task of rolling the ideological boulder uphill for so many generations?

The Street Musician in Leningrad

I encounter a man playing a guitar on the corner of a lesser street near city center in Leningrad. Hugo is talking to Dasha, and she doesn't notice as I slip away.

"You like my music? Da? You are not from here—you have Sears and Roebuck cloths—da? American? I thought so.

"Please to make a donation to a good cause—the hat is open!

"I am Vadim Vorontsov. I am a teacher, but there is no money in it. So I play for tips from rich tourists. I hope you are rich. Nyet? Too bad.

"I am playing for a dollar or a pound! You have to know where to stand, how to catch their eye—especially the lonely old ladies from America. They love me. They sometimes put dollar bill in my hat, but first hold it up and say, '*THIS IS AN AMERICAN DOLLAR BILL.*' Like I wouldn't know.

"I make vodka money here, yeah, maybe more sometimes. The police bother me. No, they don't like music. Only I get just five hundred rubles each month for teaching. Let me see—that is a hundred dollars, I think. Not much, I think. Fifty rubles from guitar, and I don't tell no one in government about that. The tax is so heavy, thirty percent for me. So it goes fast, three hundred rubles for food, a hundred rubles taxes, fifty rubles for rent. As you can see, I am a handsome single man, but there is not much left for anything else.

"Ah—pardon—a couple approaches." Vadim launches into an energetic guitar instrumental but then thumps his guitar as he watches the couple walk past without note.

"Not even a kopek—must be New Russians—cheap. That, my friend, is perestroika!

"We have nothing to be proud of, but we are not starving yet!

"Isn't perestroika a good thing, you ask? It is this way—yes, yes, yes, I think Mr. Gorbachev's belief is good—it is about freedoms. It is speaking free like you and me are doing. It is about freedom in elections and all of that. But perestroika comes, and nothing is predictable. Food is not delivered, and then crime comes. This is a huge clash of Communist control and what you have in America, what you call it? Market economy? BANG—that's it!" Vadim harshly strums a minor chord on his guitar.

"Perestroika is the head-on crashing of Communist control and your market economy freedoms. That's why Gorby has that mark on his head—banging it against the wall! Look out there, those lines—longer, longer, longer." Vadim points across the park to a line of people along the street. "And for what? There's nothing in the stores. At least with the old boys we got food.

"So you ask if I want to go to America? America, oh, that is my dream, to go to America! As you can see, I have an 'AMERICAN DOLLAR BILL.'" Vadim holds up the bill, shaking it like the old American women do. "Ah, America. Are there lines there? I will dream there are not.

"You know a lot of Russians want the New Russia. Da, it is true. But they are not necessarily the ones in power. I see very much from my place here on the street. Politics! Ha—music is much better!

"Now look at that beautiful woman coming to hear me play! Maybe not? She looks unhappy and is looking at you, Mr. American. Hmmm—I think I recognize her.

"PAR JOUL STA!

"Maybe you will remember me when I go to America? Da? DOSVEDONYA."

I drop a ten-dollar bill in Vadim's hat. This fuels a rousing gypsy piece, but—alas—Dasha is not dancing. There is the slightest wrinkle in her perfect brow, indicating her mistake. She let me slip away and talk to an unscripted character in this Russian ballet of her father's.

Noril'sk: Metals and Bones
(1996)

I want to take you to Noril'sk before we look at diamonds. To do that we'll jump five years into the future: Noril'sk in 1996—seventy-nine years since the revolution, forty years since the gulags closed, and five years since perestroika.

But what is this place, this Noril'sk? It is one black dot on my *National Geographic* map of the Soviet Union. It was a gulag. Noril'sk remains the largest copper-nickel-platinum deposit in the world. A buried treasure mined by prisoners who had done no crime—except to think freely.

In 1996 Boris Yeltsin is more than halfway through his presidency of the New Russia; halfway through his term of ruining Russia. He drinks heavily. He forgets things. His health is questionable. He doesn't understand economics. He doesn't understand environmental protection. He's forgotten what people need. The Black Mafia is thriving, and wealth is being sequestered by the few, not the many. Yeltsin scowls a lot. He knows the Communists are again taking control of the government. This will ultimately inaugurate the era of Vladimir Putin and secrecy and control of the media, only three years away. Russia will change again. But Putin—something of a self-described social democrat, perhaps more of a sovereign democrat-wannabe-dictator—will also try to salvage Russia from Yeltsin's incompetence. Putin would become his own ideological guidepost, a strong-arm approach defined by a chaotic clashing of inconsistent military, economic, financial, political, and social themes.

Still the gulags haunt the older generations. They do not let Mother Russia forget. As long as there are grandmothers and grandfathers it will be remembered.

In the midnight distance from the airport, the lights of Noril'sk reflect off the ashen underbelly of low clouds. Our bus is carrying a dozen of the company's geologic staff into the Siberian town after a flight halfway across Russia.

The huge smokestacks of the nickel smelter are eerie monoliths belching dark poisonous fumes in the sodium-lit night. Heavy-duty cranes stand like ghostly skeletal images of extinct dinosaurs. Silhouettes of colorless square buildings and spiderweb-like power lines paint a bleak and desperate image that is this remote arctic town.

"My *GAWD*," Hugo says. "I had no idea this place was like this."

Someone in the darkness says, "The company wants to buy this place?"

Another says, "Buy it! Who'd want to even work here?"

As we drive by the apartments, I notice the ones with lights on are full of green plants. The occupants have created personal forests to stave off the gloomy introversion of Siberian darkness. Along the streets are kiosks selling vodka, videos, and cigarettes—distractions, diversions, and addictions.

We check into the Noril'sk Hotel by 12:10 a.m. About half of us toast to our arrival over vodka with smoked fish victuals.

Proletariat of All

This morning in Noril'sk we eat bread, cheese, one hard-boiled egg each, and strong brown tea thickened with sugar. A small, rectangular, high-ceilinged room is our dining area, and we sit hunched over on benches along the walls in the chilled air. The food tastes good, being spiced with urgency of hunger and the shiver of cold. There's no heat because it is only zero degrees outside.

"We turn the heat up when it gets cold," one of our Russian chaperones says.

On a low coffee table one of the American managers counts out $35,000 in hundred dollar bills from a suitcase under the intense gaze of a Noril'sk Mining and Metallurgical Company representative. There are a dozen of us on this invited exploratory business and science trip. The Russians want our mining company to assess and hopefully make an offer to partnership with them. This, in their mind, would lead to a life-saving influx of foreign cash and expertise to repair and modernize all that is here in Noril'sk. For this *honor* the Russians are charging us $2,500 each—in cash—to visit and assess the mines. The Noril'sk Mining and Metallurgical Company representative's assistant recounts the hundred dollar bills, and his associate recounts them yet again.

One of our guides, Alexander Stekhin, sat next to me; his nickname is Sasha. He's a good-natured, round-faced, large-bellied geologist with thick, dark hair and an easy smile. Sasha is a geologist with the Noril'sk Mining and Metallurgical Company. He is one of our main sources of information, or at least he is directing us toward where to get the information. "That is many dollars!" he says, his eyes unblinking and focused trancelike on the currency. "That is many, many dollars! You know, it would take me, ah . . ." He looks up at the ceiling and says, ". . . ah well, a many big number of years to ever see that much." Sasha can't take his eyes off the stack of bills. "That is more than my life."

"What would you do with all that money?" I ask.

"Ha!" comes the sharp, almost cough-like response. "I would drink and screw until I die of it!" Several of us laugh at that, but Sasha is not kidding. He's a scientist, but also just past young, handsome, fun-loving, and utterly enamored with Western ways, and utterly addicted to vodka. "I hate it here," he whispers coarsely to me.

Once the financial transaction is concluded and the suitcase full of cash vanishes with the Noril'sk Mining and Metallurgical Company representative into a back room of the Noril'sk Hotel, we are told to load up into a bus.

"Today," Sasha says, "we go and look at maps and get a boring lecture. Bring much vodka. You will need it." He yawns as if punctuating what we will experience today.

In short order we are standing in the hall of one of the mine offices awaiting the chief geologist's arrival. This is where we are to be given a geology lecture before visiting the mines over the next few days.

A woman is introduced to us. Her name is Atiane, and she stands rigidly among her hardened male comrades with hands folded in front of her; she is enjoying the moment of foreign company.

In the woman's smile is a gleaming gold tooth. She notices me and her grin broadens. Atiane is wearing bright pink lipstick, with eyebrows painted sienna brown in high, surprise-like arches over pale, early winter skin. The gray stiff dress and forest green suit coat combination hangs on her sturdy frame like it might have come from the factory. Atiane's garb makes it impossible for me not stare at the contrast. She is the only woman geologist working at the Russian copper-nickel Komsomolsk Mine in 1996; one of many contradictions in this former gulag town of Noril'sk. As we wait, I strike up a conversation, asking her about her life here.

"I am here since university. Some years now," she says in response to my question. Her smile cracks the pink lipstick and bits of it dapple impossibly white teeth.

"You live in town now?"

"Of course, there is nowhere else. It is better than most . . . now." Atiane's face suddenly clouds as her smile vanishes to a thin, tight, pink line, like a scar, and her frown struggles against the painted arched eyebrows. Her body tenses. The chief geologist approaches from down the hall; percussive footsteps on the wooden floor announce his arrival. He gives Atiane a sharp nod. She looks at the group and motions to a doorway.

"In here, if you please," Atiane says, herding our group of geologists into a dark paneled conference room. The walls are ornamented with Siberian woodland scenes inexpertly painted by local talent, the table is heavily lacquered spruce, and the dull carpet is worn under the dark wood chairs.

There are no windows, not that the gray October sky would advance much solace to the cloistered ambiance. Atiane takes a military stance under a red banner with Lenin's portrait, below which is written in gold embroidery:

Proletariat of All Nations Unite
—Under the banner of Marxism & Leninism—
Under the management of the Communist Party
Let us advance to the victory of communism.

But the confident slogan and rigid posture are juxtaposed against Atiane's painted face, which rebuffs this ennuyeux Siberian post. Even so, she seems to bend ever so slightly before the stern glare of Comrade Lenin.

I am so very aware that as a visitor I will be able to leave freely.

"We are proud to be here working at this great mine, and we are proud to be here and show you our work, ask any question you desire!" Atiane announces, and then she introduces the chief geologist, Dr. Tiltyn. Soon Dr. Tiltyn is lost in a tedious and not terribly informative presentation about the mine.

Sasha, as promised, is nodding off during the chief geologist's lecture, and his head bobs, jerks up, and he looks around the room bleary-eyed. "Still talking?" he mumbles to me.

There are questions during the talk, and we ask about metal resources, things like how many tons of ore and what concentration of metals exists in the rock. All Tiltyn says is, "We have enough for our grandchildren!"

"Hah," Sasha mumbles again. "Careful, he'll make you a miner, and you'll never get out!"

Sasha hints at the separate reality that seems to exist here, the independent time line, the lack of any sense of economic imperative or environmental impact or recognition of the human need for dreaming.

Some people here don't even know where they are. At one point I pulled out my National Geographic map of the Soviet Union and showed a miner the location of Noril'sk. After overcoming the shock that I—an American—had such a "top secret" map in the first place, he said, "That's not right, that shows us north of the Arctic Circle, and we're supposed to get bonuses for working up there. This map can't be right!"

Chief geologist Tiltyn's monotonous lecture continues. I remain distracted, struggling to grasp the enormity of events here—both human and geologic. Here is one of the world's greatest natural concentrations of strategic metals. The numbers are staggering as we learn the story of how billions of tons of ore were formed in this ancient rifted land. But between the lines is the other story of how more than a hundred thousand people were forced to mine the mineral deposits.

Atiane sits in the corner feigning interest in Tiltyn's lecture; her surprise eyebrows seemingly mock all that is here, challenging the status quo, seeking identity. She represents a daub of color in the sepia world of Noril'sk.

Sasha reads my frown, "Yes, it is same as before. Nothing changes here."

"Can't people leave here, go some place better?"

"You Americans! We can't just pack up and move like in your country. Where do we go from here? We need papers, we need money and work, we need ambition, we need—we need—we need, and we don't have!"

And there it is: nothing changes here. No matter the political regime, no matter the world economy, no matter the plea for human rights—the metal must be mined, and the miners must work. It is a point-in-time existence for many. Certainly a measure of freedom has arrived in this post-Soviet experiment, and more importantly an inkling of hope. Some of the scientists here have even been able to attend international conferences and conduct research overseas. But that is not the majority. The music of progress is still just crackling static from distant transmitters that do not understand the irresistible forward momentum of such a place as Noril'sk. I will forever see a copper penny differently.

<<<>>>

Down by the Noril'sk River, long after dark, we join a group of miners, engineers, and geologists for a home-made dinner of pickled fish, sausage, ham, potatoes, and lots of Stolichnaya vodka. We immediately begin the toasts—to miners getting paid, to better ore being found, to more American dollars—that one from Sasha. Traditionally the third toast is to all the women in our lives, and then you smash the glass: the more pieces the happier they'll be, perhaps finally there will be a reason for Atiane's surprise eyebrows. The toast is made by balancing the glass of vodka on your arm and then in a rapid balanced motion tipping it into your mouth. The difficulty increases with successive toasts due to larger volumes of vodka.

Sasha says, "Here is to all of our new friends!" There are hearty agreements as glasses are drained. But then stillness overtakes the room—that pregnant moment that sometimes befalls careless conversation. Somber faces look down at the floor for the briefest of moments as we hold the future within us like holding a breath in our lungs before we can surface from this deep pool.

I slowly exhale and sense the ghosts of the gulag are silent tonight, waiting, as always, for the music to start.

Oktyabrskiy

My bedside alarm wakes me in the dark. My bed was an inflexible slab of some ancient material, and the covers thin and insufficient. The lone forty-watt bulb seems like some beacon in the shadow of morning as I mechanically dress. I hear others walking outside my door. Down the hall is breakfast.

Alexi Stekhin—aka Sasha—joins me. Today we are to continue our assessment of the mines and mills of Noril'sk and its sister city Talnakh, about sixteen miles north where there are more high-grade reserves.

"You sleep well?" Alexi asks me.

"Fine," I say, and chew on the cold ham I've been served.

Alexi smiles through a hangover from last night's impromptu gathering. "It is not an easy place to love. You know, I told you yesterday. I hate this place."

"Noril'sk?" My mind is fogged from the medicinal impacts of last evening's vodka. I could not even begin to keep up with Sasha.

"Da. Not easy. But this is where we work." He spreads some lard onto his breakfast roll, scoops it through the runny cold eggs, and takes a bite. "I love three things!" Alexi says through the mouthful of food.

"And?" I ask.

"First, of course, my wife—because I have to. Second is the famous geology professor from Canada, Tony Naldrette—because I want to; he's so smart to understand Noril'sk geology."

"And the third?"

"Ah—you, of course, because I need to! You and Hugo and all of you bring this town hope. Maybe, eh, you fix this place?"

"It will be very interesting to see the mine and mill complex," I say.

"You and Hugo and the others will study Noril'sk and Talnakh deposits. Tiltyn's lecture yesterday did not even scratch surface." He waves his hand as if in dismissal. "You will see. Irresistible wealth like nothing you dream." Sasha then bends toward me, leaning on his forearms, the smell of egg, vodka, and ham on his breath. His hair is a chaotic tangle. But suddenly his eyes are sharp and focused. He says, "But such places as Noril'sk is a great weight on the Russian heart. There is no trust because of places like this. Not everyone you meet wants you here. But do not lose heart. Me, I love the New Russia. It is our future now. You know about Noril'sk? You are learning. It is from 1935. The government needed the nickel, copper, cobalt, and platinum ore that was found—how you say—for fuel for Stalin's military and industry."

"So they brought in engineers and miners?" I ask. I too am leaning forward. I have a sense that the scene looks Bohemian, two conspirators exchanging information.

"No! The engineers back at the warm government offices in Moscow told Stalin the Noril'sk region was too cold to allow successful mine to be opened. Do you know Stalin's response? *Nyet!* So on June 25, 1935, Stalin ordered a gulag to be opened. He sent 1,200 prisoners, the first of many, to build the town and dig the mine."

"What had the prisoners done wrong?"

"Nothing!" Sasha pauses from the outburst, and runs his hand through his unkempt hair. He says, "They were teachers and philosophers. So Stalin said to his engineers, 'See, the prisoners proved you can live and work in these conditions.' I am thinking maybe some of the engineers ended up here, too, for making bad advice."

"What happened to these people?"

"Well, many died. But you will see some survivors around town. They are very old now."

So it is on this footing, we drive out into the cold October morning to see the mineral deposits of Noril'sk and Talnakh, a bus full of foreign geologists, engineers, and speculators from the mining company where Hugo and I work.

On the bus I am sitting next to our translator Ludmila Kovaleva.

She points out the window at the buildings, one partially completed. "A new project," she says, "but it is a new project for ten years. There are not enough monies to finish it. We need help for that."

Ludmila is a round-faced, pale-skinned, forty-five-year-old working woman.

"Your English is very good," I say.

"It had better be, I am your translator!" she says.

"How did it happen that you came here?"

"Oh, that was a long time—eighteen years now. There were no jobs in the south, and I went to university studying English. They needed a translator here, so I came and stayed. I was twenty-seven then, now my daughter—she is twenty-three now—is here still and working as an environmental engineer."

"That must be a challenge."

"You cannot believe how much that is true," Ludmila says. "What this place has done to the water and soil, to the air and the people—it is not good. We need help with that, too."

"Where do you start with such a huge problem?"

"I do not know, I cannot conceive of how big it is. You will see. You will see." She pauses and then looks up as we drive through a gate to one of the mines. "Ah, here we are—Noril'sk's sister city called Talnakh."

From what I can see this sister is just as hard-featured as the other.

Alexander Lamzin, the chief engineer for Noril'sk Nickel Incorporated Oktyabrskiy Mine, greets us as we exit the bus. Lamzin is dressed in a neat light tan colored suit and red tie in contrast to the disheveled and antiquated mine complex around him. He leads us into the office.

"You are privileged to be at Oktyabrskiy Mine," Lamzin says. "We are 40 percent of Noril'sk metal product—we have 1,500 miners here. And here are the good quality maps that explain everything."

I notice there are no north arrows, no dimensional scales that would provide size information.

"What is the grade of the ore," Hugo asks. We have much of this information, but want to confirm our data.

"It is very high. It is very good," Lamzin says.

"But what are the percentages?" I ask.

"They're very rich," Lamzin says again.

Alexi leans toward me, "That's right, he's right, the ore is very rich." He writes in my notebook the ore metal grades of the industrial metals, such as nickel, cobalt, and copper, in percentages and the precious metals, which are rare, in grams per ton, and then the relative percentages of these metals in terms of the global resource relative to other mineral deposits:

	Average Grade	% of Global Reserve
Nickel	1.8%	35 %
Cobalt	0.6%	14 %
Copper	4.5%	10 %
Platinum	2.5 g/t	20 %
Palladium	9.7 g/t	55 %
Rhodium	0.3 g/t	3 %
Gold	2.0 g/t	<1 %
Silver	15 g/t	<1 %

Lamzin sees Alexi scribbling the ore grades and pauses to look at the numbers. "Yes, those are the right ones, yes. I could tell you that, but now you have it."

I get the feeling he has been told to cooperate and tell these foreign scientists facts that have been state secrets for his entire career. There is a huge political-professional conflict here.

I ask, "How much of the earnings from metal sales come back here for maintenance?"

"Let me tell you," Lamzin says. "The Noril'sk Mining and Metallurgical Company earned $2.4 billion from selling these metals last year."

"And profit?"

Lamzin looks like he has stomach pains the way he wrestles with the release of information. "Yes, OK, let me tell you. After sales the company had 160 million U.S. dollars in profit. That is good I think."

"But," Alexi says, "Moscow only gives us a low platinum price—only 65 percent of the market price. That is not so good I think."

Lamzin scowls. "Even so, we still have a 7 percent operating margin, and that is good, I think."

"Well . . . ," I say, realizing they have just said they're making the smallest of profits, but that there is essentially no money for maintenance and improvements. The bottom line is the facility is bleeding money.

Alexi says, "Just you imagine—you could make it run like a Mercedes, you could make so much money here, don't you think?"

Hugo is smiling. "I think there's a lot of work to do here first. But," and he looks Lamzin in the eyes, "I see what an amazing resource you have here. World class!"

Lamzin smiles, and says, "Yes we know that already. Enough talk now—it is best we move on. Now it is time to go into the Oktyabrskiy Mine."

We follow him down the hall.

In the changing room we prepare to go underground. Soon we are fully outfitted with coveralls, jackets, hard hats, mine lights, and self-rescuer filter masks. This last item is a filter mask that converts deadly carbon monoxide to carbon dioxide should something go wrong in the mine. Carbon dioxide will kill you slowly, but carbon monoxide will drop you in just a few steps.

We tromp into the cage—a metal elevator that can hold a few dozen miners. The mine foreman sends the lift operator a signal by pulling on a bell rope. The cage seems to freefall into the black hole of the mineshaft. We are in the guts of Siberia.

There are no sides on the cage—just a railing—so we can see the rock walls of the 24-foot-diameter shaft. The lights from our hard hats are simply absorbed by the darkness below. We drop at 27 feet per second. My ears pop ten times. It is noisy—wind rushing by, metal-on-metal rattling, and loud talking in Russian.

The cage bounces on 1,800 feet of steel cable as we settle at one of the mine levels. Bare lightbulbs illuminate the chiseled rock walls, and without talking we climb into a narrow-gauge rail train. This clatters a mile down the mine tunnel.

The train stops, and we walk a half mile to catch a tramcar, and this takes us through a winding set of tunnels.

Here in the mines opened by political prisoners are a dozen geologists clamoring over the scientifically fascinating rocks of Noril'sk. Our thoughts are not of the situation and politics that forced this mine to exist, but of shiny samples and rare mineral crystals.

It is here that we see the incredibly rich copper-nickel-platinum ore of Oktyabrskiy Mine.

Between 200 and 250 million years ago the Siberian craton cracked from a rift, and molten rock forced its way to the surface. The basalt lava flows flooded the interior regions of the ancient continent, covering over two and a half million square miles. We call this the Siberian Traps Igneous Province. There was so much eruptive lava and gas lasting for tens of thousands of years that it contaminated the Earth's atmosphere. This caused what geologists call the "great dying," the Permian extinction. This was a global mass extinction event that killed over ninety percent of the planet's species. It would take tens of millions of years for the Earth to recover. I recalled the smelter fumes we'd experienced on first arrival, and how the mining and recovery of metals was once again poisoning the atmosphere, just as the volcanic event of Noril'sk's birth had. Even now the mineral deposit claims lives.

Geologists' views of how the Noril'sk-Talnakh metal deposits formed differ, but one thing is certain—the ultramafic magma rich in metals was injected into north-trending faults along the western edge of the craton. It moved upward in the earth's crust and digested metals from Proterozoic rocks and calcium sulfate minerals (anhydrite) from the layer-cake-like Paleozoic sedimentary rocks. This added sulfur to the magma, and a chemical reaction ensued. The sulfur bonded with metals from the magmatic soup. Nickel, cobalt, copper, platinum, palladium, rhodium, gold, silver, and iron hence formed sulfide minerals. These minerals, now solid and heavy, rained out of the magma and accumulated like sand grains on the floor of the huge chamber. This happened over a long period of time, and huge quantities of metallic sulfide minerals accumulated, almost two billion tons of ore. They ultimately cooled and hundreds of millions of years later would be called Noril'sk. This is how the wealth of a nation's metallic natural resources is born. But it takes people to mine it. Sometimes against their will. Sometimes because they have no other choice.

We stand in wonder at the massive sulfide wall—it glints yellow and light brown and white like polished gold and brass and platinum. Like crazy troglodytes, we charge the metallic wall and grab handfuls of samples.

But I wonder, are we that greedy? It is too easy, sometimes, to forget how this came to be. Can we find the balance between business imperatives and political dogmas and social responsibility and humanness?

Ludmila the Translator's Point of View

"It seems I am waiting all the time. Today it is for the foreign geologists to come out of the mine so I can translate some more. I don't like being in the mine. Yes, I know the miners might get more money, but I want to see the sky. Besides, a mine is not a good place for a woman.

"I am Ludmila the translator here. My job is fine. It is better than most places to work; I am told that. I have been here a long time now. But they don't pay us sometimes; sometimes for many months.

"The mining company gives us instead a plastic card to use. It is like a credit card in Europe. They give us the card to buy foods and supplies we need. Then they take that which we have spent out of the money they owe us. Very often we never see any money. And they charge us interest on the purchases. That is not fair, because we would not use the plastic card if they paid us our salaries. I do not like the way the mining company works.

"And the company won't pay for our heat or water. No! Not either—if you believe me. I have a nice apartment on Lenin Avenue, but I am not having heat there for a long time. It is very cold sometimes. It was better before 1991. At least when the Communists were in control we got paid and had heat. Now—we never know what to expect.

"And perestroika! Don't tell me about that bad idea. It is because of that crazy Gorbachev that we are in this situation.

"I do not like communism, but it is too hard now. I hear about the theories the politicians are talking about. I hear that they say it will be better for us someday. But I am not happy now. I am not a theory, I am a woman. I have to live here every day. And every day we are forgotten, well, is another day that is very hard. It is not easy transition. And I am unhappy about President Yeltsin, too. He doesn't do a good job. He forgets about us.

"Ah—here are the geologists now—and look they have their hands full of rocks. They are crazy men!"

ACT 2

We Visit Dante's Gates of Hell
(1996)

The Nadezhdinsky Nickel Smelter is at the edge of Noril'sk. It is here we meet Mr. Yuri Filippov. Filippov is the director general of the Nadezhdinsky Smelter. He stands in a tweed jacket and pressed pants as we approach. His head of blond hair is precisely trimmed. A cigarette is in his hand at all times.

"Welcome, and I hope I can present you with a good understanding of our facilities. As you can see we are working on repairs and maintenance, always a challenge here," Filippov says.

The questions begin. Filippov is ready with unapologetic answers—it is just a fact, this place needs help, and he knows it.

"At what capacity are you operating?" one of the engineers asks.

"We are at 61 percent," Filippov says.

"How does this smelter compare to the other two in the area?"

"This is the most modern," he says.

Our engineer's shoulders sag, and I can see he's mentally tabulating the needed upgrades and the astronomical price tag to fix this place. We are assessing risks here—the risks of economics, safety, political changes, and liability. Should we work in this country or not? That's a big question, and seeing these facilities firsthand—well, it's sobering.

I ask Filippov, "What do you pay the smelter workers?"

"The average is about 1,000 U.S. dollars equivalent every month. Very good pay. But unfortunately, we have not been able to pay wages for several months. We hope to soon. You know, new government, it is why you are here. Yes?" Filippov says.

<<<>>>

The first building of the complex is football stadium-sized and full of thousands of tubs frothing with concentrate bubbles coated with gunmetal gray sulfide metal. Rotating arms skim off the froth into a slurry trough and then onto the huge drum dryers. These drum dryers are twenty feet across and have a fabric over the perforated metal skin of the drum. The sulfide metal scum from the concentrate sticks to this fabric as the drum rotates through the slurry. A vacuum force within the drum sucks out the contained moisture in the concentrate. Once dry, the concentrate spalls off the drum fabric and onto a conveyor. It is then dropped into the smelter, where the sulfide metal is broken down through a reduction process. Fumes of sulfur dioxide ascend though the towering smokestack, and the pure elemental metal is left behind.

It all looks like some forgotten machinery from a lost alien civilization. Hardly so, though, since the metalliferous concentrate is Noril'sk's only means of minting money.

The first part of the tired complex seems clean and safe compared to what we walk into next. We hike a half-mile down a wide, low-ceilinged corridor designed to convey thousands of people to work each day. The air becomes more pungent, more metallic. We can taste it. The windows are soot-tinted to the point of opaqueness. On the other side of the corridor's wall are the hydrometallurgical autoclave rooms.

Yuri Filippov opens one of the heavy doors. Hugo and I peer into a massive area through an atmospheric haze. This reveals a ghostly array of pipes, suspended steel walkways, girders, and venting steam and smoke amid huge cylindrical autoclaves.

"You interested in a job here?" a voice says.

"Huh?" I turn to look into the face of Alexi. His black hair and round form jiggles with soft laughter. I am speechless, as this is the last place on earth I would like to spend the rest of my career.

"Come, there is more, the good part," Alexi says.

Hugo, Alexi, and I follow the others behind Filippov. We walk farther down this seemingly endless corridor.

The atmosphere continues to sour, and as we turn off the main corridor into the smelting works I can see the air—it has particulate and color and texture. Massive furnaces spill forth molten metal. A shower of glowing material precedes the pour into enormous buckets. The buckets hang from a moving bar crane driven along ceiling girders. Heat and acrid sulfurous gasses issue into the fathomless room from the splattering molten nickel and copper.

We all cough and wheeze in the yellow sulfuric atmosphere. All of us, that is, except Yuri Filippov. He looks at us and the faintest of smiles touches the corners of his mouth. He lights up a cigarette, inhales deeply, and then lets the smoke mingle with the smelter room atmosphere.

"You see the workers?" Alexi says, as he points to a group of men working near one of the furnaces.

The men are moving huge carts with ingots of metal to one side of the smelter works. They are apparitions in the polluted gloom. Their forms seem to glow orange from the light cast by molten metal as it spills from one huge bucket to the next. The men are dwarfed by the enormous machinery—yet I can see their muscular torsos, clothes soaked in sweat. Many of the men are wearing particulate masks, but I can't imagine they do much to cut the acidic fumes. In the pyroatmospheric environment I see one man smoking a cigarette as he moves through the room.

Filippov says, "We have 3,700 people working here. Each man working in the smelter works for three days. Then we give them two days off to recover. Then back to work." He looks at us, and smiles. "This plant produces 120,000 tonnes of nickel metal every year. Russia needs its nickel—this is how we get it."

Later, back in Yuri Filippov's office, I am still coughing and wheezing. My eyes still sting. The environmental calamity here is staggering. Globally—greenhouse gas emissions. Regionally—groundwater and surface water contamination. And locally—well, the very lives of these men and women are at stake.

Hugo is blinking repeatedly and blowing his nose. "I would say there's an environmental problem here! Where's OSHA when you need it?"

"That is what a smelter is," Filippov says. "This is how a Russian smelter makes metal for . . ." Filippov doesn't finish the sentence but looks around the room. He lights up another cigarette as a distraction. "Do you need any more information?"

Alexi leans toward me. "Metal for the people, he was going to say—this is how Russia gets metals for the people. Old school, da? Now you see the difficulty of changing Russia, da? American presidents have demanded Soviet Union to change. Then . . . what luck! The world is given Mikhail Gorbachev—maybe a miracle, da? But it comes down to places like Noril'sk as much as anywhere. We are taking generations to change—but we will. This is not just daily news headlines. You understand?"

"Yes, yes, I think I get it," I say, with new understanding.

The Gulag Survivor

I walk down Lenin Street to the Noril'sk Museum where 390 years of local history is portrayed. Sasha is with me. We look at the history together, but it is the last sixty-five years that constricts the throat and pains the heart. The gulag years are laid out in photographs behind strands of barbed wire and examples of meager personal belongings. Letters in the penmanship of the educated plead for release or news of family and friends. Many Europeans who had believed in communism ventured into the Soviet Union from Finland, Hungry, France, Italy, Spain, the Arab states, even the United States. But Lenin's paranoia saw them as future enemies, and he imprisoned them for mandatory ten-year sentences, a term that often never ended. Some even had been working for the KGB but were accused of being double agents. Could the indigenous Nanets and Dolgons who inhabited the Taimir Peninsular region have ever imagined that the harsh Siberian environment would one day be surpassed in cruelty by an ideology?

I study the black-and-white pictures of men and women and children holding shovels, dressed in worn work clothes, and all wearing dour or frightened expressions lined the walls.

In one of the corners I see an old withered man. He sat hunched over, reading the daily newspaper through thick spectacles. His skin is almost translucent, highlighted by blue veins coursing tired energy through his very being. He looks up and notices me glancing at him as Sasha and I walk along the row of pictures. The man waves me over to him. I am drawn to him as if he were the magnet and I the iron. Sasha acts as a translator so that this old man can tell me his story.

"I am Yuri. Don't look at me now. Look at me when I was young. When I had a life ahead of me. There—on the wall—is a picture of me.

"I work here at the memorial museum in Noril'sk because you must remember everything. You are here visiting mine? Yes? Now you learn what I know.

"See, I was taller. I was stronger. But that picture was taken when I was first brought to Noril'sk. The gulag of Noril'sk.

"I didn't do anything wrong. I was a teacher. But Lenin and Stalin—everybody made them afraid.

"I spent thirty-six years of my life in the gulags. After that I stayed here at the mine—no place else to go. I was shipped here to Noril'sk in 1935. Stalin said that a mine must be opened here. He made us open the mine and build the town—such as it was. It was horrible. Cold days, cold nights, cold food, and cold hearts. And now I am very old.

"I am 100 years. My back is hunched over, and my cane is my friend—I hold its hand all the time.

"They told us this is about the theory of Socialist Realism. That's what the Congress of Soviet Writers used to change the world. My world. All of this is personal. We are just people. We are just people.

"You should not forget this. There is so much irony here. Did you know that most of these revolutionists—you know, Lenin's mob—were so-called terrorists of the state according to the tsar?

Well, it turns out the tsar was right! The tsar put them in political prisons in the old Russia. Lenin, Trotsky, Stalin, Nikolai Bukharin, Maxim Gorky, Andrei Zhdanov, and many others. Sentenced to 'Katorga'—hard labor.

"So you see, this makes no sense that these revolutionists would do to me and so many others the same things what their oppressors had done. That is the horrible irony of the gulag.

"But these new revolutionists took their theory of Socialist Realism to absurd levels. They demanded that all creative things— all art and writing—and I wanted to be a writer, but that is dead long time—anyway, all of these creative things must depict some aspect of the people's struggle toward achieving the communist state. The purpose of communism we were told was to work toward a better life, but we just worked. Or they killed us. Or we took our own lives. Eighteen million!

"Before Khrushchev all creative people—men, women, children—had to serve the proletariat. They had to do so by portraying realism and optimism and heroism in their art. You must have seen these horrid concrete statues in the city? Who is like that—it is not abstract, it is just a lie. Ehhh—this is crazy, this is absurd to demand this. My brain didn't work that way—I was a daydreamer before they killed that in me. Now I am passing time. I do not have children. And the woman I loved—oh so much—I never saw her again after the soldiers came. It doesn't matter where I'm from—because that doesn't exist anymore.

"It was a very hard time here working in the mines. Nickel and copper and platinum—for what? For war, I think. You touch the metal in the Soviet rockets and our blood is in there—a human alloy in the Soviet metal. I didn't like the mining. All my bones are aching now because of the mines.

"One of the men here, Nikoli—he is dead now—but he was a mathematician. He said one day in 1952, 'Do you know Yuri, that you are fifty-five years old, and that means to the Soviet Union every year of your life is worth 100 kilograms of nickel. That's all.

"Nikita Khrushchev let us go in 1953—right after Stalin died. But some of the gulags still went on. I can tell you almost 30,000 died here at Noril'sk over eighteen years. Yes, there were 103 gulags in Russia—and eighteen million people died. Nikoli, my mathematician friend, would have perhaps said this is 1,300 people every day—eighteen million of us. We are just people.

"I must tell you about Nikita Khrushchev's grave. You know, every man holds a little bit of evil. In Nikita there is an irony. He was buried at Novodevichy Cemetery, also known as New Maidens Cemetery. This is in Moscow—that is where he was buried, not at the Kremlin, because he died a private person. He was, of course, dismissed as a general secretary. His monument is angular, black on one half and white on the other.

"What do these colors represent? Ehhhh? What do you think? It's abstract. Maybe the extremes of Russia, or the vices and virtues, other differences perhaps? Maybe so, but the irony is Khrushchev hated abstract art. His hate of all things abstract led him on a mission to destroy such paintings and sculptures in Russia.

"Now listen to me. This is the thing I love. One of the many abstractionist artists that fled the Soviet Union was chosen to design Khrushchev's monument. An abstractionist! Ha! He was Ernst Neizvestny, who had immigrated to America. Neizvestny's name means 'Unknown.' Neizvestny—this abstract artist—was asked to design Khrushchev's gravestone! Can you imagine what he thought when that request came through? You bet! And he designed the gravestone that is black on one side, the white on the other. There is no gray for men like Khrushchev. The divide is sharp—now you understand this man Khrushchev.

"I call that poetic justice. Ha! Khrushchev would have hated poetic justice." Yuri lets out a gravelly laugh, which turns into a cough. He pauses, and his face saddens, pales, and his eyes glisten with tears.

"This town of Noril'sk is so full of ghosts. I will join them soon. This city built on bones." Yuri's eyes well up with tears, and they streak down his wrinkled cheeks. He wipes them free and looks up at me and speaks again.

"And you, an American visiting me. A young geologist—I am glad to talk to you all afternoon! It's good Americans are here.

"And I tell you—please do not forget me."

114

Roger James Kuhns

The Red Russian Girl
(1991)

Now I want to take you back to Leningrad. Back to 1991 again. Back to Hugo and the beautiful Dasha and the mysterious Andre, and the search for diamonds.

Hugo and I are calling Dasha "our beautiful KGB girl." Not really KGB, we're sure—I mean the old KGB was disbanded. But the Black Mafia possibilities poke at our thoughts like a gun barrel in our ribs.

Dasha says, "Time to go. Russian Museum. You can see our culture."

Dasha is staying close to me at the Russian Museum of Arts because of my near escape earlier with Vadim the street musician. She's gliding and swaying gracefully as we walk. She says, "Red is beautiful don't you think? Tell me I'm a red woman."

"Well, that sounds odd, don't you think?" I say.

"But look here, this is the early Soviet flag. You see all the red and blue and white, the colors are those of the early Soviet flag—red for struggle always in the background, blue for hope like the sky above, and white is for purity. But red also means something else here in my Russia."

"Well, struggle is pretty obvious here," I say.

"No, no. Red in Russian is *krasnyy*, and it is same for us as beautiful. So Red Square is Beautiful Square. We keep our valuables within a red circle at home. The red chamber in our home is for honored guests."

"So whenever red is used, then it means something important or beautiful?"

"Yes, beautiful. You understand, yes? And red girl is . . ."

"Beautiful woman. Nice. Not white for purity?"

"Oh no! Red! Red Russian girl. You think I am red?"

I'm struggling here, because KGB or Black Mafia *and* Beautiful Red Russian Girl all must mean trouble. I think she is very *red*.

115

Dasha seems to read my doubt. "You think I'm KGB?" She says with a coy smile. "Everyone thinks everyone is KGB. Not KGB. This is New Russia."

"Of course not," I lie.

Our conversation pirouettes around the museum in a strange ballet. This interlude in the plot of gaining an advantage, of winning investment and taking home the monies, is so dancelike. Careful steps, no treading on toes, and no unpracticed moves. But every ballet has a tragedy.

Fields of Diamonds

Hugo and I have come to Russia to look for diamonds. Diamonds, when considered as a commodity, are globally monopolized by De Beers. Diamonds are artificially priced and happen to be in great abundance in this confused, transitory, post-communist Russia. What a good idea this is!

These are my thoughts as I wait at the Pulkovo Airport in Leningrad. Our jet to Arkhangel'sk and the Siberian diamond fields is a Tupolev II. This jet is the Soviet's answer to the Boeing 727 but has "bomber windows" in the nose of the aircraft . . . just in case it needs to multitask.

Dasha is in her field clothes—tight blue pants and a tight white top—maybe some purity today? She has a red scarf around her neck. She is dressed in the colors of the old Russian flag. The colors peek out from a London Fog rain parka. She looks great, just like one of the Bond girls.

Dasha says, "Ah, now we fly Aeroflop!" She laughs at her joke, and then holds up her flight coupon. "Do you see? Our tickets are from the Sputnik Travel Agency! We take you out of this world! We Russians are very clever, da?"

Such a statement couldn't be more accurate!

The plane smells musty, like mildewed carpet. There is no request to fasten seatbelts from the steroidal, dark-haired, square-shouldered stewardess. I'm thinking crew team, maybe an Olympic weight lifting medalist.

After forty-five minutes in the air the stewardess brings greasy green plastic camper cups with apple juice.

Through the oval port window I can see for hundreds of miles—nothing but the muskeg and black spruce of Siberia's boreal forest. Lakes. Rivers. Few houses. This is Siberia—the land that swallows people and armies.

Andre is seated next to me. Dasha is with Hugo.

Andre says, "I am starting a company. I want part of this company of mine to be a diamond exploration company. I already have all the equipment."

I say, "Really? Like what?"

Andre says, "You know, diamond exploration equipment—I have it all."

"Where did you get it, what kind do you have?"

Andre says, "You know, very useful equipment. I think you and Hugo will be pleased."

"Where did you get it?" I ask again.

"It is the best the Soviet military has to offer—I have an air force sub-chasing magnetometer I buy for very good deal. I have hydro-conductance equipment that was used to find missile silos, also very good price. I think it may be useful to find diamond kimberlites in my New Russia."

"Perestroika!" I say, and offer a toast with the green plastic cup full of apple juice.

"Wait!" Andre, pulling out a flask and opening it, tips vodka into our plastic cups. "Glasnost!"

Soon we land in Arkhangel'sk at the Talagi airport.

Arkhangel'sk is along the White Sea delta of the Severnaya Dvina River. Docks are crowded with ships. The town sprawls outward from the waterfront. One can almost hear Tsar Ivan IV's decree in 1584—*Build me a port city!*

In the outlying areas are hothouses and fields for carrots, cucumbers, and tomatoes. Dozens of drab gray or green six-to-eight story apartment buildings are home to thousands of residents. A bronze larger-than-life Lenin stands in the town square, and outward from this monument are memorials to soldiers. There is one for the rugged northerners. Even one honoring the reindeer of Siberia.

Andre loads us onto a bus and into town we go.

<<<>>>

The lobby of the Jubiley Hotel is a sorry sight. Tiled floors are chipped and scraped; the ceiling is sagging; the clerk is ashen and slow. Later we meet in the hotel's restaurant.

Dinner ambience is a cigarette smoke saturated atmosphere. Vodka flows like water, and the toasts start as soon as the vodka bottles' flip tops are taken off.

In our small group are diamond geologists from around the world—from De Beers in South Africa, CRA and Ashton Mining in Australia, and Monopros/De Beers in Canada. I am the only native-born American here.

We drink the vodka while spooning orange Russian caviar onto small crackers. We are like a tribe of sorts, we geologists. We are a bit on the fringe of the rest of the business world. We are eternal optimists, just the sort to take on challenges of working in Russia. We like the journey as much as, if not more than, the destination.

Hugo tells a story: "A bride is anxious about her wedding gown. So she goes to a store to buy cloth for the ceremony, and some more for her wedding night. She wants a special gown for that evening, you see. She tells the salesgirl to wrap the bolt of cloth around her until it measures 30 feet. 'That should be enough!' says the bride. The salesgirl asks, 'Is all of this for how many dresses?' The bride says, 'Only one—my fiancé likes to look more than find it.' And the salesgirl says, 'Ahhh—husband must be an exploration geologist!'"

A tureen of *rassolnik,* a cabbage soup with meat, barley and pickled cucumbers, is brought to the table, and we ladle it into bowls. This we sip with our vodka.

"Ah—I love *rassolnik*," says Dr. Vladimir Grib. Now Dr. Grib is a very important man here. He is deputy director of Arkhangelsk geologia Company. He is playing his part in this chapter of Russian privatization, but I think he's faking it. He doesn't want foreigners running his mines. Grib is the first to fill his bowl. Between slurping spoonfuls he says, "Now, let me tell you an old Russian proverb. It goes just like this. The hunter, it goes, likes the hunt more than bagging the trophy. The fisherman, likewise, says, 'Ah I love to fish, I just don't like to clean and eat them!' And finally another man says, 'Yes, it's like all these children in my house—I like what leads up to them!' Ha! And so you see we work—but the result I am not so sure about."

Pork chops and deep-fried potatoes in a small ocean of grease arrive at the table. We all pour more vodka into our glasses. It is the solvent, loosening tongues and dissolving grease.

One of the Russians accompanying us on the trip is a senior research worker from the Siberian branch of the USSR Academy of Sciences in Novosibirsk. He is Alexander Rodionov, and he says, "We must toast our vodka—so do it harshly so it splashes into the other's cup, so if we try to poison each other, then my poison and your poison mix. We both die, or we both live long. That is the way!"

He laughs heartily, and the vodka is flying. No one dies.

Mineralogist Vladimir Sobolev tells a story: "There is a man, Ivan, who falls in love with a woman and they have an affair. Now Ivan is a geologist and must spend a lot of time in the field to look at his rocks. Well, he goes away to do fieldwork and when he comes back his lover is gone. He waits for her, but she never comes back."

At this point all the geologists in the room look around and nod at each other, because we know what life is like in this profession.

Sobolev continues his story. "So, ten years pass, and he meets a young boy who looks much like him. So they talk and he says, 'I must meet your mother.' This he does and finds out the mother is his old lover and the young boy is his son. So Ivan asks the woman—'Why did you leave?' And she says, 'It's better to have a bastard in the family than a geologist!'"

Andre is smiling and holding his cigarette in front of his face. He knows we're the right kind of people to take on the impossible tasks before us—being part of the rebuilding of Russia. He knows if this happens, he will become a rich man. His eyes look from face to face through the veil of smoke. His gaze settles on Hugo, who is laughing and teetering. He smiles. Andre then looks at me and sees me studying him. The smile vanishes, then the glass of vodka is raised to me, and a new smile—one I can't read—appears on his face. The veil of smoke clears. We drink, bottoms up. No one dies.

Morning: my head hurts from last night's libation. Everyone looks a little rough around the edges as we prepare for our travels to the Lomonosov diamond fields of Siberia.

Andre is directing again. "Everyone! Please. We must go now, it is time to go to the airport!" He claps his hands and herds us down the hall and back onto the buses.

With all these Russians we truly have a large entourage—ten Russians and eight foreign geologists. And the beautiful Dasha, who hovers amongst us, tossing her smile to the most receptive and the most lucrative. But she always circles Hugo and me.

Andre is trying to beat the system. He says, "I can get you where you can't go. You will hear *No! You cannot do it!* I will hear, *No! You cannot do it . . . unless you really want to do it!* Nyet problem."

Promoria Town

Andre herds us like cats from Arkhangel'sk to the airport. "Hurry, hurry, we must go!"

A Cold War era Mikhail Mil helicopter rests on the tarmac; it is a big, orange Mi, an alien-looking piece of antiquated aeronautical machinery. We climb in and take seats on the benches that line the fuselage. We wait and wait.

Hugo: "I think I understand the Soviet system better now. You wait and wait until you can't do what you want to do. Then you get to do what they want you to do and that might not be what anyone wants to do!"

Dasha: "That's why the Communist Party invented vodka. So we could go through such a decision-making process and not feel any pain!"

Andre is across from me, again studying each of the faces of the geologists from South Africa and Australia and Canada. Then he looks at me. "You know," he says, "you are the American here. You are the first American to go to these diamond towns—at least on the record. You are the first. How about that! That is a feather in my hat, and perhaps yours too!"

The chopper lifts reluctantly off the tarmac. Rattling and clattering it lumbers into the gray sky like some gargantuan pregnant bug.

The White Sea opens to the horizon. This is the Winter Coast. We fly north over choppy steel-gray water, then eastward toward the Lomonosovskaya kimberlite field.

The vista is a mottled Siberian landscape. It's flat as a plank and dimpled with silvery lakes and dark-green muskeg and segmented by lethargic meandering rivers.

There is a strange silence in my mind even amid the cacophony of the helicopter's engine. Then I see people looking up at the helicopter.

This is Promoria Town. This is the Lomonosovskaya kimberlite field, an isolated and restricted place.

The landing is a hard bounce. "Now we walk," Andre says.

I imagine things would cheer up a bit if the sun was out, but on this day we follow the muddy road between drab buildings that huddle under a gray sky.

Andre says, "In here, we look at maps."

Maps on the walls, and rocks on the tabletops, and dishes full of diamonds have been put on display for us. Dishes full of diamonds—like candy. Our cameras start going off like a press conference as we all photograph the amazing gems.

Hugo says, "Getting all this down?"

"Gettin' it," I say.

Dasha says, "All these diamonds—so much wealth! It is unbelievable to me that Russia is so hungry with all this wealth here."

One of the De Beers guys, Jock Roby, asks, "How many carats is that big one, what do you figure? Dr. Grib?"

Grib says, "That one is a big one—maybe five, maybe six carats."

The De Beers guy says, "I think it's bigger. What pipe did this come from?"

Grib says, "This one, Promorskaya kimberlite."

"What's the grade?" I ask. Hugo is sorting through the diamonds and putting them in categories of color, carats and clarity. These diamonds are all uncut. Grib is watching him like a hawk.

"The grade? It is very high," Grib says to me.

"How high," asks the De Beers geologist.

"Very high. It is economic," Grib says.

"You mean, what, 50 carats per hundred tons? Or higher?" I ask again.

"It is very high, as I have said," Grib says.

Andre is rolling his eyes at Grib's answers and leans into Grib, saying, "Answer! Facts! Remember, I pay you! How are they to invest if..."

Hugo says, "We're going to have a hard time making a financial model of this if we can't get the data." Hugo's got about thirty diamonds sorted on the table in front of him.

Andre is at Hugo's side. "You approve of what you are seeing?" Andre has his smile.

"Yes, wonderful!" Hugo says. "But we have a lot of work to do over the next few weeks."

We keep pummeling Dr. Grib with questions, and slowly some are answered, but most are met with a shrug and "Next one, please!" Grib has been told for years that all grade and tonnage and economic information having to do with these mines are state secrets, and now he can't just open the doors.

Then all of a sudden Andre is announcing, "Time to go—we must move on. We go to the stock pile dumps!"

"Alright!" Hugo says, like a kid whose been told the ice cream is free.

We all scramble out of the building into the chilly air and hike across some work areas and into a fenced yard toward several huge piles of black kimberlite material. We attack the ore like mosquitoes on a bare bum.

Andre is smiling broadly; he's chain-smoking and walking among us to hear our comments and to watch our reactions.

The South African De Beers geologist and I wander off to a far rock pile. Suddenly military guards surround us. "*Nyet! Nyet!*" they yell at us with hands on their sidearms. They point back to the other piles of so-called ore on the far side of the yard.

Dr. Grib runs up and says, "Not this one," and points back over his shoulder to where the other geologists are. "That one."

"Why?" But we both really know why. The other piles of rock are not ore—there's no diamonds in them.

Grib: "It is policy! Now, please!"

The guards look stern, and we wander back.

Andre: "I should have told you about that. I cannot arrange everything."

Hugo (quietly): "What did you see?"

"Not much time," I say.

Hugo says, "They sent us to the waste rocks, right?"

"Yep," I say, and discreetly hold out a piece of the kimberlite from the forbidden pile. "We'll see what we learn from this."

Hugo nods and smiles. Geologic espionage. I drop it in his bag of samples from the waste piles.

Then Andre is yelling, "We must go! We must go! The weather is worse, we must go!"

Everything is in a hurry here. But no one is in a hurry, really. We've only been looking at these rocks for twenty minutes.

"Hurry, hurry, hurry!" Andre calls to Hugo and me. "We must hurry, if we don't get out—they may keep us here to become miners, and then—you'll be sorry then!"

"We'll never see diamonds then," Hugo says.

On the flight back Andre breaks out a bottle of vodka, smoked salmon, and brown bread. We eat and drink and laugh over the rattling roar of the big orange Mi chopper.

"Feed us and give us rocks and we're happy," Hugo yells.

But Hugo and I will revisit the diamond fields several times and gather information before we can make a decision about working here. Like so many places in the world, very poor people live near the wealth of diamond fields—and Russia is no exception.

I am fumbling with the key to my hotel room door.

The vodka does that.

There is much noise across the hall, and then the door swings open and one of the Australian geologists yells out at me.

"Hey, mate, join the paaahty!"

He's drunk, and I'm drunk, and he has a couple of Russian hookers. *Red Russian hookers!* "Naw, don't think so."

"Your loss, but look at these Soviet sweethaaarts!" he says. The dark-haired, tall, and quite attractive girls are all over this guy—undoing his pants and shirt. "Hey, mate, I'm not against progress, just keeping up the old diplomacy—if you catch my meaning?" One pulls him into the room again, the other looks at me for a moment. She smiles in a way that makes my knees wobble. The vodka does that. Then, keeping her eyes on me, she slowly closes the door.

I lean against the wall in the hallway. I hear Australian whoops of joy and a muffled, "Awe, Sheila, those are really nice ones!" Vodka does that.

But I am still standing.

Diplomatically speaking.

ACT 3

A Scientist Tries to Understand Life

Hugo and I had the name of a scientist we had met at a conference, and we wanted to meet with him again and discuss research opportunities. He lived in a small flat in Leningrad, and as we walked from the tram toward his apartment building we purchased a bouquet of flowers for his wife and a bottle of vodka for the scientist.

Upon arrival the scientist welcomed us into his home. Our conversation drifted late into the night, and I learned what it was like to be a man of science in a society so restricted. Later, I would recall the evening in his words.

"Tonight I had a wonderful night," the scientist said. "Two old friends came to visit. I met Hugo and Roger at a conference some years ago. They said they would visit one day—and they did! Can you imagine?

"I am a scientist, a physicist. Do you know what I work on? You will think it crazy. I am designing experiments in my laboratory that recreate amino acids in primordial mixtures using electricity. I think life started this way. Roger joked at me, and said it sounded like Frankenstein's laboratory. Ha—maybe so! He asked just whom I expected to make in my primordial soup. You know I told him I hoped a really smart leader would crawl out and fix Russia.

"Well, no luck so far—well, maybe . . .

"Oh, I am Volodya Ryabchuk—pardon my manners. My friends brought red roses for my wife Galina when they came to dinner. I was sorry they had to see my small apartment. My apartment is very restricting for the family—there are Galina and me, then my daughter and her husband and their child. There is one small bedroom, one small living room. I have all the walls lined with my books. There is a narrow kitchen, and across the hallway is the toilet and bath. It is good we all get along.

"I am proud of my books. They are perhaps philosophy and perhaps my physics. Galina is my music here. I put a piano here in this tiny place for her. She plays so well.

"I like philosophy. It was hard, before, to be a philosopher, because we couldn't study other philosophers. It is very hard to criticize them if you don't know what they said! With Brezhnev, Andropov, and Chernenko—there was no hope. Never a thought of what could be. But with Gorbachev, at least we can think of hope.

"Galina tells me every day she just wants fresh milk and fresh vegetables—no more books please! Books are my food too.

"My friends tonight asked me what do I think about Gorbachev's policies. Is this a good thing? Yes, I am thinking so. Maybe Gorbachev is the one who comes from my primordial soup in my laboratory, huh? How about that thought! But—all this change—it is not without much pain. Mr. Gorbachev wants openness; you have heard of this— this is glasnost policy. And it has had an earthquake affect on us all—the truth, real history, not the propaganda one that was in all the textbooks before. What is history anyway? Will we really ever know?

"I think I make it rich. I will collect these old Party history books and sell them as fantastic fiction when we have a new order here, what do you think?"

Hugo and I take the metro back to our hotel. As we walk to the train with Volodya, I ponder that this scientist - living as he does - will never own a home, will always struggle to get books he longs for and food he requires, he will never own a car, or other such things that we take for granted in America. But he has a strong spirit fortified by a loving family. For most of us, that is the basis of our lives, no matter how or where we live.

At the station we say farewell to Volodya, then, with firm handshakes and many thanks. Volodya says with emotion: "I do not say goodbye to you my new friends, and as I walk away, I do not look back, so that the memory of this evening is always without a farewell."

Hugo and I travel silently then. The metro is 15 kopeks, less than a 10th of a U.S. cent. We descend down 100 meters on an impressively long escalator. We are in Mayakovskaya Station and it is only moderately crowded at this late hour. Each side of the station consists of rows of automatic doors set in concrete and tiled walls. It is well lit and well maintained. The train suddenly arrives, doors bang open and people pack into the cars. I hang on to a hand bar as I stand near the door. It is a good ride and the train cars are in fine shape. The subway arrives at Primorskaya Station, and we board a bus that takes us within two blocks of our hotel. We are staying on one of the floating hotels brought up the river. Scandinavians entrepreneurs operate it. I refer to it as "our pumpkin", for the Olympia Hotel is a fantasyland compared to the rest of Leningrad. The overhead speakers are playing "Yellow Submarine" as we walk the gangplank onto the hotel deck. This floating Scandinavian hotel seems to flaunt the west at the very doorstep of Leningrad. I wonder what Volodya would say about this?

The Matryoshka Perspective

I am recalling our evening with scientist Volodya Ryabchuk. During our long conversation Volodya said something in Russian to his wife Galina, and she agreed. In English he repeated it: "Here is a strange place. Listen, you cannot do it. No you cannot. But," and here he paused for one of his characteristic shrugs, "if you want to badly enough, you can do it!"

There's more to these than I first thought. It seems like a child's toy, a game—but Russia is all of these personalities; like multiple personalities in the matryoshka dolls, and each surfaces for a little while now and then: this face, and then that face, and so on.

Russia would become the world's second largest diamond producer—10 percent of the market.

And Noril'sk? No buyers yet as I think back on these visits to Russia. With 300,000 people living in Noril'sk and 80,000 employees, it remains one of Russia's largest state-owned business. It is controlled by UNEXIM Bank in Moscow. The company now has significant investment holdings in Stillwater Mining Company's platinum deposit in Montana! Russia has invested in the US mining game.

The Russian Ballet

I am thinking of the stage-like drama that is all around us in Leningrad, one dream after another. Yet the music does not play to everyone's ears. The music is in hidden corners and merges with the story line of a country in transition.

Andre and Dasha collect us for a performance at the Kirov Ballet in the Mariinsky Opera and Ballet Theatre. On this evening we go back in time to when the city was called Saint Petersburg, a name that it would be known as again in the future.

I dress in my business suit and, upon arrival at the ornate neo-Byzantine hall, feel underdressed; I feel oddly sanguine in this immutable environment. This seems at once part of, and yet so untouched by, what is happening outside in the streets or on the international political stage. I wonder, could this new Russia really change?

The pillars and archways of the hall's façade are white over walls of light green. Inside I sit in the second balcony in the emperor's box directly in front of the stage. Dasha is next to me. Hugo and Andre are behind us. The many folded and draped main curtain is a rich gold interleaved with varying shades of purple. There is a large chandelier on the main ceiling, surrounded by paintings of dancing women and cherubs in flowing robes.

The lights dim, and the pit orchestra fills the hall with music. The curtain is lifted, and the ballet that Dasha says is about *sylphs*; it seemed to be an interpretation of *Giselle*. It is the story of a man about to wed, but he falls in love only to have tragedy follow, as his true lover has killed herself rather than not have him. She becomes a *sylph*, or a fairy like being, but upon meeting him again cannot stay with him, and vanishes in the new dawn. In this transforming world the fairy dream of wealth is driving the Andres of New Russia.

Andre is pressing, but Hugo is watching the larger stage. Hugo has decided we will not invest in Russia at the present time.

Dancers float and flow as if belief in the fluid orchestral strings will lift them from the travails that gravity brings.

Dasha is frowning; her tactics have produced no fruit.

On stage the protagonist meets his dreamlike fairy, his one time lover, in delicate wings and slight feminine form. There is hope—the quest so sought after is within reach. But it is not to be. When the protagonist and the fairy join, she loses her wings and fades away.

At that moment Dasha's hand reaches out and touches mine. She looks down at her own motion and instinctively draws it back.

"Oh, I am sorry!" she says. There is a tear in her eye. I am like a touchstone for her—a cultural touchstone from another reality. A glimpse of what her country could have been—of what it may become. But democracy cannot be forced. It is more of a courtship.

She looks down at my hand again and reaches out but pauses. She is not being the temptress now. She is a lost girl, the red Russian girl wishing for a different world. Perhaps she is wishing for a mirror to step through.

I realize her action is reactionary to the heartrending story on the stage before us; her guard fell away for a moment, and she was just a woman lost in the ideal romance of the ballet.

I realize how much she doesn't understand me, and how much I don't understand her. But how much, really, we are alike. Playing second fiddle in a large orchestra.

I look over my shoulder. I can see Andre now, his face a mask of frustration as he realizes Hugo is not yet in this Russian world.

The protagonist on stage has doubted his station in life; he has overstepped his natural boundaries because of his emotions.

Andre does not see the similarity.

On stage the man dies of grief in the end.

The ballet dancers and mimes portray the story; it is in this hall and on these streets and in the heart of Russia.

Dasha touches my hand again. She holds on.

CROCODILES IN THE DESERT

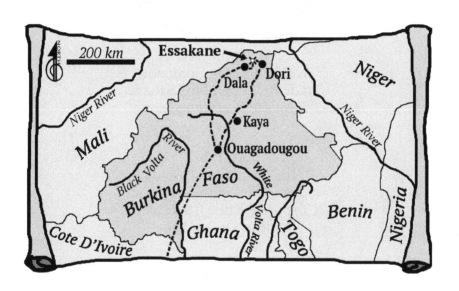

ACT 1
Hugoed
Explorers
First Steps into the Sahel
The Orpaillages' Gold Fields
Madani Explains the Dogon
Wrong Shampoo
String Theory—Loose Ends
The Left and the Right
"Shadow of a Doubt" song
Madani's Well
President Blaise Compaore
Trade Routes and the Sahara
"Theory of Everything" song

ACT 2
The Bartering of Gold
Crocodiles in the Desert
Corporate Knife Cuts Deep
African Dream Dies

ACT 3
Hugo's Last Meeting
Death of Dreams
"Out of Control" song
Oasis

ACT 1

Hugoed

I called it: "Getting Hugoed."

It would go like this: On any given Friday, usually at 6 p.m., as I was trying to get out of the fourteenth floor California Street San Francisco office, I'd hear, *"Raja!"*

"Yes?" I'd call back two doors down the hallway.

"Raja, you still here?" Hugo Dummett was a big man with unbounded energy. "Raja?"

"Yes, Hugo, I'm still here."

"Good. Come in here for a moment, I've got something for you."

And that is how it would start. One time he said we were going to Russia the next day, pack your bags tonight. There went the next three weeks. One time he said I had to go to Venezuela to look for diamonds—but that's another story. On this day, though, he had something else in mind.

"Go to Africa, Raja, find me some gold. Put a team together. Let's do what we do so well." Hugo's grin was wide, friendly, offering a glimpse of his good nature. His eyes were alive with the adventure he knew he was offering.

What we did so well was find things. We were explorationists. We were members of that small club of geology people who have, at once, the good fortune and the misfortune of exploring the world for buried treasure.

"You want me to go to Africa? Where in Africa?"

"All of Africa," Hugo said. He sat back in the creaking leather chair and then let out a laugh that embraced his offer—a laugh that seemed to punctuate his feeling that this offer was just too good to pass up. Hugo's big toothy grin, jowly face, and a great head of salt-and-pepper hair gave him that slightly larger-than-life demeanor. He had the enthusiasm of a child on an adventure! Now, Africa was special to Hugo—he was born in South Africa and subsequently immigrated to Australia and then on to the United States. But he had an African heart.

"I've made a decision, I want you there," Hugo said. He stood up and walked toward me with his hand out. "I know you'll say yes, I need you there right now." And he shook my hand that I had somehow extended to him. Hugo said he had another job for the really good geologist working out of this office and managing that part of the world at the time. In exploration our jobs were dynamic; there was no surety in employment or position. But now the deal was sealed, and I hadn't even said yes.

I thought of all the people I needed to talk to. It looked like my son and daughter would be spending summers in South Africa. But, characteristically with Hugo, there was no time allowance for decision making—he couldn't imagine anyone would say no to such an offer. It was a forgone conclusion: Roger is now General Manager for Exploration in Africa and the Mediterranean.

And that's how it started.

Explorers

Today I am at the edge of the Sahara—in the Sahel, that edge land, the shore to the Great Desert. This land of mirages—visions that fool the eye, the mind, the soul. I have heard some strange things about this desert—odd myths of crocodiles and aliens and restless nomads on the Harmattan wind.

I am watching a nomadic Tuareg on a camel ascend the tall dune. He is heading into the desert. I can see no destination from my vantage point.

No destination. Hmm. My meeting with Hugo many months earlier comes to mind. What do you put down as your destination, if your destination is everywhere?

I am like a fluid on a flat surface, moving outward in every direction. I am tracking across this physio-mental landscape seeking purpose, trying to understand linkages. I am humming along with the cosmic hum.

I am not a rich man. I am not poor either, but I never would have had the resources to see every corner of the world had I not been given these jobs by Hugo Dummett. Some people advised me to get as far away from Hugo as fast as possible—"He'll only mess up your life; he just cares about himself and his own goals," they'd say.

But they didn't understand Hugo. His ego, although large, wasn't his principal driver. The need to discover was what moved him so. This uncontrollable part of his nature that pushed him to his limits was the reason for his many successes, and it took him away from his family too.

The need—the urgency—to discover was almost maniacal, always on his mind, always pushing him—and there I was at his side, because that urge was in me also. People who don't have it don't understand it. The need to discover grabbed us and shook us like a crazy wild thing, and we were driven to learn of the world, to explore the rocks, the jungles, the deserts, the very continents in search of gold and silver and platinum and copper and diamonds—all sorts of resources. But we discovered much more than that. We discovered the grand panoply of human culture, the beauty and ecology of the planet, and the intricate workings of the global community and economic imperatives. We learned what sustainability really meant.

Hugo, though, was really a drifter in this grand universe. He'd worry over not seeing his family and then book another trip without checking in with his wife. He'd island hop from one project to the next, one city to the next, one continent to the next, and get lost in time zones, jet lag, meetings, and strange hotels. I was right there with him.

I knew if I had been born a thousand years ago, I'd be on some crude ship sailing off to see what was over the oceanic horizon. And I knew Hugo would have been right there with me. We were explorers, and in this century it just happened to be for metals.

Hugo and I traveled the world together for more than a decade. But he could never believe how fragile, how fleeting these amazing jobs of ours were. Nor did he really believe how fleeting, in fact, was life. We would see that soon enough, for this journey he and I embarked upon would lead to many endings.

First Steps into the Sahel

I fly across West Africa. The Sahara Desert unfolds below me. The pale rusty red dunes of the desert sand are like fossilized ocean waves that stretch to the horizon. Here and there the faint trace of an ancient riverbed can be seen. The blanket of sand mutes occasional outcrops. This was once wet and lush and fertile when glaciers blanketed Europe not long ago, geologically speaking. That's what the souls of the people who live here remember. But the Sahara does not think of the comfort of humans. It is just what it is. It is a hot, dry, baking breath exhaling across a population of dreamers.

Now I find myself committing years of my life to exploration, management, and team building in the regions entrusted to me by Hugo: Africa and the Mediterranean.

The Air France jet descends to Ouagadougou's international airport—I have arrived in Burkina Faso—"the land of upright men." The population here is half Muslim and most of the rest have animistic beliefs. Christianity is a minority. As I flew across the Sahara and into the Sahel, the land became dotted with rude adobe huts and simple sheet metal and brick houses. The airport building is the color of the desert. When the Airbus doors open I am hit with a blast of hot, waterless air.

It is late in the day, and Madani Diallo and Serge Nikiema are there to meet me at the baggage claim. Madani, from Mali, is a good and clever man. He has learned a way to maintain his ethics while working within the temperamental milieu of West Africa, where government behavior is inconsistent—often corrupt, always slow. Madani is a reserved man. He has a friendly, handsome, roundish face and wears glasses. His black skin blends with the geometric brown pattern of his shirt. Madani was awarded the highest civilian honor from the Malian government for helping find a gold mine.

Madani brings a global view back to West Africa, having earned a PhD in Russia; he is my West African manager.

Serge Nikiema is a young, energetic, string bean Burkinabè. He's so skinny that his wife says when he turns sideways there is no shadow! Serge's big smile and easy laugh help one get through the toughest times. Serge earned his PhD in geology from the university in Paris. He's also a really good guitar player.

The streets are crowded and dusty and full of earthy smells. Goats are bleating, human voices merge to create a din of human sound. The cadence of humanity is compounded by the buzz of mopeds and grumble of untuned trucks. I love it—this is my kind of town.

Morning in Ouagadougou comes too soon. I watch the orange glow in the east—the solar engine begins its daily routine of fueling the desert. Burkina Faso is a landlocked French colonial remnant, and one of the poorest countries in the world.

I go down to breakfast with Madani. Serge lives here in Ouagadougou and meets up with us later on.

"We have much to do, much to show you," Madani says. "Our geologists are anxious to meet with you and plan for continuing the exploration programs. They are used to the other manager's ways and need to learn your ways. But mostly we will be in the field, to the north. It will be hot, very hot. And dry, very dry."

Madani and I pick up Serge Nikiema and leave Ouagadougou. The way out of town is dirt street after dirt street. Each street is lined with small open kiosks—like newspaper stands—that sell all manner of goods. The scooters zip by as tall, slender, black women in wonderfully patterned bright blue, yellow, orange, green, or brown print wraps walk along the road. They have bowls of provisions balanced on their heads. The men are solid and good looking, although their clothes are faded and worn.

As we leave town the one-story earthen brick and sheet metal houses give way to a parched Sahel terrain. The main tar road turns to pale brick-red dust, and we enter a remote and relentless world. Donkeys and goats and cattle are being herded along. A dilapidated truck has dozens of live goats tied down on the roof. Mothers walk along the highway with babies on their backs in a kangas sling or held to breast or balancing on hip—all the while with a jug or container balanced on their heads. I think there is a danger of forgetting just how harsh this land can be when zooming through it in a Land Cruiser. I mention this to Serge.

Serge says, "Oh, we will have many flat tires and probably run out of gas, and maybe water—we will remember then how *très difficile* my country can be!"

Serge's life and career have pulled him up from the poverty of this country. He is highly educated, and he brings the future's potential to the present day. Serge is a tenuous string that can be cut by bad politics, bad business, or natural calamity—drought, global warming, disease, famine, and the like. But like most explorationists, he is an optimist.

The terrain is geologically ancient. Underfoot are slivers of the Proterozoic Birimian greenstone belt—a series of ocean floor basalts and continental sediments. A thick, iron-rich, red weathered layer, called a laterite, has developed on top of these rocks. This weathered rock is so fully depleted in nutrient elements that crops do not grow well, a fact exacerbated by the scarcity of water. We stop often to examine rocks in the hot, hazy afternoon. The haze is from the Harmattan, a parched, gritty Sahara trade wind that dries up the land. This same wind can spawn hurricanes in the Atlantic and drive them on into the Gulf of Mexico. Another thing here is that wildlife is rare—it has been hunted to oblivion or driven away by drought.

By dusk we arrive in Dori. This Sahel town has wide dusty streets with adobe brick buildings and the occasional corner shop. At the north end of town we go to a small hotel. Here we're given simple rooms and eat skinny chicken and wash it down with beer. There are no lights in the town, and the heavens are aglow from the billions of brilliant stars. One cannot help but look up into the unknown. My mind wanders into this universe above. We sample it sitting here on our planet as Earth spins, watching the stars move and wondering about what planets may orbit these distant suns.

Many spins ago there were dinosaurs here. That was the Cretaceous period, and the number of Earth's rotations to this day would add up to sixty-five million years. Now we are in a new era, what ecologist Eugene Stoermer and Nobel Prize-winning chemist Paul Crutzen have coined the Anthropocene, in which humans have significantly impacted Earth's natural systems. And the Sahara and its bordering Sahel are one enormous experiment in how terrain and people respond to climate change and how the industriousness of humans changes the climate itself.

But back in the Cretaceous . . . well, that was when this was a humid tropical environment. It began weathering and leaching the rounded tired hills of the two-billion-year-old Birimian craton. That was when the blood-red laterite began forming. All that is left of those days are small patches of the stuff on the highest tabletop buttes and ridges. Even the bones of the thunder lizards were washed into a young Atlantic Ocean.

I get Hugo on the satellite phone. Children from the village watch with wonder as I set up the suitcase-sized satellite phone box—an icon of mid-1990s technology. The kids laugh when they hear Hugo's voice. It's a wonder! It's also a seven-hour time difference; Hugo is in San Francisco. Late at night for us, afternoon for him—so he feels like talking.

We talk geology. But he wants to know how the team is doing, and with great excitement asks, "Is everyone fired up?"

Then I call my kids. Matthew is ten, Madeleine is eight. The conversation goes like this:

"Hi, it's Dad. I'm in the desert."

"Hi, Dad," Madeleine says. "Why are you in the desert?"

"I'm working here, remember we talked about West Africa?"

"You should get out of the desert. Aren't deserts really hot? Are you thirsty? Are there snakes?" Madeleine asks.

Then Matt asks, "If you're in the desert, how can you call us on the phone?"

"I'm on a satellite phone."

"Like Star Trek?" Matt asks.

"Sort of. It talks to the satellite and the satellite talks to you."

"Okay. Could you just beam home then?" he asks.

"I'll try."

The next morning we need to repair a flat tire—just as Serge promised. We find a tin shack functioning as a service station. Beer bottles filled with petrol are for sale on a wood box out front. We buy a case of gas for the truck from the attendant, a lanky fellow with piercing dark eyes that reflect his passion for fixing anything mechanical. He looks over the dusty Land Cruiser, walks around it, admiring a machine that cost more than he'd make in forty years. I roll the punctured tire toward his shed. "Deux heures," he says, and Serge and I lock the vehicle and wander off for a walk in Dori.

Drifting on the breeze we hear the rhythmic beating of djembe drums and the bright notes of the xylophone-like balafon. Serge and I instinctively turn toward the diaphanous polyrhythmic melodies. Our pace unconsciously and metronomically quickens as our conversation latches onto music. The narrow dusty streets are filled with the cacophony of a nearby market.

We turn a corner around a mud brick building and walk into a small herd of cattle that stands at one corner of the market square. We push through the herd and the music grows louder. A quartet entertains the market shoppers as they select tubers and dates, spices and vegetables, strips of dark red beef, and woven cages filled with skinny chickens. The place is the definition of chaos, but the music provides an underlying harmonic order. The music is like a series of strings holding this reality together. Here is heartbeat music that everyone seems to sway to. Children dance and mothers rock their babies to the beat as they go about their shopping. Two djembe drummers, a balafon player, and one kabosse player and singer work passionately at their music. There is a basket in front of them for tips, in which one woman places an orange and nods at the singer. Meanwhile, arms are flying at blinding speeds as mallets strike the wood slats of the balafon and the drummers beat the goatskins of the djembes with lightning hands that are driven by the motion of their whole body: arms, shoulders, torso.

The guitar-like kabosse player sings melodic lines that twin the instrumental notes—like a call-and-response—it is all very fast, very lively, and about life and love. Serge translates the local dialect; it is a song about a man who couldn't win the heart of a woman, no matter his efforts . . . *do I have to cross every desert and every mountain for your love?*

Well, we all know the answer to that!

We return to our truck. Our tire is repaired. I pay the equivalent of about 50 cents. Soon Serge and I and our small team of geologists are on our way again to look at more of the ancient rocks of West Africa.

The Orpaillages Gold Fields

On the flat horizon is a low pyramid-shaped hill with a flat top. This is a heap of rock from the crushing and milling of gold ore. This place is called Essakane. Our company is in a joint venture with a Burkina Faso national company. We are exploring the area around and on Essakane.

Essakane is now a boomtown because gold was found here. The Burkinabè and people from all the surrounding West African countries have come here to mine the gold. Some are here because drought has made it impossible for them to subsist in their homelands. Others just hope the dream of riches will come true.

Essakane has been here for thousands of years, and is within the Samo ethic region of modern Burkina Faso. It was an agricultural area before the Sahel began drying up. There is evidence that the town was burned hundreds of years ago. Archaeologists suggest people were captured and sold as slaves here. It has a dark past, one that is overlaid by the current hunger for gold.

Artisanal mining started in the region in the mid-1980s, spurred by the discovery of quartz gold veins at the surface. The locals quickly learned from their Malian neighbors how to scrape out the loose lateritic material, pick through the quartz, and find gold.

On the low hill I walk among the thousands of artisanal miners. They are digging pits, shafts, and trenches along the quartz veins. Some have excavated their tenuous diggings 180 feet into the earth. They climb down into the six-foot-square areas using only crudely cut hand and footholds in the lateritic walls. A miner will leave his shirt or shoes outside the hole to let others know he's working below, and if not collected by sunset, then the family knows he's in trouble. The artisanal miners emerge from the depths, squinting in the bright light and covered in dust and mud. Their black bodies are blotched with white, yellow, and red clay.

The wives and children, dressed in bright print kaftans and wraps dulled by the dust, collect the quartz and laterite material hauled up by the men. The women winnowing the gold ore all have their children working beside them. Several suckle their infants while working; others have the babes asleep on their backs in a wrap, the Sahel sun beating down on them. When the winnowing is done, they balance a metal pan full of the concentrate on their heads and carefully walk back to the artisanal milling compound to have it crushed to a fine dust and washed to further concentrate the gold.

Meanwhile, up on the hill the men descend back into their pits for more ore. The surface of the hill is riddled with what looks like thousands of bomb craters from the mining. The hill also stinks with the acrid scent of urine and the foul pungency of human feces. When the urge comes, they squat and dump, then continue to work. The hot, heavy air is nauseating when the wind catches the smell.

In the artisanal milling compound the hand-cobbed and wind-winnowed ore is brought into crude booths—hundreds of them—demarcated with woven mats and straw walls. Here men, women, and children use crude mortars and pestles, some made from a drive shaft or pipe or an elongate rock, to further crush the quartz. This material is examined for larger nuggets. The smaller dusty material is then panned in chocolate-colored water to concentrate the gold. Throughout the compound is an eerie symphony of dull clanging sounds from metal on stone and a scraping, shushing sound as hundreds of people pan the fine rock dust.

When the gold is gathered, it is brought to the end of the compound where a low table awaits. Day in and day out, children, women, and men are recovering small aliquots of gold. Behind the table is a man with a tin balance. First the gold is poured into a small tray, and then it is passed over a magnet to collect the magnetite, which is removed. Thusly concentrated, the gold is put into the balance. For counterweights ad hoc gold buyer uses a matchstick for the equivalent of 0.1 gram, a 1 CFA franc coin for 1.0 gram, and a 10 CFA franc coin for 5.0 grams. CFA is the West African *Communauté Financière d'Afrique* designation for coins in 1-, 5-, 10-, 25-, 50-, 100-, 200-, and 500-franc denominations. The CFA franc is a fraction of the value of a French franc. But a 1 CFA franc coin weighs just a bit more than one gram, about 1.3 grams, so there is a some measure of skimming going on by the ad hoc gold buyer in Essakane.

The weighed gold is then put in a bottle, and the miner is paid in cash for the gold at a mid-1990s rate of about 4,000 CFA francs per gram, about $282 per ounce.

One of the gold buyers tells us that the artisanal miners produce about a half ton of gold per year. This is twelve thousand ounces, or about 2.5 ounces per person per year, and there are about 5,000 people mining gold on the site. The average income from this gold mining is $700 per person per year. They work ten hours per day for half a year; some stay all year. That's about $0.25 per hour wages—not that great, but three times the average Burkinabè income of $250/year.

The deposit has been very heavily worked for almost one hundred years, but especially in these past few years. From our calculations we determine that the artisanal miners have removed 177,000 ounces of gold by hand—that's almost 20 percent of the nearly one million ounces in the entire deposit.

By nightfall we've found another guesthouse in a small town nearby. It seems as if we've been time-warped into prehistory. The village is in a state of constant disintegration and rebuilding, each house being built on the weathered remains of its predecessor. Many of these towns occur on low hills that rise above the surrounding Sahel, but that is because of the lasagna-like build-up of ruins on ruins in these historical settlements.

As the chicken last night was literally skin and bones, I have the fish tonight—carp, small but tasty, and couscous with an onion tomato sauce. That with local beer finishes the night.

After dinner Madani, Serge, and I look at the stars and talk of gold and adventures, of family and home, and how we try to balance these realities. We have many questions, but few answers.

Madani brings up the curious world of the Dogon.

Madani Explains the Dogon

This is what Madani tells us:

"There, that star, that is Sirius—the Dog Star, the star of the Dogon people. They are there, just over the border in Mali. Not far! Look up in the sky at that bright star. It's Jupiter; can you see its four most prominent moons? No. The other bright star—that's Saturn; can you see its rings? No. Not without a small telescope. Look at Sirius again. Can you see its companion star? Not with the naked eye. So, how could the Dogon people in Mali know about these things over a thousand years ago?

"The Dogon have a controversial belief. Well, it is not controversial to them, but it is controversial to scientists! Controversy often means that science and proof are countered with emotion and assumption or philosophy and religion. There are many cultures and religions that have beliefs in the supernatural, and maybe the superscience. We try to explain, we get close, but contradictions, lack of provable data, ambiguities . . . well these all plague us.

"So it is with the Dogon belief in the Dog Star—Sirius. These people, the Dogon, seem to know a lot about this star Sirius. They have been here for nearly four thousand years, and for a long time they have known that Sirius has an invisible companion star. This circles around Sirius every sixty years or so, according to the myth. Is it a myth? How would they know this? You can't see it with the naked eye. They also know about the rings of Saturn and at least four of the moons of Jupiter—how would they know that without a telescope? They didn't have a telescope. Who told them?

"Some have interpreted the Dogon knowledge as coming from aliens from Sirius, or somewhere up there—some say they were kind of like amphibian beings or fish people. The Dogon call these creatures the Nommo. There are many myths that mix humans with animals. But what is even more interesting is they have a ceremony that is practiced only once every sixty years—the same time it takes for the Sirius companion to make its orbit. The Dogon calendar has a sixty-year cycle. It doesn't make sense with the Julian calendar, which is Earth's rotation around the sun, or the lunar calendar based on the moon's cycles.

"This—the Dogon of Mali—is one of the puzzles of the Sahel. Now, of course, we know Sirius has an invisible companion. Astronomers have confirmed this. Sirius is a binary star system."

One MIT professor in physics once said, "They [the Dogon] have no business knowing any of this!" (Kenneth Brecher, "Sirius Enigmas," in *Astronomy of the Ancients*, 1979).

The Dogon also claim there's a third star with Sirius and Sirius B. Astronomers haven't identified that one yet. What if they do? What does that mean?

Did amphibious aliens visit the Dogon people in West Africa thousands of years ago? The Dogon believe so, and they don't care what you think about that!

Wrong Shampoo

Ouagadougou.

I had a meeting with the Burkina Faso Ministry of Mines' Zoungrana Etienne on one of my trips to Ouagadougou.

I woke up early to get ready for the meeting. I looked around for some shampoo and found a small bottle of the stuff in my hotel room. As I lathered up I notice it smelled, well, like strawberries and something else, like strawberry bubble gum. Great. I washed it out and tried to get rid of the dainty aroma.

At breakfast I could see Serge trying to figure out where that curious strawberry bubblegum smell was coming from.

Right after breakfast we drove over to Minister Etienne's office. Zoungrana Etienne is a compact man of modest height with a strong featured round face. On the right side of his face are some long, wide vertical scars. These, I am told, are from tribal scarification ceremonies of initiation into adulthood. They are common to the Boni village areas—and I realize this man may have ancestry related to those people I had met in French Guiana not too many years ago. The scars of ceremonial tribalism contrast with the air-conditioned, neatly appointed office that exemplifies modern technology.

Well, Minister Etienne and I shook hands and began to discuss mining leases, environmental care, and mineral opportunities. I notice he would look around now and then and seem to sniff the air. Then he'd frown—unable to identify specifically the source of the strawberry bubblegum aroma. We talked for a while, and although the air conditioner was on, it didn't work too well, and my sweat seemed to intensify the presence of strawberry bubble gum. Finally the meeting concluded, and when Minister Etienne shook my hand, he leaned toward me and caught a whiff of the shampoo. He tipped his head slightly and frowned.

What could I do about that? I felt like saying, "Oh, that, why it's my strawberry bubblegum shampoo—do you like it? Can I have a mining permit? Please?"

String Theory—Loose Ends

I'm noticing there are an awful lot of loose ends in this business, too many questions, and so many overlapping and repeating histories. And I'm thinking about these Dogon—this desert, these people, their unseen planet, the apparent timelessness of the landscape, and stranger things. Recently we have been hearing strange rumors of crocodiles in these thirsty lands, and I wonder how such animals fit into the larger picture *here*. How is it all connected—really? It's connected—because it's . . . here. But what are the strings, and who is pulling them? What are the strings that stitch up this fabric of our reality?

Physicists, astronomers, biologists, geologists, many philosophers and *religionnaires*, and my mother are pursuing a deeper truth. They seek a fundamental theory for everything—the Universal Equation! Can we understand chaos, diversity, order, and beauty—and in doing so understand what drives us? The Universe!

Astronomers know there is dark matter out there where the Dogon's aliens came from. Some researchers say that over three-quarters of the universe is dark energy. We know this because when we look up there we can't see it! I'm looking up at the stars, but most of "space" is dark.

So the physicists came up with a theory that we can't test, and we want to apply it to the Universe—most of which we can't see. I thought my job was hard.

There is this theory about strings. String theory is based on ideas that remain experimentally unproven after thirty years of research: supersymmetry, additional spatial dimensions, and some special gravity conditions are necessary components to this theory.

The force of gravity that we feel, according to string theory, arises from hypothetical gravitons. One more thing we can't see. Also there are many dimensions, alternate realities—the usual stuff of science fiction. So—most of the universe we can't see, lots of neatly strung together ideas—not a bit of it can we prove. In this reality I can certainly believe these Dogon myths!

I always need extra dimensions—it's where my luggage resides when it doesn't show up at the airport!

The Left and the Right

Sometimes when Hugo visits it seems like he flies in from another dimension—certainly another reality. Hugo brings sobering doses of news from the head office in Melbourne, Australia.

The years have been trickling by. We've had some success, but we are also working within declining world markets and a wavering global economy. The company always wanted a mineral resource to be bigger and richer. The old adage in the business was that if a geologist finds an ore body, the engineering and economics will carve it down to size. The truth is that we are in a very competitive, costly, risky business. This means we have to find high-value metal deposits that are easy to mine at relatively low costs in countries that want to work with us. A world-class deposit can shoulder all of these requirements.

My team has found a number of gold deposits, but they average between one million and five million ounces of gold in the ore. The company is now saying they want gold deposits that contain ten million ounces. This is because it is more cost effective and easier to permit and manage the mining of a single ten-million ounce gold deposit than to mine multiple one- to five million-ounce gold deposits in multiple countries. Our odds for success diminish astronomically as the size and grade demands increase by an order of magnitude. My team is frustrated, because management had said we should bring them one-million-ounce gold deposits. We've done this, but now the rules have changed. In all of this Hugo tells me:

> "Raja, our old friends in corporate have been misbehaving. We're tightening our belts, I expect. You know they went ahead with the platinum deposit development, and that's not working out. We'll lose a billion dollars on that one. Some of the other projects that should not have gone forward, but did, are also not doing too well. There's a gas condensate project—we're losing money on that. Then there's the bad copper company merger—we probably paid two billion too much for that one. The board is simply afraid of going ahead with some good projects—they just don't know what to do. I don't think they trust us and, well, we don't trust them. Sometimes our discoveries get locked into a room in Melbourne, and the number crunchers and planners make conclusions without ever knowing what it is really like out here.
>
> "I know people are wondering about our company's commitment here, the minister of mines, even the president. We need to be straight with them—that we're in it for the long haul; look how long we've been here already.
>
> "Talking about politics, you're not really

supporting Bill Clinton? How can you? He'll shut us down. Gotta have a guy who supports the mining industry. But careful what you wish for. You might get a bleeding heart liberal in the White House again—and that just isn't a good thing for us. One more thing? Try to move a little more to the right—would you?

"I know! You're telling me about what the local miners have done out here. I've seen it; it looks like a thousand bomb craters. But we can't fix that. We didn't do that. We have to conduct business that improves these peoples' lives. We'll do better."

Hugo, Madani, Serge, and I keep talking numbers. Madani recalls when the company came to West Africa, starting in his home country of Mali. Oliver Warin and Jim Bratt were the innovators at the beginning, and they brought on Madani and Samba Toure and many other local geologists and administrators. But times have changed in the discovery world. Hugo mentioned that the newer gold discoveries are lower grade. In the 1980s the average discovery grades were commonly over 0.15 ounces per ton. In the 1990s this dropped to less than 0.1 ounces per ton. That might not seem like a lot, but other factors add to the challenge. First, the money we spent on exploration to find gold averaged between $15 to $20 per ounce. With gold hovering at about $300 per ounce in the late 1990s, that meant the mining costs had to be kept down. The catch-22 is the total value of the ore once all the costs of exploration and mining have been figured in. The company looks at this in detail and then decides if the profit is worth the risk.

So, I scribbled down some very generalized notes to illustrate what we were talking about in terms of simplified costs:

Price of Gold: $300 per Troy ounce.
Size of Gold Deposit: 1 million ounces at an average grade of 0.09 ounces per ton.
Ideal contained value: $300,000,000.
Ideal value of a ton of ore: $27, which means each ton of ore has 0.09 ounces gold.

150

Percentage recovery of gold: 91%, which means 9%
      of the gold is lost in the recovery process.
Recovered value of a ton of ore: $24.57, where
      recovery is 91% of ideal value.
Corrected contained value: $273,000,000, or 910,000
      ounces recovered.

Discovery cost per ounce:	$18.00	(6%)
Mining costs per ounce:		
Development	$44.00	(15%)
Capital Costs	$33.00	(11%)
Admin. & Gen.	$16.50	(6%)
Direct Mining	$167.70	(57%)
Tax & Royalty	$13.80	(5%)
Total All-Up Cost of gold:	$293.00 total $/ounce	

Exploration & mining cost - life of mine: $266,630,000

After cost earnings: $6,370,000, which translates
into *only a 2.4% rate of return.*

As we talked I could see Serge's shoulders sag, and Madani
looking off into the distance. We have found a number of deposits
that total over 7 million ounces of gold, but mining them would
require at least four separate operations. Hugo noted that when all of
our exploration started the gold price was over $400 per ounce and
that would mean the deposit would have a rate of return of over 25%
($364,000,000 recovered value). A number like that justified the
investment. But the drop in the gold price during the 1990s and the
lower discovered grades meant a reassessment of what was profitable
in terms of the investment risk of time and money.

But the odds were increasingly stacked against us. We knew the
numbers, and the statistics that said only about fifteen percent of the
deposits discovered were larger than ten million contained ounces.
We also knew that newer discoveries were being made in old and
existing mining districts. That meant that new areas, which we called

grassroots exploration, were becoming harder and harder to find. We might look at a thousand properties, and only ten would be worth drilling, and only one would yield some kind of gold deposit. Even as our technologies improved and cost controls were better understood, our jobs were literally like looking for a needle in a haystack. All of the metals we use for civilization are found this way.

Serge said, "Does upper management even know how difficult it is to find a gold deposit?"

"I tell them," Hugo said. "But when you are in the air-conditioned board room on the upper floors of a skyscraper looking at a ledger full of numbers, well, a lot of that is not greatly appreciated. Besides, they say that we were hired to do this job, no matter how difficult."

Hugo's visit is circumspect, and tinged with foreshadowing. We are explorers. That's what we do. But we are also stewards of the land and need to enrich the communities in which we work, and that's what we've learned. Serge and I argue ecology with Hugo. For more than twenty years I've been balancing on the blade of the mining industry—working behind the scenes to input environmental land practices while trying to influence more responsible mining behavior. The progress is akin to walking up a steep sand dune. You'll make it eventually, but there's a lot of sliding down that slippery slope. I had been working on Hugo for years. He was bending to accommodate ecology—reluctantly. But he loves the game more than anything.

Serge tipped his last beer, but even after several he still looked sober on account of the evening's discussion. Madani finished his last Coca-Cola. Both men pardoned themselves to go to bed. Hugo, though, didn't feel like sleeping. He slept so little. I had shared enough rooms with him in desperate mining towns to know he'd get up at three in the morning to work. He'd make a bunch of phone calls to people in different time zones or catch up on some reading. Or take a late night chocolate break—one of his main sources of contentment.

So tonight we sit in the calm heat of northern Burkina Faso, while sipping another beer.

"Hugo, this is why we need to be careful here—better stewards of the land, better diplomats, better humans. Serge and Madani and their staff see us as so rich that we hardly care how much money we spend or how much something costs. Madani and Serge have both been to San Francisco, and they know what it's like. The average income here in Ouaga is about $200 a year—and in Marin County about $200,000 a year. You and me—we can expect to live eighty or ninety years, but here—lucky to make fifty. Few here ever finish a high school equivalence, let alone college—not so in the United States or Australia. There is virtually no medical insurance here—but you and I have that well covered. And transport and housing—you've got an SUV, the locals here might have a donkey or a moped."

"I know," Hugo said. "But our mines will bring wealth. We have got to find bigger deposits."

"True. For a while—then what?" I replied. "And if we pull out, if we can't keep our word to the staff and their families? We've brought them prosperity for now. But even this prosperity is at risk because of the decisions by the board in Melbourne. We don't have the equation right for the universal applications of equality, wealth, sustainability, things like that."

Hugo nodded, and said. "You know I travel almost all the time—like you. I get lost in this world of travel; I see these things all around the world. I know what you're saying. But we must fight the battles we can win. Let me worry about Melbourne. You got a great bunch of guys here. You know what to do."

Hugo and I had hundreds of days and nights traveling, and to a large degree we felt a bit nomadic. It is then we question what drives us so. This human need to do something—the quest for an unknown "thing."

Hugo would sometimes doubt all of what we were doing. "Sometimes, Raja, we're just puppets on a string. Sometimes, Raja, the maps don't help us."

Shadow of a Doubt

```
      A         E
```
Got a map without a highway
to a place that I don't know.
Been around this world so many times.
It's wearing down my soul.

Refrain:
```
   A    B       E      B   A
```
And I'm trying to remember
what this is all about.
This life will leave you stranded,
with your shadows and your doubts.

You know I've walked so far
the road wore through my shoes.
Standing here with empty pockets
listen to this same old news.

Refrain

If you talk about emotion
then you're talkin' 'bout some tears.
Try to possess what you cannot own
will make you old before your years.

Refrain

Madani's Well

WATER!!!

Serge stops the Land Cruiser near a water well that is surrounded by about a hundred women and children. The women are filling up five- and ten-gallon plastic containers with water. The kids are splashing and laughing in the cool fluid between their mothers filling the containers. There are smiles and laughing on this hot, brilliantly sunny day. The water looks like liquid diamond as it sparkles in the unforgiving light—it is the most valuable commodity around.

I follow Madani to the well. The kids are having a blast pumping water. Madani talks to the women—and suddenly everyone lets out a great cheer and begin singing, and their arms go up and they circle all around me. The women put their hands on my arms, my shoulders, on my hat—they touch me gently, patting me and smiling and cheering.

"What's this?" I call to Madani over the din.

"This is the water well you paid for. Now they don't have to walk ten kilometers for water! I told them you are the one that gave us the money to drill the well."

"But you drilled the well, Madani—it's to your credit!" I say.

"No, Roger—I could not have drilled this if you had not given me a budget and trusted my judgment—it is you who did this good thing," Madani says.

"Okay—well, it's all of us then!" And I took my hat off and bowed to Madani.

The women cheer even more, and some of them pat my balding white head—laughing the whole time. One of the kids comes up to me with his hands cupped and full of water—grinning he splashes it on my shirt.

And we all get soaking wet in the dry Sahara sun.

President Blaise Compaoré

Serge has set up a meeting with the president! President Compaoré of Burkina Faso. For this we go to Ouagadougou.

Hugo has just flown in from San Francisco for the meeting. Serge and I pick him up at the airport, and within an hour we are at the door of the president's palace.

Blaise Compaoré. We had heard a lot about this man. Not all of it peaceful.

An aid to the president meets us at the door. He directs us down a wide hall and into a broad open area that has a set of couches arranged in a square in the middle of the room. The windows are open, and the air conditioning is on full blast. Hugo, Serge, and I sit down as directed by the aide and await President Compaoré. Serge has a big smile on his face—meeting his president, this doesn't happen every day.

And then, after about an hour's wait, President Blaise Compaoré enters the far end of the room. Alone, and with a steady pace, he approaches us directly. Today he is dressed in a traditional white Burkinabè *tuntun fani* kolokore, a traditional cotton-silk long robe that is embroidered with fine golden silk strands. He is also wearing a traditional white and embroidered pillbox cap, or *pugulugwili*. Compaoré is of the Mossi ethnic group, which is the majority in Burkina Faso, and well understands the etiquette and ceremony. He is sending us a message of Burkinabè national pride. The three of us stand to welcome him. Compaoré is tall, stern, confident, and handsome. In 1996 he had been in power for nine years. The president shakes our hands and then motions to the couches. We all sit down. Formalities are spoken and introductions made.

President Compaoré says, "I am told by the message from Dr. Nikiema that you are finding gold and wanting to mine this gold in my country. Are things going well?"

"Thank you for your time, Mr. President," I say. "We wanted to let you know of our operations and seek any advice from you that you wish to share."

To Hugo and I the president says, "Do you know what Burkina Faso means? It means the Land of Upright Men." Compaoré paused and looked at each of us closely. "My advice begins with a question. What are your intentions regarding our upright men?"

Hugo: "Our intentions are to mine gold and conduct good business."

President: "And improve and employ my people, I hope."

Hugo: "Yes, of course. Dr. Serge Nikiema is an example of our commitment."

President: "And you are spending millions of US dollars?"

Hugo: "Yes."

President: "And you are employing many?"

Hugo: "Yes, we have ten employees right now in Burkina Faso."

President: "Not enough! We need thousands of jobs. Thousands!"

Hugo: "If we succeed, that will come."

President: "Thousands of jobs?"

Serge's eyebrows go up. Serge is not a poker player. He recalls the conversation about the company's new demands on the size of discoveries needed.

Hugo: "If the mines are large enough."

President: "And you—your company—it is very big. I looked at the information. Your corporate leaders understand Africa. Yes?"

Hugo: "They do."

Serge's eyebrows go up again. I'm biting my tongue. The president sees Serge's expression.

President: "I'm sure they do. But those men not from here seldom understand our ways. So you will stay here as you promise? And you will bring jobs to the people?"

Hugo: "That is our wish."

Serge's eyebrows go up again. Hugo's reply is not a lie, nor is it a truth—but a wish. His reply is corporate vague . . . "who is this "our"—is it the corporation or is it the three of us?"

The president studies us for a brief moment, but it truly seems like an eternity. He is sizing us up. Compaoré is used to sizing people up. He came into power on October 15, 1987, in a bloody coup during which the existing head of state, President Sankara, was killed.

Compaoré had publicly stated, "This death was an accident." No one believed him. Compaoré overturned Sankara's policies and instituted what he called the "Rectification of the Burkinabé Revolution." Compaoré refused to investigate the murder. Two other major revolutionary leaders were soon "eliminated" so as not to create problems. The UN Human Rights Committee would ultimately issue a condemnation of Compaoré's failure to investigate the murders. But the killing would continue. Reporters in the media who criticized Compaoré's policies were taunted, and one would be killed in 1998, again mysteriously, and again no investigation.

After the seemingly timeless pause, President Compaoré broke into a smile. "I understand you. All is good." And he stood up, shook our hands, and promptly left.

And here we stand. The empty space before us; the impression of the hand of a president still felt in ours. This hand touched by the blood of his predecessor and the blood of others.

Trade Routes and the Sahara Desert

Today Serge and I are in the field mapping quartz veins and rock types. It is hot . . . 114 degrees Fahrenheit. There is no shade. And Serge just keeps on going. I've got northern European genes in my makeup, and this heat is really testing me. We've been in it for days, and we have been drinking a lot of water. But still, some days my urine is dark yellow-brown—a sure sign that my body is drying out.

In the distance I can see several Tuareg walking before their camels. Serge looks up and wipes some sweat from his brow. "Maybe a small caravan," he says. "There aren't many of those left, they're being replaced with modern transportation."

Dromedary camels are the Tuareg's principal means of transport. The camel's physical features seem to beg us to evolve into desert-tolerant creatures. Their long eyelashes keep sand from their eyes, and if that fails a double eyelid brushes away sand and dust. They have thick fur that keeps the heat away from their skin. Their big feet let them travel easily on the sand, and their slit-like nostrils close during sand storms. Their temperament is bad, though, and they spit and bray and bite nearly everyone but their masters.

Serge says, "And the oases of the Sahara are not as many as before. No one knows why the lands are drying up. It looks like those Tuareg come from where the crocodiles are."

There are rumors of crocodiles in these dry lands— but crocodiles here in this desert? We see no water. The oases draw upon the fossil water in deep aquifers filled during two million years of greener times during the continental glaciation and more moderate northern Africa temperatures.

Beginning almost three thousand years ago, incredible camel caravan routes were set up that relied on the oasis communities for water, sustenance, and security. The caravans were well organized and led by knowledgeable, well-paid Berber guides. The typical caravan had a thousand camels. But some combined five thousand or ten thousand camels, all plied with goods bound for North Africa: gold, ivory, iron, and slaves. Scouts went ahead to secure oasis water and safe routes and to avoid bandits. On the return trip came salt, cloth, beads, and metal goods. Some of the slaves returned as trained slave soldiers to serve under the West African tribal powers.

But in 1591 Moroccan troops attacked Timbuktu and other Malian trading centers. The infrastructure was all but destroyed and never recovered in terms of natural cultural progression. Lean times were the fruits of these conquests. By 1890 the French had arrived— an invasion of the Sahel. The colonial yoke was put around the necks of the West African empires. Attempts to revitalize or modernize infrastructure had failed by the early 1960s when these colonially defined countries acquired independence. National boundaries stopped the colonial projects.

The new governments pushed out the nomadic people, such as the Tuareg, and even railed against Tuareg nationalism.

In the new era of nationalism, arose new markets for West African raw materials. In this era, President Compaoré rules. It is within this context that my team of African explorers was working.

I was driving through Ouagadougou yesterday, which made Serge a bit nervous. The streets are crowded with bicycles, pedestrians, animals, and weaving vehicles.

These roads are the crossover of realities—a donkey next to a $30,000 Land Cruiser; a geologist with a GPS unit and satellite phone next to a Tuareg who navigates by the sun and stars.

When I pulled into the Hotel Le Silmande, Serge exclaimed, "I am so surprised, we made it! You did very well!"

During my many trips here I feel like I've connected my universe or reality with Serge's. There I go again, thinking about all the realities and how to connect them.

Theory of Everything

What did T. S. Eliot say? Something like: "Einstein, Newton—what were they thinking?" I could say the same thing about exploration geologists! But we're all trying to string things together.

Theory of Everything

```
G                        C/G
```
You've got your reality and I've got mine.
Let's tie it all together with a simple piece of twine.
You may have odd dimensions I won't say a thing.
```
G                            C/G          D
```
But every part of you is part of the whole; connected by these strings.

Refrain:

```
        C               G
```
Everything is one . . . universal equation.
```
        D           D7              C                   G
```
Doesn't matter 'bout time or space . . . to get to your destination.

I crawled out of a wormhole you made a funny face.
All I do is change my shape in your fabric of space.
You warped and stretched me; so I called my quantum mechanic.
He said, "It's all chance—just tossed the dice."
But string theory is a panic.

Refrain
Bridge:
```
            D                       C               G
```
We got photons and electron and galaxies, neutrons, gluons and stars.
We got fermions and tiny sparticles, and morons driving cars.
We got hadrons and gravitons and super nova it's a new phenomenology.
We got klingons, debutons and dark matter, in this astronomical
theory.

Let's do a space and time fling in a gravity well of tiny little things.
I've got dimensions a-plenty of vibrating energy strings
I guess its my idea of just communication of being
Got the big bang, a bunch of black holes; it'sthe theory of everything.

Refrain

Everything is one . . . universal equation.
Doesn't matter 'bout time or space . . . to get to your destination.
Gravitational transportations; Emotional transmutations
Atomic morphological investigations; Career choice retributions
Physio-ecological insurrections; Relationship insurrections
Geo-seismological transformations; Black hole suck-you-dry corporations
It's an energy sensation.

END: *I can't prove it, you can't prove it, but we believe it is true.*

ACT 2

The Bartering of Gold

Hugo calls me one day while I am in the Ouagadougou office. "Raja, I need you to sell all of our West African gold assets—all the discoveries, all the mineral licenses. And don't tell your staff. Keep it as quiet as you can, as we don't want people to panic."

Don't panic? Don't tell my staff? Across Africa I had 350 people working for the company in 14 countries with five offices. Trust, respect, honesty, and the vitality of our teams would be compromised if I did not bring my managers into this discussion. Madani would be the first person I would call.

Hugo explains that the company's board of directors have pursued too many bad deals and projects. The fallout is consolidation, reevaluation, reorganization, reprioritization, rebudgeting—and, for the staff, the dreaded word . . . retrenchment—being laid off. The fruits of corporate disasters are now cascading down upon my remote African teams.

The moment I said to Madani and Serge that we need to joint venture or sell our discoveries they knew. They knew we were out of business.

Crocodiles in the Desert

Even though we are selling our gold assets, we continue to look for more—a bigger prize. With our explorationist's optimism we hope to avert the impending corporate disaster.

Serge, two others, and myself wander across the Burkina Sahel. The river courses are bone-dry dips in the landscape where hungry, dead-looking trees await the rain.

We drive south to a place called Dala. This is the place, Serge tells me, that crocodiles are rumored to live in the desert. We see no water anywhere. Every depression we pass was once a water hole or pond but is now dry and hopeless. Serge and I find it nearly impossible to believe that there could be crocodiles here.

We park our Land Cruiser and walk into the village. This prehistoric place of rounded stick and reed huts is set along a small dry pond below huge rounded rocks. We are told that during the rainy season there is water here for two months. Then it dries up as a dusty basin for ten months of the year. During the dry season the locals pull clean cool water from a forty-foot-deep well tapping the fossil water beneath the desert.

Serge asks one of the older men if there are crocodiles here. "Yes, yes," the man says and points to the dry depression. Serge smiles. "He says the crocodiles live in the pond!" Serge talks to the man some more and then tells us, "Oh, he says the crocodiles are only there for a month when the water is here, but the rest of the time they go up into the mountain—up there to the rounded granite mountain behind the village. That's what he says, but I told him crocodiles don't inhabit mountains. He says they do."

Serge talks to the man some more, but we are directed to the village center to talk to the holy man. "We must get permission to talk about the crocodiles and see where they are," Serge tells us. He shrugs and smiles in disbelief. "I cannot believe this—crocodiles in the desert!"

As we walk toward the center of the small village a crowd gathers and follows us. The children walk with me, hold my hands, and smile up at me.

The holy man is ancient in appearance. His wrinkled face and body is almost mummified, and his eyes are clouded and there is white stubble on his face. He smiles, many missing teeth, and reaches up to shake our hands from his seated position before one of the huts. His contact is more of a touch and hold than a shake. The holy man nods at us as he listens to Serge describing who we are. He considers our request to see the crocodiles.

The holy man talks for a long time to Serge. He points to the sky, he points to the dry pond, and he points to the mountains. Serge tells us, "He says there are crocodiles here. They have been here forever. But now the water is rare, it used to fill the pond for more than half the year, but now only one or two months. So the crocodiles cannot survive if they stay in the pond. The holy man says they crawl up into the mountains. It is unbelievable. He says they go into a cave."

The holy man gives us permission to go up to the caves in which the crocodiles hide during the dry months.

We walk up the rounded rock hills, led by a dozen locals who see this as a fun diversion from their normal desert tasks. Elephant-sized boulders are strewn about. Into the rocks we climb, through narrow paths, up steep slopes, and between narrow rocky passes. The locals keep telling us this is the path of the crocodiles.

Serge and I look at each other—we can't believe a crocodile would crawl thousands of feet up a dry rocky mountainside. Yet the locals insist it is true. Finally we reach a sandy open area that ends at a rocky overhanging wall. At the base of the cliff is a low deep cave. One of the villager's points into the cave, and tells Serge this is the place.

"That's where the crocodiles go, that's what he insists," Serge says.

I look closely at the sand ahead of us. And I can see the distinct impressions of a crocodile's clawed feet. There are also tail drag marks. As I look more closely I can see a half dozen different-sized footprints, each set with its own distinct tail drag marks.

All of the tracks continue into the low dark cave. I get down on my stomach and peer into the cave. I angle the mirror on my compass so that I can shine light into the cave. I hand the light back to Serge and ask him to the reflect the light as far into the cave as he can. The grotto I enter is a low, cool, dark space; it is too low to move on all fours. I can smell the water in the air—and realize there is water deep inside this mountain. Water that the crocodiles smelled and followed into this cave. On my stomach I crawl into the entrance; a very mild animal smell is in the air. Listening closely I can hear faint indistinct noises far inside the cave. I drag myself a bit further into the cave.

The tail drag marks are deep and the claw prints larger than my hand. My body is blocking the tenuous light reflected from the compass mirror Serge is holding at the entrance. I suddenly think—*What if I run into one of these crocodiles?* I back out of the cave.

The locals gather around Serge and me as I stand up and brush off the sand. I nod to the local men; they are right. We have witnessed an incredible proof. These signs of crocodiles are evidence of the last large animals in a now defunct ecosystem. Their habitat has all but died as the Sahara expands and dries out West Africa.

Back in the village we thank the holy man. He smiles a broad smile and nods acknowledgment. He tells Serge that the crocodiles are sacred—they are not killed and seem to live in the reservoir during their brief respite from the refuge cave. The holy man tells us that the crocodiles live up in these rocks without harming the locals or livestock.

One man tells us the crocs eat frogs, toads, and dirt. He says sometimes goats go missing.

The Corporate Knife Cuts Deep
(1999)

I have been flown to Australia for urgent meetings. Hugo is worried the company is going to feed him to the crocodiles! The corporate leaders have decided to eliminate our global mineral exploration. This means just about everyone will lose their jobs. Hugo wants to meet with me and the other seven general managers who oversee all the exploration regions of the globe and work out a transition plan. I am not sure what kind of "transition" plan can be made . . . more like abandoning ship!

The days growl by like we're doing time in a prison camp—we can't leave, we have to make this transition plan, and there are the seeds of revolution in the team. We have cut our geosciences staff by over 70 percent and our support and technical staff by over 90 percent. It is so hard, going one by one, deciding the fate of our friends.

The group's team dynamics begin to break down. Some are working behind the scenes to undo Hugo's career. They are the backstabbers and are end-running Hugo. Hugo is a stubborn man and doesn't always see the shortcomings of his team. He tends to trust, and this will, in part, lead to his undoing. Meanwhile, teams all around the world die. Scientists are let loose to find new careers.

The corporate facilitators say it is just business. But it is not. It is always about people, for without people we have no reason to do business. This is personal, these are our friends, and this is where we have spent our years, our lives. Now the corporation just draws a line through a name on an organizational chart. It is clear to me that the most dangerous crocodiles are not in the desert, but rather in the boardroom.

In a matter of weeks the iron-fisted hand of a dispassionate board puts tens of thousands of people out of work around the world.

Hugo and I spend time together, and at one point tears well in his eyes. "It's all gone. This is such a waste of good people. We've been thrown out like so much trash."

The African Team Dies

The last few days have been the worse days of my career. Back in Cape Town I have to tell my staff that our jobs are gone. I talk to each one. There are gasps from some of the people as they realize what has been decided. So many personal histories impacted and so many dashed dreams. I would help many get new jobs.

People are being dispersed to the wind. The global metal markets have fallen and the collateral damage is people. The company has to protect its stockholder value, or it too will cease to exist. There are whispers of the company merging with other huge mineral companies to strengthen their market share. None of that really matters to most of my African team; how do you explain to your wife and children in

Burkino Faso that a decision made ten thousand miles away for global market reasons means you have no job. A few will stay on, but most will find work elsewhere. We are all exhausted. Months of meetings, reorganizations and budget cuts, and planning and confrontation all come to this conclusive end. My body just caves in. The company has created its own black hole, and now it has gone supernova, dispersing us like stardust.

Hugo tells me I should accept an offer to move to Australia and help with acquisitions and other business in this now very different company.

And then Hugo tells me—"Things don't look good for me. We found the diamonds in Canada, the gold in Africa, and this is how they thank us. I hope you stay, this company needs you."

My job . . . this job, is like a mirage in the desert. It wavers and fades . . . it is unreal.

It is not real.

When parallel universes collide you get a big bang; that's what the string theorists say. Like I said, the mind wanders. Like in physics, as in business . . . when things improperly interact you get a big bang because all that energy has to go somewhere. In this case it is human energy.

ACT 3

Hugo's Last Meeting

A week later I fly back to Australia. I am with Hugo in his new apartment in Melbourne.

"They want me to be here. They want to keep an eye on me. They really want to let me go," Hugo said to me. We are sitting in his small living room at dusk, looking out through the twentieth-floor picture window at the city of Melbourne. "See, it's not so bad," he says unconvinced.

Hugo is like a caged wild animal—far from family and friends, far from exploration and adventure—a captain without a ship. Captive in the nest of those corporate masters he just never really got along with.

"I just can't play this game," he says. "I tried so hard to save all these jobs—we lost just about everyone. I don't know whom to trust. You're the only one. I don't know about the others. They are the backstabbers. I thought those people were my friends. What has happened here?"

The problem is that people forget business is personal.

Never *not* hear the music.

The Death of Dreams

It's dark. It's hot. It's late. It's time to fly again.

I have one last trip to see Madani in Ghana. One of his helpers stopped me in the now empty office. He thanked me for helping find him a new job. We had been able to place just about everyone. Then he said, "Do not deny reality—even mother has to die someday."

Madani is without work. Serge will stay on in the significantly downsized company. I have declined a position in acquisitions and will move on to some other reality.

Serge says, "We are like the crocodile. Remember them—we saw where they lived in the desert where they shouldn't be! Now we retreat to some place that is better for us. We wait for the rainy season so we can drink water again. We are patient."

But Hugo is gone. He has moved on to a small exploration company. Two years later tragedy would strike—his truck would roll over while he was driving alone in the platinum fields of South Africa. He would have fallen asleep because of jet lag and pushing himself too hard. He would be found a day later, lying on the African soil that was his birthplace.

A life captured by the urgencies of an explorationist.

A kindhearted, bighearted man who spread himself too thin, who was, really, out of control.

Roger James Kuhns

Out of Control

D+G   Dsus   G+D/C   G+D
Picture it now,   clear in your mind.
F   G
A road long and dusty—left far behind.
You travel it now, asleep at the wheel.
Whisper last rights: The Dream It Is Real.

Refrain:

Cm   Am   G   Am
'Round the world you go out of control.
'Round the world you go spinning alone.
'Round the world you go out of control;
spinning alone, out of control, out of control.

The beating heart is the measure of life.
Push it too hard into the night.
So many know you, but not all that well.
The road is your mistress, that's where you fell.

Refrain

Instrumental interlude
Am G Am G Am G Am G
D+G Dsus G+D/C G+D

Ship in the desert; no Captain on deck.
Sea of illusion; sea of regret.
How can we find you drifting this way?
Soldier of fortune, no sheltering bay.

Refrain

Oasis

I remember . . . I *remember* . . . I REMEMBER!

There is a deep hole in the desert that was dug by hand and lined with rock to keep the sand out. Nevertheless, when the winds sweep hot air across North Africa the sand can build up and threaten to bury this hole, at the bottom of which is clear, clean, cool water. The wind blows so hard sometimes that the well moans, deep flutelike baritone sounds, as if staving off the creeping fingers of sand that threaten its very existence. I have heard chanting in the desert and wonder if it originates from such a place—people mimicking the sound of the wind?

Today I find myself by the well, but there is no wind and the sun is blowtorch hot on my shoulders. My two traveling companions and I have come to refill our canteens and rest under the suffering trees. Our Land Cruiser causes some notice by five Tuareg nomads who are also visiting the well.

The Tuareg have arrived on their camels, and the men have tethered the beasts to various bushes to keep them from wandering off. Everyone is thirsty.

One dusty old man, as brown as sunbaked leather, sits by the well. A cotton *riga* shirt under a faded indigo cloak hides the man's bony frame that hints of his thirst and hunger. Yet, there is no complaining here, not in his wizened brown eyes which seem to focus somewhere in memory's distant recesses. He squints his eyes in the moment's caustic sunlight and watches us as we approach the well. It is no one's, it is for everyone to use.

The afternoon sky is blindingly bright, so much so that colors seem faded out. In this light humans take on the characteristics of leafless trees stranded at this meager oasis. The Tuareg men are here waiting for the heat to drift west with the afternoon sun. Each man possesses a bag sewn from goatskins enclosing personal treasures and tools used for desert survival and practicing stubborn faith. Several of them hide their expressions with indigo head cloths. My thirsty expression is easy to read, only shaded by my fedora, which is dirty and ringed with dried sweat.

We walk sluggishly to the well and note the rope. Tugging on it I can tell there is not a bucket. Angling the small mirror on my compass, I shine sunlight down the well to estimate its depth. All eyes are on me. I guess it to be fifty feet deep. I also discover a fifteen-foot deficit in the rope's length. No bucket in any event. This makes us even hungrier for the desert's water. I raise calloused fingers to my chapped lips and my tongue seems to remember the emotion of cool, clear, clean water. It is more important than food. It is more important than anything.

My companion produces a length of rope from his backpack. One of the Tuareg stands up in a single fluid motion, empties his goatskin bag, and offers it to us—its use obvious. We tie one end of the rope to the bag—bucket fashion, holding it open with crossed-sticks. Then, I pull up the existing rope and join the ends. Down the well goes the makeshift bucket. Glad smiles welcome the splash, as if to announce: just enough rope.

Many hands come to assist as miracle water is tasted and saved to goatskin canteens. The sound of water being poured is desert music.

There is a shuffling of the pad-like feet of the dromedaries; they smell and hear the water. A thirsty camel can drink thirty to forty gallons of water in ten minutes.

We drop the bucket a few times for ourselves and fill our canteens. We'll leave it to the Tuareg to water their camels.

But we have water now, and this brings on an impromptu feast of dried meat, dates, and hard unleavened bread that is shared all around. The orange molten sun deforms into a mirage horizon. Our mortal bodies are revived. Once cloaked faces are now visible and animated with discussions. I do not understand the spoken language, and my friends only catch the occasional word. But it does not matter.

I close my eyes and become, for the briefest of lifetimes, a welcome companion to a lost time in an unmapped place with ageless men who share a moment because of the need to survive.

Time drifts, and we find the evening upon us as the sun escapes below the horizon without fanfare. The older man in the Tuareg group has a presence about him. It seems to me that he is the desert's own child. An amulet around his neck holds a passage from the Qur'an.

This nomad, this faithful man of the desert, unwraps a bundle that protects a bulbous half of a calabash gourd. It is covered with a goatskin, with a stick attached to one side and a single drone string. The lute-like instrument is ornamented with small, white cowry shells, leather tassels, and inked design work. Warbled chanting and singing ensues as the droning of the lute gives the still night air a haunting quality.

The wind in our lungs is like that of the land—vibrant, warm with life, and singing of Allah's gift of giving up the desert water.

I am the stranger here, from as far away as the others can barely imagine—an alien of sorts, as unbelievable as crocodiles in the desert. The spirit of my friend is alongside me now. We are strands of string in these crossover realities. But we are not so very different tonight, and we know this to be true, and in that realization is peace.

I sing my own lyrics to a shared melody heard only once but remembered forever.

Roger James Kuhns

DREAMTIME DOWN UNDER

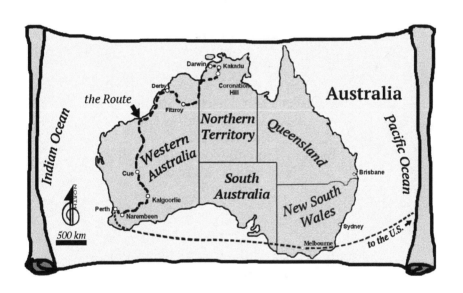

ACT 1
Dreaming
Paddock
Oliver
Paddock
On the Road
"Any Time You Like" song
Back to the Paddock
Oliver
Back in Time

ACT 2
Oliver's San Anselmo Studio
Back in Time Outback
The Sculpture
Back in Time to Coronation Hill
Nineteen Years Later
Dreaming

ACT 3
Twenty Years and the San Anselmo Retreat
Back in Time Again
"Outback" song
Forward Twenty Years
"Expectation" song
Dreamtime
A Vision of Oliver

ACT 1

Dreaming

Dinney is a ragtag, dusty, soil-colored and down-to-earth Australian Aboriginal dreamer. I met him in the Northern Territory. He was always giving me advice; good advice I might add. It is from Dinney that I learned to play the didgeridoo. But more than once he would say to me: "I was just dreaming. This is what I dreamed . . ."

So it was I found myself traveling in Australia. It was 1988, and I had just flown into Perth on the coast of the Indian Ocean in Western Australia. Perth might be the most remote city of its size in the world. Within hours I had met up with my colleague Geoff Woad—we both worked for a large Australian mining company, and I'd been sent Down Under to help him figure out the geology of a newly discovered gold deposit. Soon we were driving east of Perth in his field truck, headed to the project area outside the small town of Narembeen.

The first thing I wanted to see upon arriving in Australia was a kangaroo.

Geoff's truck had these huge bars across the front grill. He called them "roo-bars" and said Australians never slow down for 'roos—they just bounce them off the bars.

It's a three and a half hour trip to Narembeen from Perth. Keep going east or north, and it gets drier and drier until you're outback! The eucalyptus gum trees give way to farmland—mainly wheat and sheep. The first 'roo I see in Australia is roadkill.

Paddock

We arrive in the late afternoon. The town sign says, "Welcome to Narembeen—a Tidy Town." Not sure what a Tidy Town is, but it did look tidy.

We pull into the Narembeen pub, café, bed and breakfast—an all-in-one business in this small Tidy Town. By the time we're settled in, it's the dinner hour—a meal of lamb, potatoes, cauliflower, and peas.

We are here to explore gold properties, particularly in the ancient geologic region called the Western Gneiss Terrain—which is a kind of composite of overly cooked and deformed rock. These are old rocks—some of the oldest on the planet—and they've got gold in them. I will be helping Geoff work out the geology and economics of the gold mineralization on a property owned by what I'm told is the "little off his rocker" Farmer Gault.

The land is much like Kansas, except there are sheep instead of cattle, eucalyptus instead of cottonwood, and kangaroos instead of deer. Native animals tend to hop instead of run—that's the motion you see in your peripheral vision.

Oliver

Oliver Warin was well into his fifth decade when I met him; crazy wild salt-and-pepper hair, a bushy artisan mustache, bright inquisitive eyes, and severe untamed eyebrows.

I'd been introduced to him for the first time just a month ago at a company meeting; he came up to me and said, "You're that good! So says the exploration grapevine." Oliver grabbed my hand and held it with both of his. He leaned into me so our bodies touched and whispered, "But around every corner is the next best thing, so never rest on your laurels!"

Oliver is a blend of Balzac, Milk, and Oz . . . all the intensity of Balzac, the sense of human justice of Harvey Milk, and—I'd say—the whimsy of the Wizard of Oz!

Oliver grins at me—it's almost *caricaturistic,* too animated, too full of energy, too enthusiastic. My new mentor, although I didn't know it at the moment, was the quintessential Renaissance Man: a concert pianist, sculptor-artist, and world class geologist—born in Britain, seasoned Down Under, emigrant to America, but a citizen of the world. "So it's off to Australia you go!"

He opened the door to the world—and I jumped through!

Paddock

We wake up at 6 a.m. to a bowl of Australian Weeties—bran flakes strongly resembling pressed cardboard. I heap granulated sugar on them for flavor. At night dinner is home-cooked, and we're given only one choice each evening; even days are lamb, odd days are beef—always with lots of peas and mashed potatoes.

Each morning, after the cardboard breakfast, we drive in the tray-back (flatbed truck) out to the Gault farm southeast of town; long days out in the windy, cool paddocks. Geoff is a young fellow, even tempered, handsome, and soft-spoken.

Geoff is good with his "fieldies." One of the fieldies, named Stuart, needs watching—so says Geoff. "Stuart, a dangerous lad, that one; fancies himself a swagman of sorts. But he's never been out of Perth before. Not too much upstairs. Kuhns, chase away them jumbucks before that troublesome lad Stuart has his way with them!"

Roger: "Jumbucks? All I see is sheep . . . Oh."

Stuart: "What 'ave you got against sheep?"

Geoff: "Look at them, Stuart, they're watchin' ya and shakin' in their woolies, they're fearing for their dignity because of you, Stuart."

Stuart: "I want to go home. I miss my girl." (He was wearing a cowboy hat with cork hanging from string all around the brim—to

181

keep the flies out of his face. He looks ridiculous, but it seems to work. Thing is, there aren't any flies out today.)

Geoff: "You miss your girl? That's your problem, cobber. The life of a geologist is a lonely, desperate, miserable, thankless existence Stuart. Didn't anyone ever tell you that? That's why you make those jumbucks as nervous as a snake crossing a highway full of road trains! Life wasn't meant to be easy, lad! Show some backbone—not that other bone!"

Later that day Stuart put gasoline in the tank of a diesel truck. "Wha'? Wha'? I didn't know—how'm I s'posed to know?"

Geoff: "Didn't they teach you to read at university. Look here—this says, 'Diesel Fuel Only' right here on the side of the truck!"

Stuart: "Yeah."

Geoff: "Did you see that?"

Stuart: "Yeah."

Geoff: "Stuart. Stay away from anything mechanical, electrical, combustible, living or nonliving!"

Stuart: "I can still see my girlfriend?"

Geoff: "I don't know, what species is she?"

Stuart: "What you mean by that, she's a girl."

Geoff rolls his eyes. Stuart says, "You want me to fill up the other vehicles?" Geoff rolls his eyes again.

Now Narembeen and our little gold property are west of the geologic mecca—that golden city of Oz, that geologic dream land called Kalgoorlie. An unbelievable amount of gold has come out of the Kalgoorlie mines. Geoff dreams of discovering a new City of Gold. But for now Geoff and I are just out standing our field on this cool morning.

I tell Geoff, "I feel a lot more like I do now than when I first got here."

I'm looking at the field office, which is an old farmhouse that was previously used to store hay and wheat, so the place is full of mice.

Geoff says, "The mice are a good sign because it means there are no snakes in the house."

This morning the pile of drill core logs and field notes on my desk start to move. I carefully lift up some of the pages to see if there is a mouse trapped under all this paperwork. Not a mouse . . . I am holding my hand lens pretty close to all these eyes; eight eyes—amazing. It's a big spider—twelve inches across! It moves one of its spiny hairy legs out toward me. Kind of like it's testing what's there. I've got my insect field guidebook open and say to Geoff, "It's a Huntsman, it's an *Isopeda vasta*."

"Kuhns!" Geoff says, "What are you doing with that spider?"

"Hey, this is a huge one, like a giant crab! It was under my drill logs."

"Yeah, and they're deadly and they jump!"

"They jump?" And with that I perform an acrobatic leap from my seated position, into the air, landing three feet away from the spider. Geoff is smiling. I think he's scoring me a nine-point-five on the move.

"No. But you sure can! And they're not deadly. But that one is."

I'm not saying a thing, but I am getting jumpy again. I look to where Geoff is pointing on the far wall. There is another spider dangling just above head level. Spiders are not my favorite creatures.

"That's a redback," Geoff says, rolling up a magazine as he talks. "The females bite—fancy that—and it's deadly; gets your neurotransmitters." Geoff smashes the spider with a rolled up magazine. We now have colorful, neo-splatter impressionistic insect artwork on the walls.

Meanwhile the Huntsman has retreated and is now out of sight. I still have my *Deadly Critters of Australia* guidebook open and read a bit more. I learn that one enemy of the Huntsman is *Cryptocheilus bicolor*—the spider wasp. The wasp hunts the Huntsman, flying around as the spider rears up defending itself with its long legs. The wasp is trying to get on top of the spider's back. It is like a gruesome dance, and ultimately the wasp dives in like a Huey helicopter and lands on the spider, hanging on as it adjusts its stinger. Now in place, it stings and immobilizes the spider, then lays a single egg in the spider's belly. When the larva hatches it feeds on the still-living, stunned spider. What a way to go.

Need a sci-fi plot where something pops out of your belly, maybe an alien? Just go Down Under for ideas.

On the Road

Hired a car today to go on a short road trip.

I drove up the West Coast—I needed to see water! The land quickly transforms from the sere inlands to open bush after passing the vineyards north of Perth. The vineyards hug the coast where the moisture resides, and thoroughbred horses graze in the paddocks.

I go through the small town of Two Rocks. This begins the Coral Coast on the Indian Ocean—white sandy beaches and people swimming with dolphins—what a place.

I want to live here!

I drive right up to the sandy berm of the beach where the road stops and the Indian Ocean starts: gentle waves, blue water, blue sky, and naked Australians. There's a dozen of the beautiful people sunning and swimming and running and romancing on the sandy beach. I've found paradise!

I want to live here!

I tear off my clothes and jump into the Indian Ocean and run on the beach. I've been working for a month in the Australian equivalent of Kansas. This is more like it! I try to blend in—but I've been in Narembeen and my skin is white and theirs is tan. I've got a Narembeen tan—like a farmer's tan. One very attractive woman looks me up and down and says, "You need to do something about that!"

I want to live here!

Any Time You Like

F   Dm7   Dm   C
I've been calling this warm place home.
I'm living on this sandy southern shore.
Got no shoes, but I still got soul.
The ocean beach is my only floor.

> *Refrain:*
> Bb   Gm   C
> You can stop by any time you like.
> Bb   Gm   C
> There's love in the water; love at night.
> Gm   Am
> All you gotta do is leave those blues at home;
> Gm   C
> Take my hand—you'll never be alone.

I used to work in an office park.
Weren't no trees, just mushrooms in the dark.
Every one's poppin' blood pressure pills.
Slaving to pay that stack of bills.

> *Refrain*

We all make choices, some are mistakes.
Sometimes we toss our future to the fates.
Your alarm clock's ringing way too early;
Stop and take a breath, you're living in a hurry.

> *Refrain*

Let me take you forward one year; we'll go back to the paddock in a moment.

Oliver and I are traveling together. Our tickets put us in business class; the wine comes with the reservation. I am on the aisle, he at the window. Oliver likes the natural light, which seems to set his great head of salt-and-pepper hair all a-glow. He has his sketchbook and pencil in hand. We're on a long flight to Melbourne from San Francisco, and he's sketching the flight crew. He's focused on one of the stewards.

Oliver leans into me and says, "This is a good looking lad. I always hope my model will allow me to wander around in his mind, turning over stones to see what he's all about. Sometimes a parallel energy clicks, and I exactly capture the soul of the lad. I try to find what is unique, different in a person. That's a clue to what evokes loyalty in a friend, sparks the eye of a lover, or forges courage to the unsure."

He pauses and looks at the progress on the sketch. Touching up a bit on the nose and the line of ear and jaw, he nods to himself.

A stewardess, lean and spry, smiling and filling out her uniform, leans in and says, "Drinks, gentlemen?"

"A red for the both of us," Oliver says. The stewardess pauses and leans over me to glance at Oliver's sketch. "Very good likeness of Peter," she says, and moves to the next row as Oliver smiles a thank you.

Oliver's glasses are low on his nose, and he looks up with his eyes to his unsuspecting model, then down to the sketch through the bifocals. He talks as he sketches.

"Roger, we are wanderers! We wonder at this world, we explore it, and we can't help ourselves. It is so hard for non-explorers to know this."

The stewardess returns with the wine, and I take both glasses so Oliver can continue his sketching. I take a sip of the cabernet sauvignon. It's from the Hunter Valley region of New South Wales. Up and coming.

Oliver's mind is wandering as the sketch fills out to the likeness of the steward. He has been concerned about relationships, something I'm not too good at.

186

"You know when I came out my wife didn't seem to really hold it against me." Oliver looks over at me; a whimsical smile crosses his lips. He is now looking at me, and flips the page of his sketchbook to a clean sheet. He studies me a moment, and continues. "We had our two kids, and well—Roger, hold that pose—well now we cohabitate as friends. The sex in the marriage was long gone, but the love of friendship was still there—we were a family still, of new sorts. So we decided to share a life of partnership and, I suppose, convenience. But love was the foundation. She has immersed herself in her own professional life. But I tell people that if they don't know my wife, they don't know me. Very true, that. You see, Roger, we must be careful to nurture love and not fall into hate. Falling into hate is the end."

We fall silent for a bit, and then turbulence seems to announce our approach to Melbourne.

Oliver looks at the quick sketch he has drawn of me, looks up and smiles. He says, "There, I think I've got you!"

Back in the Paddock

I walk everywhere on the property. Geoff drives, and on the rainy days often gets stuck in the mud. He says it's safer to drive because of the snakes. And in fact I find one! I'm watching this very big snake, very scaly looking. I've got my *Deadly Critters of Australia* field guidebook out and am keying it down.

"Kuhns!" Geoff says as he drives up in his truck. "What are you doing with that snake?"

"Identifying it. It's huge—must be eight feet long!" The snake isn't very active on this cool morning.

"Kuhns! What color is it?"

"Kind of a brownish, with some black in it. Got it! Mulga—*Pseudechis australis*. It's a—oh, a king brown."

"Kuhns! Step away from the snake!"

I am reading about the snake in my book, and I look up and say to Geoff, "Hey Geoff, these are deadly."

Geoff says, "Kuhns, that's the second deadliest snake on the continent, only after the taipan. And it's the third deadliest in the world. Get in the truck, Kuhns, before that thing gives you a kiss!"

<<<>>>

Every bit of land has someone who knows it, or claims to own it. Cliff Gault claims this farm.

"You don't want to tangle with that mad farmer Cliff Gault," Geoff says.

"Why not?"

"He's crazy—mad as a cut snake. I told him we needed to cross the paddock with the drill, and he gave me such a murderous look. He ranted to distraction—I feared for my life!" Geoff says melodramatically. "You know our schedule—we have to drill every day, even when it rains, and that means we get bogged down in the mud of these fields—it just is the way it has to be."

Geoff and I drove up to the house to see Cliff Gault. I thought I should meet the farmer since Geoff was scheduled to go home for the weekend. Cliff and his son were in one of the tin barns shearing sheep.

Cliff Gault looks up from the shearing—clippers in hand and piles of wool all around him. He shakes his head, and bends his body back to shearing sheep. Cliff is a willowy man with a lined, tanned face and a long crooked nose. He frowns as he shears the sheep, and his agitation shows in the pink dots that appear on the white-gray wool as the shearing clippers sometimes nick the skin.

Cliff lets the sheep go, having received its close cut, and looks up at the two of us. He says angrily in a heavy duty Australian accent, "What's the trouble now?"

Geoff says, "We just wanted to have a chat with you, Cliff, and let you know that we are not finding as much gold as we hoped . . . "

Cliff is looking at his shoes, and has his hands in fists on his hips. Shaking his head he interrupts and explodes, saying, "I told you! I told you bloody all there wasn't no gold there!"

"Well, maybe, but we need to move to another part of the paddock . . . "

Cliff roars another interruption, "And destroy my paddock some more, cause topsoil erosion. That's what's wrong with you and all of *yous*—you're ignorant, you're bloody arrogant and ignorant spiny-legged bastards, and you're, God all Christ, so bloody ignorant . . . God all bloody Christ, can't you see that a hundred points of bloody Christ rain will make mud!" He grabs another sheep his son has brought forward for sheering. The sheep bleats, and resigns to the rough shearing of its coat.

Geoff, so soft-spoken and considerate, tries to defend himself, saying, "But Cliff, you . . . "

Cliff looks up again, one fist holding a mop of wool to hold the sheep still. He cuts off Geoff again, all but screaming and waving his other fist that is clutching the shears, "You're so bloody arrogant, all of you, bloody Christ can't you stop working when it rains, it's winter—you should have planned, I told you this would happen."

As Cliff Gault's rant continues the sheep in the barn just stand and watch, some fluffy and unsheared, others naked with bloody little nicks from the clippers where Gault was shearing a bit too vigorously. The son stands looking at his boots. I think his expression is much like that of the sheep.

Geoff says, "Cliff, this is Roger Kuhns, whom we've brought in to help. He's an expert from North America. He'll be looking after things for a few days while I go to Perth . . . "

Cliff interrupts, "Perth again, bloody Christ, all you do is *ya-de-da* in Perth. You just stay here and finish and quit your bludgering around so you can git off-a my property. I can't be bothered with a sook."

Geoff is anything but a sook – a whiny person; just the opposite in fact. But Cliff is just too worked up. We just stand there and watch him.

Cliff bends down to continue the shearing. He is shearing the sheep very fast and ferociously now; around the legs, the ears—nicking the skin now and then so that some of the wool is dabbed in pink.

To emphasize an insult he shakes the pointed clippers at Geoff. "You *ya-de-da* spiny-legged..." He lets the words trail off. Farmer Gault's ears are red like glowing coals.

During a second pause in the ranting I ask, "Could I ask a question?"

Cliff looks at me with some surprise. He takes a breath and looks us over, and then says, "Why, yes."

I ask, "Would it be okay to come to the farm and ask you if it was too wet to work on days it had rained and make sure you know we were shutting down and not eroding your soil?"

Cliff stands up, and I can see his shoulders relax. We watch as a conspicuous transformation occurs. His crimson ears begin to return to normal coloring; his shoulders relax a little. Cliff unclenches his fists as color returns to his white knuckles. He sets the clippers on a nearby box. In a calm, conversationalist voice he says, "Why that would be rather polite of you. Yes, that'd be good."

We chat about communication for a moment, and his son looks up at us – now in the present, and now less tense as well. I shake their hands and wish them a good day. Geoff does the same.

Geoff and I depart back to the tray-back truck, and once inside the cab he says, "Whew—you worked some magic there, mate. I thought he was going to shear the both of us for a moment!" Geoff is clutching the wheel like it's a lifeline. "Kuhns, I am officially putting you in charge of all public relations in dealing with wacky Farmer Gault."

Days drift by in the field, and in the evening we are back at the Narembeen Hotel. We eat most of our dinners here, and Matilda knows how to cook lamb. Well, that's just about all she knows how to cook. We've had lamb and potatoes and peas almost every night since I've been here.

The invariability of the fare benumbs the taste buds. I am succumbing to culinary anxiety. I suggest dishes that could be created in the humble Tidy Town kitchen. Matilda listens to my proposals and nods politely while holding a frown that suggests such a consideration would require grand technological innovation. I just want lasagna. But each evening when I am at the pinnacle of comestible expectations, and most vulnerable to an esculent calamity, Matilda proudly presents to us yet another large plate of lamb, potatoes, and peas.

Geoff says to me, "Hey cobber, ya *gotta* love the lamb." He pauses and then reinforces his statement, "What I'm saying is you *gotta* love the lamb. It's a survival thing out here." Then he looks at Stuart and says, "As a food, Stuart, not as a friend. Now behave yourself and *bog in*, mate."

My geology has so far indicated that the gold grades and tonnages are not enough to warrant the upcoming million dollar payment to Farmer Gault. We're drilling a new area this week, which, if no gold is intersected, may kill the property.

Cliff Gault stops by late Saturday, as I'm finishing work on one of the drill holes. He is in a friendly mood, and loading feed into buckets to distribute to the farm animals. Cliff is wearing multi-pocketed trousers and a weatherworn green and brown plaid shirt with more than a few holes. He wears a hat whose rim is rumpled and crumpled all around, with a dark finger smudge on the front where he grabs it to put it on or take it off. The smudge is the same color as the earth on the tan hat. The air is heavy with earthy and manure odors, but the pleasant breeze on this clear day brings in enough fresh air so that it is a good working farm presence. I ask him about his farm.

How many sheep? "1,800."
How many acres? "3,600."
How many years on this farm? "These days it seems like forever!"

No one from the company had yet taken the time to just chat with him, he tells me. We walk the paddock, and he talks about his life, the trying times, how the land was more important than a million dollar payment. He talks about how he can't be bothered by the government or the big corporations, and he's all buggered because of it. Cliff then mentions how he misses a normal life with his wife.

I ask him about that. We stop walking, and he rests on his haunches; one hand goes to the soil, and he picks up a hand full bouncing it gently in his hand. This earth is his touchstone to reality. He looks down at the reddish brown soil and is quiet for a long moment.

Cliff says, "She's got the cancer. It's got her bad. She won't recover. I don't know if I can continue here, but I don't want to leave. My son might not continue on here, so it might just end up being me."

This explains so much. Here is a quiet, rural family in ultimate distress, and along comes a big, seemingly heartless, and maybe a bit too pushy mining company expecting this simple farmer to comply with their contract without argument. But the human equation was missed. He is tired and frustrated with the mining company, but—as it turns out—not the people.

Cliff says, "Yeah—I'm probably too hard on that young lad Geoff. I can see he's a good kid. He's just got a lot to learn about people. Life's too brief to go about it as a spiny-legged bastard!"

As we walk I talk about the geology we've been finding and about the ancient history of the rocks. I tell him the land was once a series of volcanic islands surrounded by a sea. But billions of years ago the islands were pushed up onto a continent by tectonic forces and then buried many kilometers down. This cooked them and folded them, and the hot fluids moved gold out of the rocks and concentrated it in pockets and veins to form the gold deposit.

"Well, I never," Farmer Gault said. "That is bloody remarkable. Can't never tell about a rock."

"Just like people some times," I say. And Farmer Gault slaps my shoulder in a friendly fatherly way, like I am now versed in something important. We walk at a quicker, more positive pace back to the barn.

Cliff shakes my hand and says, "Your fair dinkum."

Over the next few weeks Geoff and I conclude that we need a larger gold reserve to make this mineral deposit economical as a mine. We found gold, but just some that spilled from the end of the rainbow, not the rainbow itself. It seems Mr. Gault will be able to keep his paddock intact.

Geoff is at wits' end again. "That bloody Stuart put gas in the diesel truck again. You can tell Stuart is a level-headed geologist—he drools from both sides of his mouth!"

In the town, at dusk, I see an Aboriginal man walking along the side of the road. He's a dark, round man with a wide nose and a bowlegged gait. He is wearing only shorts and has a kangaroo tail over his shoulder. I wave at him. He nods.

"What you gonna do with that?" I ask.

"'Roo stew, mate." He looks at me through his deep brown eyes. His smile is wide and white, and a stubble of a beard follows his jaw line.

"I haven't seen many kangaroos around Narembeen."

"Roadkill, mate; right off the roo-bars—still fresh."

And I'm thinking—that might not be such a bad addition to our dinner fare at the Narembeen Hotel. I am dying for something besides lamb and have been asking Matilda the cook if she'd make lasagna—I'd kill for lasagna right now.

She said, "Yeah, tell me how to make it and I'll make it!"

I actually drew a sketch of the multiple layers of pasta noodles, tomato sauce, meat, and cheese and gave her all the ingredients. It looked like a geologic stratigraphic column. I labeled the layers, for scientific accuracy, and to the sketch added a scale bar and an arrow indicating the up direction.

My mouth has been watering all week. So tonight is the night, and Matilda proudly carries out a big deep dish of lasagna. The dining room, in it's simple purity of worn white walls and chocolate box paintings of outback scenes, seems to tremble ever so slightly with expectation. In my mind's orchestra section I hear John Phillips Sousa marching band music. This is all very exciting.

Everyone is watching Matilda.

Matilda cuts into it, I see a green pea pop up. Hmmm. I sense worry rumbling in my psyche. The band music is paused. A furtive bead of sweat glistens on my brow. In the distant reaches of my addled piquantified mind I think I hear a tremulous drum roll.

Matilda cuts out a mountain-sized serving and hands me the plate. I sharply inhale, for I see no sauce of tomato—I am speechless! I can smell the lamb. My eyes search for a melting of cheese. The stratigraphic layers are thus: potatoes, peas, potatoes, lamb, potatoes, peas, potatoes, lamb, and potatoes. There is one thin layer of lasagna noodles as a capping, as if it was a frivolous afterthought. The dish is topped off with a sparse sprinkling of cheese, a dusting as rare as rain in the outback.

In the orchestra section of my mind I hear the slow, sad, declining cartoonized *wha wha wha* sound effect of a failed endeavor. I am, I realize, witnessing an outback lasagna. I've been thrown back into the culinary stone age.

Oliver

Let me take you forward two years. I'll bring you back to Narembeen momentarily.

But now Oliver and I are traveling again. I've met up with him in Melbourne. We're in a quiet diner with a modern metallic motif and small jars of vegemite on the tables next to salt and pepper shakers and sugar packets. The room smells of grilled sandwiches with a hint of vinegar. The view out onto the street is of a bustling Melbourne day with powerwalking "suits" clutching briefcases and sporting VP haircuts, bicycle couriers, slow-moving camera-toting tourists, and locals not in a hurry to get where they are going. Cups of coffee have been filled and drained and filled again. Oliver is sketching on the paper place mats as we talk.

"I'm troubled about our executives. They don't seem to really see us. It is not so obvious how we're seen or perceived by those around us," Oliver says. "It is along the lines of: *To be is to be perceived.* We want to be seen and perceived by our lovers and mentors and kin and friends. Not that the corporate chaps are really any of those. But we need to be seen. It's seeing what is there in our lives and drawing what we see in our own way. There is so much acting out, posturing— you know—body language tells you if your lover is being genuine, honest or false. We've all been there! And what they say—you know it's harder to understand—easier to misunderstand—so we tend to misunderstand, some even get used to that state of mind—a state of, oh, disbelief. They don't believe what they see. If we can't see the person we're talking to, well, we misunderstand; we disbelieve what they are. We need those visual cues. That's their outer display." Oliver pauses, and smiles at me. He's been sketching me again. And then says, "And I've almost got yours—not bad."

Back in Time

Today Geoff and I drove from Narembeen farther east across the increasingly dry landscape to the goldfields in Kalgoorlie—four hundred kilometers.

At one point we stop at a rocky outcrop that rises from the great flatness. The first thing I noticed was the curvature of the Earth—the far side of my old horizon. I stood upon the small monadnock and surveyed the outback. It was vast and lonely and desolate. It was a land of quests—for metals, for Aboriginal dreams, for understanding biologic isolation, and for some a new shore.

A region such as the outback is still home for somebody. We found several Aboriginal hunting tools near one of the hills, and holding them I realized that tools such as these had not changed in tens of thousands of years. Timeless, and true to their given Latin name, *ab origine,* the people *from the beginning.* The simple stone tools, although ancient in appearance, could well have been used the day before in this land so full of sameness and subtlety. Perhaps that was why the Aboriginal people remained unchanged for millennia, for there was no need to deal with new natural challenges—they had mastered their environment, their home, from a subsistence point of view. Certainly they had impacted their world through the use of brush fires, and some suggest this helped accelerate the drying out of Australia.

I saw two kangaroos hop out from cover and then sit back on their tails to look us over. Again the feeling of timelessness overwhelmed me. The geology was old; the people were old, and the animal life unique. This, the globe's smallest continent, was the result of isolation generated millions of years ago when Australia drifted away from its continental neighbors.

The land, the passive and stable craton of Western Australia, has been so steadily weathered down over the ages that it possesses all the relief of a plank. On that surface have accumulated the products of erosion, a substance known as a deflation lag. Along this surface hydromorphic concentrations of iron and manganese oxides occur, giving the desert a varnished or gravely blacktopped appearance. When disturbed by a truck tire or boot, the lighter colored underlying material is exposed, marring the native character of the desert. Much of the outback is paved with billions of white quartz pebbles and black maghemite nuggets. The land has been exposed to erosion since the Proterozoic—a billion years ago—and variably buried by relatively recent Tertiary gravel up to 450 feet thick. Quartz is so common in the pediment because it is all that survives the erosion; all else turns to dust.

<<<>>>

We move on, and ultimately arrive in the city of Oz. Kalgoorlie is a solid dose of reality! Kalgoorlie is a gold mining town. It's city limits dribble off into desolate outback like a sweat stain on a hat brim. Small, economical tin-roofed houses are the normal things here.

Mine head frames and crushed rock and clay tailing heaps are all through the town, integrated amongst the buildings and streets as if planned by some drunk architect. This is the realm of world-famous gold deposits; it's called the Golden Mile. Miners have pulled out more than fifty million ounces of gold from Kalgoorlie, and there's years of mining to go! This means they've mined so much rock that the equivalent volume is roughly that of *five* Empire State Buildings!

The historic Golden Mile, part of the well-endowed Norseman-Wiluna Greenstone Belt, occurs in the Kalgoorlie area. This belt of metamorphosed and dismembered volcanic and sedimentary rocks extends for over 500 miles in a northerly direction as part of the Archean Yilgarn craton of Western Australia. The area is host to the ultimate treasure hunt—nearly all the clues are buried, and the land lacks relief to even pretend to offer rock exposures. The outback represents a geologic, geomorphic, hydromorphic, and biomorphic environment perfect for practicing geochemistry and geophysics. The Australians developed an ingenious geochemical method to search out the faintest traces of gold at the surface that might indicate great wealth at depth. The method is called *bleg sampling*, from *b*ulk *l*each *e*xtractable *g*old.

The bleg method mimics the gold recovery process used at many mines. A one-to five-kilogram sample of deflation lag or stream silt material is collected, crushed, and subjected to twelve hours of cyanide leaching. The purpose of the cyanide leach, which dissolves gold, is to remove all the gold from the sample, thereby creating a uniform geochemical database. More traditional analytical methods often yield incomplete recovery of gold that would translate into a variance in the results, which are sometimes difficult to interpret. Since all the gold would be extracted from a given bleg sample, even low concentrations of gold, as long as they were greater than the regional background values, could mean the telltale presence of a significant gold deposit at depth. We found one such deposit based on a three parts per billion gold anomaly. Under the series of anomalies 400,000 ounces of gold lay hidden within the folded quartz veins. Such a low surficial concentration is not much gold. In fact a three parts per billion gold concentration can be likened to finding a pinhead-sized piece of gold in a moderate-sized house. It is not an easy thing to do, but the bleg method provided a new way to look at ground that had been explored in the past by traditional means.

<<<>>>

I've been wandering around town and meet up with Geoff on a dusty street corner.

"Kuhns, you old goat, what are you doing wandering around down there?" he says.

"Just out and about to see the town."

"Kuhns! You were in grave danger down there!" I love Geoff's sense of humor and his sardonic delivery. Now we're on Hanaran Street. "Stick to this street—there's plenty of pubs and honest sheilas. Now, where you were by that ugly excuse for a building—that's the brothel on Hay Street. You could have been captured, Kuhns! A tender young American like you is no match for a Kalgoorlie sheila—she'd have done horrible and sensuous things to you! Yeah, mate, over there—that's trouble waiting to happen."

Geoff continues, "Now, look one block farther down on Hay Street—see that building? Well that's the authorities—the cop shop, but they changed the name of the street in that block to Brookman Street so the *ladies* and the cops wouldn't have the same address."

This is not the Narembeen wheat fields—this is Kalgoorlie, and it exists on the edge of desperation! It's a *"hot, dry, desolate . . . so let's dig a hole and work in it"* mentality! It is a metallic culture of gold hungry Australians who will trade a nugget for a beer and vice a versa. Now I understand why they sent me to Narembeen first—I needed to bolster my Oz culture and alcohol tolerance!

Later, we meet at the historic Boulder Block Hotel. In the pub room is an old, still-open mine shaft. It's fenced off, but deep and dark and cool. This would be dismantled because the land would be consumed by Kalgoorlie's Super Pit in a year or two, a pit dug for gold and ultimately reaching over two miles long, a mile wide, and over 1,500 feet deep.

The proprietor jokes, "Yeah, mate, if ya didn't settle up on your room back in the day, we'd toss ya in."

I'm thinking . . . how many people are down there? I'm glad we're staying at the Palace Hotel in town. Then I hear: "Vell—you vant to see down der? It is very deep!"

And I whirl around to see this big, tall, baby-faced German guy standing over me. I step back from the shaft.

Geoff, next to me, says, "It's the redoubtable Herman the German! I see you two have met!"

"Ya," says Herman the German, "I am meeting you now." His boyish grin conveys his sense of the place: unreal, fun, wild, untutored, and unrestrained. It is pretty clear this guy does not like boundaries. Dressed in a tan safari shirt with buttoned epaulettes and oil and hydraulic fluid stained and faded bluejeans, he fits right in with the Kalgoorlie vibe.

And now I remember who this guy is, he's the man that owns the drill rigs we were using at Narembeen. Geoff calls him Herman the German. But I never met him in the land of the wheat fields; he was always in the Land of Oz.

Geoff says to us, "Dinner at the usual place?"

Herman the German says, "Ya; vee go to da Mexican—sink it's best."

Herman the German is twenty-five years old and a new immigrant to Australia, a boy engineering genius. Self-taught, he ended up in Kalgoorlie as a topsider, which is a driller's helper. Soon he was financing his own rig, and now he's a millionaire.

So we gather at the only Mexican restaurant I've seen since I've been in Australia. The motif is confused Spanish-Central America-Mexico-Texas artifacts and paraphernalia dosed with outback stuff like walking sticks, didgeridoos, hats with corks dangling from the rims, and a stuffed crocodile. They use mutton in their burritos and are playing Greek party music over the speakers. We are very south of the border! I mention this, and Herman the German responds.

Herman the German: "What border?"

Roger: "The Mexican-American border. In the US we say this kind of cuisine is from south of the border."

Herman the German: "Oh, zees kinds of problems I love."

Roger: "You mean the actual distance?"

Herman the German: "Ya, zis is very interesting." And he looks around the room and spots a map of the world on a far wall. "I go check." And off he goes. Moments later he is back. "I zink we use unt Haversine equation."

Geoff: "Obviously!"

Roger: "Should we just measure it off the map?"

Herman the German: "Zee math is more fun. It is zee spherical law unt cosines. So I got our location here in Kalgoorlie and I got the latitude unt longitude of Tijuana in Mexico. Will zat be suitable?"

Geoff: "That's what we would do." He has that entertaining grin on his face.

I nod in agreement. Herman the German is all the genius Geoff had told me about, and I instantly like the guy.

Herman the German: "So…" and he starts mumbling and scribbling on the placemat. "Let me see, a cosine times sine of latitude here times sine of latitude at Tijuana plus…" This goes on for a few moments. "I have it. We are 14,550 kilometers away from south of the border."

Roger: "Well, Herman, that's as the crow flies, but how far directly south." I peer at his notes. "Tijuana is at 32.5 degree north, and we are at 30.7 degrees south."

Herman the German: "Ah, ya, I see what you mean." He scribbles for a moment. "Ya, unt zis is zee answer, we are 7,036 kilometers south of your border."

Roger: "So, with one kilometer equal to 0.6 miles," I scribble the math on the placemat, "that's about 4,371 miles. So we're over four thousand miles south of the border. The food had better be really good!"

Geoff: "And that's how Herman the German's mind works." We all laugh at that, and almost every day we would have some discussion involving problems solving and engineering solutions like this with Herman the German. I love brilliant people who are self taught.

Herman the German: "Ya, I love verking math problems!"

Geoff: "Herman is working himself to death drilling so much this year. Eat more chili peppers!"

Herman: "Ya—good to verk hard. Vhat doesn't kill us hardens us. I like to be hard! Now vee moost have beer!"

Geoff waves over the waiter and says, "I'll have a Swan."

Waiter: "You'll have an Emu, mate."

Geoff: "Right, I'll have an Emu."

Waiter: "Good thing, that—we're out of Swan and everything else t'day." He turns to Herman the German. "What can I get for you?"

Herman: "Ya, vat ist cold unt imported?"

Waiter: "My wife—but she's outta town. Emu?"

Herman nods. "Vell—your vife is an emu?" He smiles broadly at his own humor.

Waiter: "No, an emu's got more sense than the missus!" The waiter looks at me: "Where you from? I know where he's from" (pointing to Herman the German).

Roger: "America."

Waiter: "Where in America?"

Roger: "Minnesota."

Waiter: "I don't know where that is, what's it next to?"

Roger: "Canada."

Waiter: "Ah yeah, d'ya know Martin Hamilton? He lives in Canada, I know him."

Roger: "Nope." I just shake my head; North America is a big place with a lot of people.

Waiter: "What can I get ya?"

Roger: "Emu."

Waiter: "Bob's yer uncle. Ya catch on, ya 'mercans aren't such the drongo." Then he yells over his shoulder, "Brenda—a round of frothy ones for these weary foreigners here!"

Over the beer and food we talk more about the land situation, and the on-going fight.

I learn that the Australians operated under the concept of *terra nullius*—"land belonging to no one"—the idea that land was not occupied before European settlement? It wasn't until the 1990s that this began to be resolved.

Later that night, walking through the center of Kalgoorlie, and watching the locals in the pubs with yellow light flooding out into the streets, I can see why this town attracts those wanting to get far away from civilization. Yet it is for civilization the gold is mined, and mined by some of the world's largest corporation. I've seen this before, elsewhere, this dichotomy born from the dream and the reality, the need and the want, and the aliquot of idealism each of us possesses.

I think of the Midnight Oil song: "How can we sleep when our beds are burning?" The lead singer, Peter Garrett, is a lawyer and humanitarian and musician. A bald, lanky, imposing and confident white guy who helped bring the human rights issues of the Australian Aborigines into the mainstream. In his concerts as the front man for Midnight Oil, he would dance in stiff and jerky movements, like he was being punched.

Years later in 2007, no longer in the band, Peter Garrett became the Minister for the Environment, Heritage, and Arts through an appointment by Prime Minister Kevin Rudd.

ACT 2

Oliver's San Anselmo Studio

Forward into time again, and I am staying in Oliver's second-floor guest room in the studio out behind his house. The space outside is cluttered with his clay forms of men and women. The sculptures, his universe—some unfired clay, others fired, and one bronze—show Oliver's world, the musculature and expressions of the human spirit and body.

I see the mortality in some of the unfired clay sculptures that are slowly eroding back into the earth. Maybe someday the clay will be reclaimed and reshaped by another artist.

Oliver says, "And here we are again, you and me. Now hold that pose. Yes, just there." As Oliver talks he sketches on a pad of paper, now and then looking at me, his impromptu model for the afternoon.

"I've just got to get into the moment, the art of it, the focus, the *able to do no wrong* courage to pursue the fantasy." He says. "God! Think of Rodin working in his studio. That man knew his way around the human body and the human soul. Brilliant work! But, my God, the sculptures—the slightly larger hands, the pained faces—like the Burghers of Calais. You can tell those men are doomed to die. Rodin captured their life force and their absolute mortality. It is this kind of focus we are looking for in our new challenges . . . something we can sink their teeth into.

"I want your opinion on something I'm working on. I call them my Sermons for Business. The first sermon is about FOCUS, the second is CHALLENGE, and the third is TEAM & MOTIVATION—we both know a lot about that! Fourth clearly must be EXPLORATION—but of course in the sense of exploring all of our abilities. But my last one, the last one—the hardest sermon, I call HATE IN CORPORATIONS.

"Hate. Think of it. Have you ever said, 'I'm falling in hate!' We've all said we're falling in love.

"I am very pained that I see hate growing now in the old exploration group I left behind. Already the shallow ones are elbowing for power now that I'm gone. They're sharpening their Brutus knives—all meant for my poor successor Hugo. Alas!

"I feel very dramatic today. Is it an emotional front for my true fear of my impending retirement? What if I become unknown and unappreciated? I feel like I'm on the bridge of a new ship without a crew—this lofty new perch is no longer corporate, it is familiar—yet somehow not as full as I dreamed it would be. Sometimes a pursuit is best when you don't have quite enough time to get lost in it."

Oliver sits and sketches a moment, pausing to look at what he might add to his drawing: a line, a shade, a curve, all to capture the subject, not just re-create the image.

"Right—I think I've got you. Enough of the sketches. I think it is time to sculpt you, lad—put you in clay for once and for all!"

Back in Time Outback

Got up at 5 a.m. Geoff and I are in the small mining town of Cue in the Murchison area of Western Australia. Every day—lots of geology.

In the morning, before breakfast, I'm up doing my tai chi. I slowly move through the forms, breathing, feeling nature . . . but I notice something on the floor. Oh crap. It's one of those deadly redback spiders. Okay, it has a right to be here too . . . I tai chi away a bit; just going to move over here . . . it follows. Okay, I'll just breathe; peaceful thoughts in my head. Eyeing the redback spider—okay, tai chi. And my foot comes down on the redback like a ton of bricks.

Off to breakfast, and then back on the road.

Dust, dust, dust. I again think of the album *Diesel and Dust*. Peter Garrett knew what he was singing about.

Several vehicles are headed our way. We can see them many miles off. Great rooster tails of dust in their wakes, and undulating superheated mirage shapes to the vehicles. I could only think of—*Oh shit, it's Mad Max . . .* What if it happened—we'd never know!

Because of the great distance it takes the vehicles a half hour to reach us. And it's not a few vehicles—it's a road train—a truck pulling four trailers in a thunderous dusty passing on the outback. We have to stop and wait for the dust to clear as we are enveloped in the road train's trailing opaque storm.

After a day of geologizing and walking about, we arrive back in Cue. The hotel is old, sloping floors, non-square doorways, and sagging beds. And the cockroaches are big here . . . Jurassic Park big. If you need a sci-fi plot, just come Down Under and outback!

Into the pub we go for a cleansing. We meet up with Fiona, one of Geoff's fieldies working in the area. Geoff introduces her to me as "That Bloke Fiona!"

She shakes my hand and just about breaks my fingers.

I'm drinking a lot more now after a few months here. The beer seems to dissolve the dust that clings to our throats. You blow your nose, and it is brownish red from the stuff. We are becoming one with the outback; more beer to cleanse the body. And we need food.

Time for a burger on the barbie out back.

The waitress asks if I want a salad with that? Sure. This burger is huge, with a fried egg on it, in addition to layers of onions, tomatoes, cucumbers, pickles, lettuce, pickled beets, and cheese. The salad is actually on the burger. It tastes great.

That Bloke Fiona orders a couple burgers. Fiona is a maniacal *Star Trek* fan and periodically blurts out, "Warp factor nine, Mr. Scott!"

Geoff and I are not sure why she's saying this. Maybe it's the outward manifestation of some internal conversation that has occurred because of too much time all alone in the outback. I guess she's conversing in her own fantasy with Captain Kirk!

Fiona takes a huge bite of the burger, and egg 'n onions 'n pickled beets 'n sauce all fall down her open shirt into cleavage!

Geoff eyes the situation, and shouts, "Beam me up, Scotty, it's becoming hazardous down here!"

Now Fiona is a bloke-type sheila. She is ruggedly cute, outback seasoned, and verbally coarse. Fiona has been outback a long time, and the sun and the beer and the crocodile temperament of the blokes has *learned* her some unfeminine habits. Fiona doesn't wear underwear, which in itself isn't anything to be troubled about. But sometimes her posture reveals more of her than we need to know. Right now she's got a knee-length skirt on, it's cool on this hot day, but one leg is comfortably resting on the edge of the table as she drinks her beer.

The bartender eyes the situation: eyebrows go up, eyes get wide, and he says: "That's what we need more of in here, free-spirited sheilas!"

Geoff says, "Warp factor nine, Mr. Scott!"

Fiona toasts with us all to that one.

The Sculpture

Let me take you forward twelve years—my continuing visits to the San Anselmo artist and mentor's retreat—Oliver has done a sculpture of me.

"Now don't you go wondering about the likeness," Oliver says. "The importance of a sculpture is that it is not a replica of the person, but an idea of them—to gain something of what they are. I want people to look at this and say, *I like that one—that person.*"

Roger: "Do you think it's me?"

Oliver: "In a fashion, mate; maybe a bit more brain in the brow."

Roger: "And a smaller nose." I hold up the sculpture and stare into its bronze eyes. There is a resemblance, but there are some liberties here. "Don't you think I look like Lenin? Vladimir, not John."

Oliver: "Well—you do instigate unrest!" Oliver takes the sculpture and holds it while talking.

"The sermons are coming along. I'm struggling with this Hate in Corporations bit. It's so obvious but really quite difficult to finish without depressing everyone. I think also that since I'm watching it happen in the company—well, it's painful. Well it's none of my business . . . I'm retired! But it's much like peeking over the hedge. I'm no good at rattling around the walls in my retirement; I'm better at the concepts than the writing up and publishing, as you know. Roger, you and I are dreamers—thank the stars for that!" Oliver kisses the sculpture. "You've lost your body, Roger! Oh—there you are—strike a pose. We're far too busy dreaming to get anything done these days!"

Back in Time to Coronation Hill

I am sent on a solo trip to the Northern Territory. It takes me through the remote town of Derby, which Geoff said was "the asshole of the north!" And through Fitzroy Crossing, which Geoff said is "three hundred kilometers up it!"

Derby is a place crowded with odd-looking baobab trees, whose fat, bloated trunks taper rapidly to a chaotic array of pale branches looking much like the tree was uprooted and stuck back in the earth upside down. White-barked Ghost Gums formed a strange open forest with the baobabs and ten-foot-high termite mounds. In the parched atmosphere pink galahs and snowy cockatoos flitted among the bony-branched trees. The Derby waterfront was unbecoming—a muddy salt marsh with one jetty extending into the ocean. Since the town lacked a levee, only small boats visited, and hence the town's growth remained stunted. In the distance dolphins leaped and chased each other in the clear water offshore.

I drove onward and out to an exploration camp called Pillara in the Kimberley Hills—small lumps on an otherwise flat horizon. It was in this remote land that geologists had discovered a lead and zinc deposit called Cadjebut.

Pillara camp near the Cadjebut deposit consisted of ATCO trailers in a settler's circle. A satellite dish provided television reception, and Ping-Pong and pool tables provided additional diversions for passing time, but aside from work there was not much else to stimulate the unimaginative mind. At night the dingoes howled and yelped as if to belay their own forlornness.

This is an Aboriginal land. They have been here for tens of thousands of years, whereas the British arrived in the Kimberley region in 1879, bringing cattle, sheep, and a forced future. The Aboriginal people brought fire to the outback and in their own way significantly changed the face of Australia through uncontrolled burns. The cattle barely survive here. They feed on the sparse grasses and spiny spinifex. Spinifex sticks and stabs the uninitiated hiker, and its barbed ends offer a painful lesson to stand clear, yet the cattle feed on the stuff.

In all of this dryness, there was once an ocean here. Its quiet, warm waters, which lapped passively along an indented coastline, are remembered in the rocks. Along Geikie Gorge on the Fitzroy River are now grand exposures of four-hundred-million-year-old Devonian limestone. It was here that great reefs became fossilized and offer mirror images of the Great Barrier Reef which stretches for 1,250 miles along the modern Queensland coast in the Coral Sea. Within the canyon walls that cut the reef are fossil corals, brachiopods, spherical algal oncolites, and great accumulations of reef front breccias.

Ghost Gums line the river, and in their white bark seems a reflection of the pale limestone and the snowy whiteness of the cockatoos.

The weathered gray limestone stands as fluted pinnacles carved by eons of rain and water flow. But as the ancient ocean grew wider hydrothermal waters rich in zinc, lead, and silver seeped up growth faults and reacted with the limestone. The metals precipitated from the acidic solutions as they buffered the carbonate rock, filling cracks and pores in the fossil reef. Over time enough of the metals accumulated to make the deposit that geologists ultimately discovered.

Such deposits speak of evolving waters and aging ocean basins and the reactive geochemical processes between fluids and rocks. The same process occurred in Ireland, Tunisia, Missouri, and in the Canadian Arctic, among other places, and all were sites of ancient seas where limestone reefs accumulated and zinc was ushered into them. As geologists we are often searching out the ancient shorelines of unknown seas.

My destination is one of the company's most remote projects, called Coronation Hill. Here I meet up with Dean, the project manager. This place is amazing—low, rolling, forested hills and Ghost Gums just outside Kakadu National Park.

The camp manager has constructed a fenced area about four feet square and six feet high. He's been filling it with all the empty beer cans, and it's nearly half full—there's thousands of them in there. We're having steaks on the barbie next to the can enclosure.

"You guys been here a long time?" I'm eyeing the cans and wondering about the math—time or volume.

"Naw, there's just bugger-all to do but empty stubbies and Fosters," Dean says.

"What you gonna do when it's full?"

"Call in Guinness, I expect."

"The book of world records?"

"Naw, the Guinness beer wagon—so we can celebrate proper-like."

There are about a dozen Aborigines working in camp for the company. Here I meet Dinney—one of the older guys, white hair, lined and weathered face, but bright eyes and an easy smile.

The Jawoyns are the main tribe here and have historically taken white English names based on whom they work for. For example, if Dinney works for Tom Taylor, he might be called "Taylor," and so might other members of his family. So there may be several men named "Taylor" who work for Tom Taylor. Dinney's full name is Dinney Taylor Jakamarra.

Dinney tells me the mining company is trying to work on a sacred site. He says that within the area is one of the haunts of the being of bad luck and evil—so named "Buja." Dinney says that the being—seen by the Aborigines in their dream sequences—can cause bus accidents, medical emergencies, mine calamities, fires, and all sorts of things.

Fourteen Years Later

Oliver says, "I've taken some of my work—some of the sketches and one or two of the busts—into one of the San Francisco galleries. They said they'd get back to me. I don't know if I have time for that—for promoting. I mean, really, everyone is an artist these days. I didn't think of this aspect before retirement, I just wistfully thought someone would say *My God—brilliant! You must show in our gallery.* Well, it's not like that. Here, sit. Let me draw you. Let's talk. I'll put on some Beethoven, maybe your record—that'll get the juices flowing!"

I stay at the studio that night. Alone and in the illumination of a single corner lamp I study the busts and torsos Oliver has sculpted over the years. This gallery has the presence of friends and acquaintances, of lovers and students; Oliver's universe like stars in the night sky. . .faces in his studio. They stare into the darkness of heavy silence as if they know something about this space. I feel the timelessness here has shifted, that mortality has infused itself into the pores and grain and fibers of this place. It is a disquieting paradise, a dream realized but coming slowly apart from malignant forces. I cannot sleep. I sit all night in that chair and am awaken by a touch on my arm in the morning.

It is Oliver, with a cup of coffee. "Come, have some breakfast—did you not sleep?"

He rests a hand on my shoulder as we walk out of the studio, past the sculpted faces—all staring out into something, some place, or some universe: the other side?

Oliver says, "Some days I feel—I feel everything. I don't know if we're meant to, it almost overwhelms me."

Dreaming

Dinney was playing his didgeridoo. The vibrating basso pulses filled the air and almost seemed to rattle one's bones.

Dinney says, "My name is Dinney Taylor Jakamarra—you can tell my names are not all from the same place!"

"Look, mate, there's no real word for it in English—dreaming is close. But what we experience is more than that. So to properly describe it make a new word that has these ideas in it: visions, revelations, realizations, insights, understanding, endless time, ancestors, mythical creatures, and all that is known and understood! What would you call that? Ha, mate, yur in dreamtime.

"It's through this that our ancestors—and now us—understand life and our place within the whole, the entirety. It is how we began and where we're going, how we behave and why—and why not! All these animals here—they tell us about the earth, and we have that understanding with them in that way. Now, I'll still jump like a wallaby when I step on a king brown—I'm not stupid, and maybe that's not the best animal to have a dream with, but—there ya go!

"Think of it like you're juggling three balls—one is this human reality of people, one is the land—physical world—and one is the creator's world. Creation is all about understanding these relationships.

"You gotta understand this land thing. It's not ours, it's not anybody's—but we need it. The land threads us to dreamtime from this reality. You snip those threads—well—then it's not connected between the here and now and dreaming. That's one reason we are all out of sorts about it—this taking the land. Now I'm not going to tell

211

you what I dream—that's personal. I will tell you all the creators are in these rocks and trees, and they're watching you and me. All the time. They live in this world. And why not? I bet they're mad as a cut snake about all these goings on.

"I think the problem in all this is we know the creators are in the land, and everybody else sees it as a way to make money."

Dinney picks up the didgeridoo and starts playing. The sound is enduring and haunting, and sifts through my very being. I am dreaming.

ACT 3

Twenty Years and the San Anselmo Retreat

With our common company life behind both of us, Oliver and I still talk a lot—but I sense a frustration in Oliver. I had gotten so very busy with this new thing—sustainability. Oliver wanted me to stay in geology, to figure out Earth. I told him I felt I'd done much of that and now wanted to help figure out how to sustain it.

I was planning a long overdue visit to the San Anselmo retreat. Then he wrote me this letter:

> Wednesday, April 16, 2008
> Dear Roger,
> Just a quick one before I get into the rest of the day—I'm sitting around in a dressing gown still at eleven in the morning! All is reasonably well.
> The surgery—which will mean three or four days in hospital—is slated for 23rd of this month, a week from today in fact. I have cancer, and have not wanted to burden my friends with this. But it is fair to tell you—I must tell you. They will take out the offending lymph node—and in fact a good deal of the lymph system of the right side of the neck and the salivary glands at the back of the right cheek. After a healing period of about a month, I shall be up for short radiation treatments.
> Give a call—we've more sketches to do, and geology to argue about—and this new sustainability thing. But I must say, I'm not feeling very sustainable these days!
>
> Affectionately, Oliver

My daughter Madeleine once told me, "Dad it doesn't hurt when you fall; it only hurts when you finally smack into the ground."

But later, Oliver writes:

> Roger, the effects of the radiation and chemo are gradual but now are pretty drastic. I have NO ENERGY, Absolutely NO TASTE and Absolutely NO APPETITE, and my mouth is hugely sore . . .
>
> And yet they want you to try to maintain body weight! I live on some stuff called ENSURE—each bottle of which gives you 350 calories. I stuff down some porridge in the morning (very hard going) and a very light scrambled egg at night—but all else is Ensure!
>
> So it is really just a question of surviving through this final week—and being able to LAUGH at the ludicrous mess I both LOOK and FEEL!!! . . . At the moment for instance I have only beard on one side of my face and long white hair over about three quarters of my head—the rest is pink and smooth from the radiation!
>
> Very much looking forward to your visit.
>
> Affectionately, Oliver

Back in Time Again

Dinney says, "I notice this mining company doesn't understand the environment. I am a friend with nature. I don't cut it or dig it up so much that it dies or can't heal. It is through the song, the dreamtime, that I understand this.

"The project manager here keeps saying he wants to develop a working relationship with me. He puts his hand on my shoulder—like a friend; right. He just wants to get me to tell him where the sacred sites are, because there are minerals in the ground there—that's one reason the land has energy. But I won't tell him where these sites are—NO! Because he doesn't want a relationship—not in the dreaming sense—we don't know what will happen if you dig up our sacred sites.

"There's a lot of magic out there, and if you don't pay attention to it you could crash your car, or have a tree branch fall on your head.

"That's the thing—here in the outback—it can drive some people crazy. You think you understand your dreams—but you don't; you've just gone crazy, mate, you've just gone bloody crazy."

And I realize maybe Dinney is right, as I look back at all the traveling, all of the dreaming, all of the running, and all of the lost time. And I can't save my friend.

Outback

D   A   G   bar A
I've been outback way too long.
Down under these heavy weights.
It's time that I better "get up and gone."
I'm like a wave about to break.

Refrain:
G   A
I'm on this island and I'm going insane.
Been around the world, but what have I gained?
I'm on this island and I'm going insane.
The years are slipping, but the dream is the same.

I caught a boat to the Freemantle shore
on an Indian Ocean breeze.
But these memories followed me once more
in the land of the endless Dream.

Refrain

You can walk about here all your life.
You can talk about how spirits are free.
Sometimes words can cut me like a knife.
Is this the window through which I will see?

Refrain

Interlude…I scribble my chord notations.

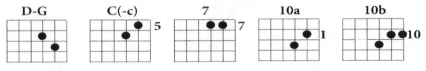

Refrain

I pack up the rented yellow Toyota 4x4 and head up the Kakadu Highway to Cooinda. The rolling hills host eucalyptus forests and occasional grassy fields. Water buffalo pose along dirt roads near Kakadu National Park.

I embark on a short journey through the yellow waters of the upper Alligator River—misnamed because there are only crocodiles here. The boat is a slow-moving flat-bottom job.

Crocodiles sun themselves on the muddy banks and occasionally snap their jaws when we come close. Their defensive reflexes are not to be argued with—they have survived through the eons like almost no other animal. Several emerge slowly, floating silently to the surface right next to the boat, to investigate our passing. They hiss warnings and occasionally slap their tails in the mud. Our eyes meet—crossing the genetic river of time—three-hundred-million-year-old crocodile realities with those of my million-year-old human origins.

How is it that one species becomes dominant for brief moments in time, while others endure essentially unchanged. It begs the question of dinosaur extinction and crocodile continuance, of clashing cultures and the right to survival of the most advanced and of the fittest, or perhaps the most appropriate, those prone to adaptation. I ponder all of this while floating.

In human terms, great grandparents acquired land, leaving behind what they thought would be wealth and security for their offspring and subsequent generations. All was done at the expense of the indigenes. Now to get this right, the colonial offspring must give something up—right the wrong of their forefathers. What is fair? How far back do you go to place blame, and how do we learn to forgive and live in some kind of harmony? Maybe at our level of evolved being, that is impossible for us to do on a global scale. Australia may be an unwitting and blatant experiment in which such questions may, in time, be answered.

The long, flat-bottomed boat skims across the marshy environment. Birds are in abundance—cockatoos, sea eagles, kites, petrels, egrets, and spoonbills—amid the tall eucalyptus, mangrove, palm trees, and stands of bamboo. Around one bend in the river we came across the large jabiru, with its huge bill and black plumage, standing still hawking for fish. We spotted a Jesus bird, also called a lily walker, which *walks on water* from one lily pad to the next.

All along the muddy banks, especially under cover of the overhanging vegetation, are crocodiles. I can't take my eyes off of them. The locals call them "salties." *Crocodylus porosus*—or big old saltwater crocodiles. They love to eat everything. They get big, too—thirteen feet long is still pretty common. These monsters swim forever out to sea—you'll spot 'em miles off the coast from here on the northern shore up to Papua New Guinea, Indonesia, the Philippines, and all the way up to India! You can't outswim them—they go up to 20 mph!

Biggest one I heard about was just about twenty-three feet long. That one weighed about three thousand pounds. Now you got your average dingo weighing in at thirty pounds—do the math; that croc is equal to one hundred dingoes! And maybe about fifteen full-grown tourists who were fishing too close to the shore. You can't see into that muddy water—they could be right there!

Dinney told me about the crocs when he heard I had gone in a boat.

"These crocs have been around for hundreds of millions of years." Dinney said. "They're real survivors! I've had crocodile dreams—those are fair dinkum. You can learn a lot from a saltie—patience and tolerance, and letting yourself get swept up in the tides and times of life.. Letting go, that's the secret, following our innate instincts. Let nature feed you.

"Now the salties scout the coast and the estuaries and rivers and billabongs for food. They'll really defend their territory. Some of them are a hundred years old, they say.

"In the wet, you'll find the salties in freshwater, and then in the coastal areas during the dry.

"They'll eat anything—'roos, wild pigs, dingoes, fat tourists on the beach, cows, monkeys, sharks, fat tourists in the water, wallabies, goannas, water buffalo, fat tourists sleepin' in their tents.

"They'll jump ya, drag ya down, roll ya around some, crunch ya ta death with them monster jaws. And then you're not doing too well. I seen one pull a full-grown water buffalo under—the buffalo struggled up, and the croc snapped and crushed its skull in its jaws. I tell you, life can be hard.

"So, mate, you gotta be careful to mind the salties—life is too bloody short. You know what's right, and you know what to do. Maybe it's best sometimes to just live on instinct. Life is too bloody short to worry otherwise."

I had to know this *homeland* better. At Nourlangie, east of Arnhem Land—where no white man can go—is a place of magic. Aboriginal rock art can be found tucked under reddish and black manganese–streaked escarpments of sandstone and conglomerate. At one instant a three-foot-long monitor lizard slowly crossed the path as I walked among the rocks. The monitor flicked a devil tongue as it paused to look at me, and I felt a rush of ancientness, a feeling heightened by the Aboriginal artwork. The petroglyphs were painted with white, red, and black mineral pigments—fundamental colors of the earth. There was neither blue for sky nor green for vegetation, such long-lasting pigments being hard to find. On the water-worn rock the artists had depicted beings of lightning, evil, and fertility. Also illustrated were social activities such as dancing.

A most common motif was the outlines of hands, those from both adults and children. I touched the home rock of these people and gained incipient feelings of their innate quest to try and understand what was around them. Oddly, and perhaps naïvely, I felt an additional understanding because of my knowledge of the geology underfoot. There are older stories in the rocks formed before mankind walked the Earth. Some of it seems mystic, perhaps, but I felt the explainable story through my science as interesting as any myth and, in fact, more satisfying. Nevertheless, it is a quest of understanding . . . a *forever* quest across time.

Forward Twenty Years

Oliver writes:

September 25, 2008

Roger—I spend most of the time each day half asleep on a couch in the family room, or in my studio . . . I find it very hard to find the energy to do anything else . . . Even reading is too much.

Then when my Deidre gets home from work we go for a slow walk that takes twenty minutes or so—which is about all I can manage.

Still . . . I'm hoping that in a few weeks I shall start to get energy back and be able to do more—Art, Geology you know, the sermons! I am, in fact, getting some more geological thoughts—Just as a relief from thinking about my physical and medical condition I think; but I just can not start trying to put them down on paper yet!

Sorry to have so much tough news—but the final prognosis seems to be getting—definitely—much better!

Affectionately, Oliver

In the months that followed we talked on the phone, and he said please come soon.

I book a flight.

But time races by. Time is a strange thing. It is compressed, slowed, accelerated, distorted—all in our minds, maybe in our physics. Maybe they're the same.

But my sojourns to Oliver's San Anselmo studio retreat were over. I had boarded my flight; I had flown west from the Midwest. I had called his home. Deidre answered, and said Oliver was gone; December 2, 2008. He was seventy-seven. I missed Oliver by two days.

The cancer took him so quickly, and Deidre told me the last of it was so very cruel and painful. Had he been retired ten years? It seemed like another lifetime one that was too bloody short. The artist's retreat is empty.

Expectation

Em   C
In the morning you rise out of bed
Walk through this house all alone.
This is not what you thought it would be about
As you turn over each and every stone.

   Refrain:
   F   G   C
   But this love is not the same;
   F   G   C   Am
   When your body leaves your soul so far behind.
   Is this unreal expectation here?
   Walk to my window one more time.

Good morning this soul of the farlands.
You stare straight into the sun.
Will you stop and rest with me a while
Before you have to run, run, run away again.

   Refrain

You wrap around me like a fine silken sheet
To relieve my weariness.
Then you go like a ghost on the wind.
What am I to do with this?

   Refrain

Dream Time

The didgeridoo is playing. I can hear it. Back in time, and outback again in the past. I am done for the day, and the Southern Cross hangs in the sky like a jeweled pendent. The stars are gaudy in their brilliance; no moon, a black palette for the illumination of countless suns. My God! How many up there are looking out on us from their point of view with the same wonder?

There is a yellowish glow on the high ground a quarter mile from the camp. Sparks meander star-ward like living things, only to fade and fall invisibly in the night. I am drawn to the fire and hear voices talking—muted laughter, but good-hearted laughter. I walk through the grove of gum trees and to the edge of the firelight.

Faces all turn toward me. I recognize the Aboriginal workers. They've gathered on this perfect night to talk. Dinney looks up at me. He cocks his head. Then waves me into the circle, friendly and casual—no fanfare. I sit on one of the dry eucalyptus logs that form benches around the fire pit. Mostly the men are talking quietly among themselves in Jawoyn.

After a time, when he's decided I'm not going to intrude, Dinney leans toward me. He says, "This is every night. This is what we are. It's quite nice, don't you think? These blokes all know you are with the company. These men all know the company wants to mine our sacred sites. We work for the company, too—but we won't tell what we know. We need jobs; the world has changed. It is all unbalanced. I feel the world is shaking. Shaking and trembling."

Dinney turns his face to the fire, and I watch the light play across the deeply folded and creased skin of his cheek, jaw, and chin. His white hair holds a yellowy cast from the firelight, and above his head are the stars of the Milky Way—they seem to be exploding out of his being into the heavens. There is one world in the fire that is so bright it washes out the stars, it washes out everything. But there is the other world in the stars, it's the universe - it is everything, and that you only see looking away from the fire.

My whole person feels as heavy as lead and at once as light as an ascending spark from the flame. We are the ascending sparks—bright until we fade and fall back to earth; like a clay sculpture weathering back to soil.

The night air is dry, cool, unbelievably clean and clear. I stare up, letting the fire warm my neck and chin. I don't know if I'll ever have a dreamtime like Dinney's—or even be able to comprehend a dreamtime that he speaks of. But I dreamtime: I dream of the crocodiles—those massive timeless survivors; I dream of the connecting spirit worlds and people. It is not accidental, these people I meet.

I watched the sun rise from that spot. I was alone then—that's me. The crew had work to do and had left hours ago. The coals in the fire—like the nights stars—had faded. In the distance I could hear an engine start up.

It was time for me to hit the road again. I can't wait to see what's over the next ridge!

A Vision of Oliver

I remember. Oliver is sitting in his favorite chair, in his San Anselmo retreat, that artist's studio and mentor's nook to which I have come to so many times.

Oliver says to me, "Roger, hold that pose." He picks up a pencil and begins to sketch. "Remember, mate, there is so much more out there. Tell the story of the journey. Roger, I wonder what's next?"

Oliver keeps sketching. And then he looks up at me. His smile in that instant is everything to me.

Oliver says, "There, I've got you."

Roger James Kuhns

WORKING UNDERGROUND

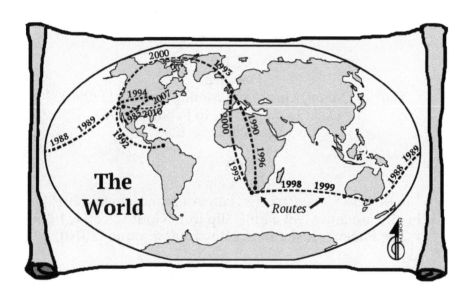

ACT 1
Underground—South Deep (1993)
Getting on the Roller Coaster (1980)
The Rosetta Stone Part I: The Language of Management (1993)
Ass End of the Business (1985)
The Roller Coaster Gains Speed (1988)
The Rosetta Stone Part II: The Styles of Management (1994)
The New Wild West: La Salvacion, Venezuela (1992)
Nelson Mandela Stops By to Chat (25 March 1999)

ACT 2
Derailed
Hartley: Metal, Music, and Money Revisited (1990)
The Dalai Lama Comes to Jo'burg (1996)
The Tech Help Desk (2007)

ACT 3
Daylight
The Rosetta Stone Part III: Gangs of Management (2010)
What If Humanity Got a Pink Slip from God? (Dec 31, 1999)
The Phoenix Rises: Lucky Boy Underground (2010)

ACT 1

Underground—South Deep
(1993)

I am thinking of the 8,860 feet of rock above me: over a mile and a half thickness of solid rock. On the ride down in the mine elevator my ears popped twenty-nine times. The rock is glistening, almost greasy-like under the strain, and it wants to explode into the open spaces to release the pressure, right where we are crouched. I can hear tiny popping and cracking noises.

Now and then we hear a dull muffled *pop* in one of the other passageways. "Rock burst," says Jock DeVilliers, the mining geologist.

The working space is about four and a half feet high. The height depends on the thickness of the gold-bearing rock.

We walk deeper into the mine, down crude wooden ladders and cement steps and past whining drills. Dozens of black miners labor at breaking rock to expose gold ore. We talk loudly over the incessant noise of compressors and engines.

At the working face are more black miners. They stoop in the low space and only wear hard hats, shorts, and mine boots. It is so hot they've removed their coveralls and piled them against one of the support cross piles. Every four to five feet are cross piles of lumber that hold the space open; like wooden pillars that are slowly, over time, compressed as the manmade grotto closes in. The sweating bodies and straining muscles convey exhaustion. This cavity in the earth is deep, hot, dusty, crowded, noisy, and dark.

This is the South Deep mine owned by—Johannesburg Consolidated Investments, aka "Johnnies." Geologist and friend Frank Gregory, my boss Hugo Dummett, and I are doing a review of the geology in this South African mine. There's great wealth here in these so-called Witwatersrand gold deposits that gave rise to the city of Johannesburg. Here it is rich if you're in on the management of the mines. It is powerful, because of the money. But the politics of inequality in the apartheid era is the rule of the day.

Somewhere up above these deep mines Frederik Willem de Klerk is secretly negotiating. F. W. de Klerk would be the last state president of apartheid South Africa, but with whom is he negotiating? We find out that it is with Nelson Mandela. It seems F. W. wants Mandela's help in transforming the teetering racially segregated country to one that is more of a democracy. But will that change how these companies operate?

Mandela was released from Robben Island prison in 1990 and would be elected president in the first all-race elections 1994; that's just about one year from today.

It's like a hundred years ago here in the South Deep mine. There are 4,000 employees and 1,800 contractors underground on any given shift. In the same district is the Savuka gold mine, which is 12,391 feet deep.

The rock is so hot that it burns you if you lean on it. The air temperature is 108 degrees Fahrenheit. This far down in Earth's crust one feels the natural geothermal gradient. Here rock temperatures climb as high as 140 degrees Fahrenheit. My coveralls are soaked with sweat. I'm roasting under my hard hat. Ventilation fans force refrigerated air down the mine tunnels, and when we happen upon a vent we instinctively point our faces into the artificial breeze. But very little air circulation exists back in the nooks and crannies of the mine where the interesting rocks can be found. So it's hot!

Suddenly a loud BANG! Someone cries out, "Rock burst!"

I am hurled backward as my body is peppered with rock fragments. Some of them are stuck in my skin on my hands and arms and legs. My hardhat and safety glasses saved my life, because I had been looking down at a rock the moment the rock burst occurred. My hard hat took most of the hit.

I'm sitting on my butt and pulling glass-like pieces of angular quartz out of my skin and thinking, *How did I get here?*

Okay, there is something else on my mind. I find myself pondering the question: What are the top five worst things that can happen on the job for an underground miner?

1. *A cave-in is the worst.* Rocks coming down all around you. Maybe right on top of you . . . maybe just blocking all the tunnels so you can't get out. Yeah, that's number one, the worst. Entombment.

2. *Explosions and fire.* Yes, when things explode, that is pretty bad.

3. *Flooding is pretty bad.* That'd be my number three: flooding and underground mudslides filling up the tunnels. Imagine: first you sense that air is being pushed by something—you feel it on your skin before you hear it. Then the sound of water, a lot of water, or the sloshing of mud. Then the visual of a frothing wall of muddy water fills your spotlight view illuminated by your mine light. Then you're in it, underwater, gasping . . . Yeah, that's bad.

4. *Deadly carbon monoxide gas.* Not breathing is really bad; it's like drowning but not in water—suffocation.

5. *And then there are rock bursts.* Kind of like buckshot in the face if you're in the wrong place at the wrong time. I've just experienced one. These sometimes lead to cave-ins: my number one worry.

The tally is grim: 70,000 South African miners have died underground in the past one hundred years. On top of that, more than one million have been seriously injured. This results in a terrible running average of about thirty people killed or seriously injured every day for the past one hundred years. During those one hundred years, from 1893 to 1993, over 1.4 billion Troy ounces (45,020,100 kilograms) of gold have been mined from the South African gold fields, according to the JCI geologists. That's about 1,310 ounces per death or injury. This year, 1993, an ounce of gold is worth about US$360, or about ZAR1,177 (ZAR is the South African rand, and the exchange rate is US$1 = ZAR3.27). So each death or injury is equivalent to about US$470,000. That might seem like a lot, but the miners never see it. I am told by one of the mine foreman that the average monthly pay varies from $100 to $300 a month. In addition to the low wage, there is no job security, what with migrant labor coming in from all over Africa, and there are health concerns, such as silicosis, a lung disease caused by quartz dust from crushed rock. The scene is grim enough, but the human cost is a tragedy.

So why am I here? Why am I going down underground? I didn't know it was going to be like this. And I ask myself again, why am I here?

Getting on the Roller Coaster
(1980)

College in Beloit, Wisconsin, and Pullman, Washington, and Minneapolis, Minnesota, zinged by! I studied geology. Got a bachelor of science and a master of science in geology, and a doctorate of philosophy in economic geology. There were early resume-building jobs. The common complaint among graduates was "All the potential employers want us to have experience, but how can I have experience if I'm looking for my first job?" I wanted to be a dinosaur digger . . . no jobs. I wanted to study volcanoes . . . no jobs. I wanted to work in environmental geology . . . no jobs.

So I took a summer position with a mining company. Good pay. Interesting work that I was really good at.

My quest is to understand how Earth works.

But the reality of it is I'm just trying to find daylight. . . the Big Understanding!

The roller coaster left the platform.

Roger James Kuhns

The Rosetta Stone Part I:
The Language of Management
(1993)

Have you ever received a memo from upper management that just didn't make a lot of sense? There is a reason for this. The language of management and human resources is a different language than what most of us speak. Good news, we've identified the sacred management text of the ancients: the Rosetta Stone.

The Rosetta Stone was discovered in 1799—it has Demotic script, Egyptian hieroglyphics, and Greek. This unlocked a language that was dead for more than a thousand years. The human resources department immediately appropriated this language.

Do you know what the Rosetta Stone says? Some scholars report that it's a record of kings and gods. It has words like *most glorious*, and *pious*, and *civilized*, and *beloved*, and *generous*. Sounds like management! It includes phrases like "revenues and taxes," and "prosperity," and "cavalry and infantry forces and ships," and "great sums of money and corn," and "gold and silver." Sounds like human resources and accounting!

So the Rosetta Stone is really a management book written by the ancients to convey the language of management and human resources.

We need a modern Rosetta Stone. If we imagine the Demotic, the hieroglyphic, and the Greek equivalents in modern speak, we get something like the following, demonstrated in three memorandums, each being reinterpreted in the next script.

First, the equivalent of Demotic script (an ancient Egyptian script): This was the legal and administrative script of the ancients, the language of managers and human resource people. The first version, the HR version, of the memo from a London meeting is as follows:

233

MEMORANDUM
TO: All Employees
FROM: Stephen Glich, HR Department
SUBJECT: Policy Updates

The human resources department wishes to inform FTEs of new QA/QC requirements in all SLPs designed to enrich your CP with S.M.A.R.T. goals using our new vision-oriented GPM system that is endorsed by the CFO and compliant with all RSAs, PPs, PEMHPs, and IRAs, except for those FTEs who have been reprioritized. Remember, our business is people!
Drive Our Vision Forward

The translation:
The human resources department wishes to inform full-time equivalents of new quality assurance/quality control requirements in all staff-level positions designed to enrich your customer performance with Specific Measurable Actionable Reasonable Timing (SMART) goals using our new vision-oriented Global Performance Management (GPM) system which is endorsed by the chief financial officer (CFO) and compliant with all retirement savings accounts (RSAs), pension plans (PPs), postemployment medical health plans (PMHPs), and individual retirement accounts (IRAs), except for those full-time equivalents (FTEs) who have been reprioritized (laid off). Remember, our business is people!
Make Us More Money

Second, the hieroglyphic equivalent (an ancient Egyptian glyph): This was the script of royalty, priests, and government officials. Today's equivalents are the CEOs and presidents. They re-pen the HR memo into this:

234

MEMORANDUM
TO: All Employees
FROM: Rudy Di Screpant, CFO
SUBJECT: Driving the Mission

As we embark on a new fiscal year it is important to convey to all of you how much we value the time and energy you give to fulfill our mission of greater profits, and our vision to innovate and improve and build better what we already build and sell. We have scheduled some new and fun workshops to help you help us better realize our vision. We implore you to work with our skilled consultants who will help you help us optimize your teams for our gains. It's a win-win! An invitation list will be sent to those participating staff. The good folks in Human Resources will also make sure your retirement benefits remain safe and sound. Remember, our business needs people!
Drive Our Vision Forward

The Greek equivalent: This was the language of the sciences and arts, of the common employee and the wise scholar! So Sidney, up in processing, read the HR and CFO memos and sent this out to his colleagues . . .

E-MAIL
TO: Jean, Anne, Matthew, Mandy, and Jacob
FROM: Sidney
SUBJECT: Uh Oh—Heads Up Again

Hi guys, what's up? Just a heads up on the latest memo-chatter. Did you hear we have more team building stuff to attend—but only if you're invited. Yeah, it's after hours—no overtime on this one. Someone got a vision up their backside. Oh, and there's more paperwork, and they say it's not going to effect our benefits, but you know it always does. And there's a rumor going around some of us are gonna get laid off. They're calling it team optimization and being reprioritized. The consultant is the guy who wrote that leadership book, and loves to downsize organizations. Remember, the boss said it's not personal, it's just business, even though you spend all of your waking hours working. Meet you all at the pub after work. This requires many beers and resume preparations.

Drive Our Vision Forward (toward the cliff).

Ass End of the Business
(1985)

I travel to Guanajuato, Mexico, to look at silver deposits. It is a dry landscape well above 6,000 feet elevation. Cactus and Joshua trees dot the hot and dry pastel earth: a *buena vista* of yellow, brown, red, and orange hills.

The town of Guanajuato is marvelous; it wraps around the eroded flanks of a fault-block mountain. The streets wind down the slopes between rows of two-and three-storied Baroque houses with steel-rail balconies. The stucco walls are white or, less commonly, earthen red, green, pink, and even gaudy pastel blue. The streets are narrow—one car-width. Huge, ornate, castle-like churches abound in the town. There is a bronze statue of a conquistador on horseback. There is a stone monument to silver miners. A square is dedicated to revolutionary soldiers.

Guanajuato is here for a specific reason. When the Spaniards entered Mexico in the 1500s, they discovered silver. Some of the mines, such as the Valencia mine in Guanajuato, have been worked continuously since the 1700s. And now the earth is riddled with mine tunnels, so much so that I think it whistles when the wind blows. The mines stretch over a half mile from Guanajuato in the northwestern extensions, through Valenciana, Cata, Rayas, and Promontorio to the southeast. Over a billion ounces of silver have been mined here. The land immediately north of town is cluttered with new mining claims and new mine workings for more than four and a half miles from west to east covering the northwest-trending silver vein systems. This place is a treasure chest. The wealth here must have driven the first conquistadors crazy as dreams of silver in the New World were realized.

I find a small silversmith shop down hill and southwest from the Cata Mine workings. The artisan wears thick glasses and is working the metal into beautiful crosses, rings, earrings, and miniatures of animals.

I drive out of town following a lead to look at a new silver find the shop owner told me about. He scribbled "Hector B. La Valenciana," and sketched a map. He also said the miner calls his tired workings Hidalgo, named after Father Hidalgo who was important in the struggle for Mexican independence. The silversmith said Hector believed…wished…it had potential and that a local family was mining the old workings on a very small scale. He told them I might stop by. This kind of mineral find is called a grassroots prospect. So I drove north on Highway 110 towards the old mine workings just southwest of the really productive areas. Dust rose around the rented truck like swarm of some living earth, and I stepped out into the heat of the day.

I walk over to the hillside adjacent to the mine workings. There are just a few Mexican miners, family members no doubt, and all are in a good mood. There is much talking and laughing under the hot summer sun. I ask around and find Hector, and show him the note. My Spanish is not good, but Hector's English is passable. We shake hands and he leads me to his small, possibly illegal operation.

This is a homemade silver mine. Rock has been dug and blasted and hauled out of the earth. A vertical shaft is nested amongst the piles of angular rock like a black hole in this small universe. The rock is colored tan, yellow, red, orange, and brown from the weathering of metal sulfide minerals; this rust points to the metals.

I look at the shaft. There is a rickety diminutive wooden head frame with a pulley and hoist system suspended over the hole. I can see a tired-looking frayed rope dangling into the depths. It is taut and moving: someone is coming up on the hoist.

I notice there is a statue of Jesus at the lip of the shaft. He stares down with an expression of love and concern at the miners. The miners kiss the statue before entering and upon exiting the mine.

I glance behind me at the lift mechanism. I follow the rope from the miner in a bucket, through the pulley, and look along the horizontal length of it right at the south end of a northbound donkey. A boy with a stick is urging the donkey to walk forward and lift the miner and ore out of the shaft.

I look at Hector, and he gives me a wide smile, as if to say, "We have it all figured out!"

Many hands reach out to help the miner out of the bucket as he arrives at the surface. The miner looks like he weighs about a hundred pounds. There's about forty pounds of rock in the bucket. And the metal bucket is at least twenty pounds. The miner kisses the Jesus statue and pats the donkey. The donkey stands there, breathing heavily with a bit of foam showing at its mouth, fighting gravity against 160 pounds of man, bucket, and ore.

This family operation is a mom-and-pop management situation. From Hector's point of view, the matriarch forces bring some measure of safety and sustenance to the miners. The patriarch, Hector, provides the organized labor and intuitive goal setting for the operation. They are motivated by the fact that this silver deposit could hoist them out of poverty and give them futures never dreamed of. To me this seems like playing the lottery. This is a people-oriented goal-driven family business.

"Okay, you go now!" says Hector, my new entrepreneurial prospector friend. He looks at my expression . . . I'd say I had a look of calm doubt, a "do I have my will in order" kind of expression. I borrow a hard hat, which has an antiquated battery operated light attached.

"Okay," I say, and I grab onto the wooden head frame, which creaks and shifts slightly, and step over the darkness into the rusty bucket. The rope yields slightly, making that discomforting creaking noise ropes make when under strain.

The bucket swings a bit, and I look along the rope at the ass . . . is it the donkey, or is it me?

"Okay, amigo, *ándale!*" I can see the boy with the stick now standing in front of the donkey and pushing him backward. The rope gives, the bucket bounces, and I am lowered into the shaft step by donkey step in jerky movements. Down I go.

My headlamp casts a yellowy light on the rusty rock, as the surface light becomes just a bright glow overhead. I can see several outlines of heads peering down at me. Some one yells down in an enthusiastic Mexican accent, "You're doing fine, amigo, so is the donkey!"

After about a thirty-foot descent I hit bottom and look down a five-foot-high tunnel. There are a couple other miners down here. I can hear them speaking in Spanish over the clinking of their hammers as they break out chunks of silver ore. There's a box of dynamite sitting on the floor. A third miner is hauling bags of ore from deep inside, conveying the hard won rock to the bucket staging area. A fourth miner is next to me to meet the bucket. He fills the empty bucket I was standing in with hand-cobbed ore. Someone up-top yells "Ha!" And the bucket jerks upward as the donkey leans into the load.

These silver mines are like jewelry boxes. The silver minerals below the rusty oxidized surface yields a beautiful array of ruby-colored pyrargyrite, silvery gray argentite, and native silver that grows out like curls of hoary frost. The rock is quartz-rich and hard as can be.

One miner wants to show me what he's been chipping out of the rock. It's a hollow space, called a vug, and the walls of the vug are lined with half a dozen different very small silver minerals. It is beautiful and rich and rare, like nature's own Fabergé egg turned inside out.

The miner says, "This, amigo, is what is at the end of my rainbow."

After a couple of hours of mapping and sampling I return to the rusty metal bucket. I have collected at least twenty pounds of rocks. Me, 165 pounds, and the bucket, 20 pounds, and my samples, 20 pounds, gives me cause for concern. The boy tending the bucket assures me that the ass upstairs can haul my ass out of this hole.

He yells up. I hear a moment of braying. The rope tightens. Strains. And slowly I am jerked upward toward the light of day. This is like some weird birthing canal, like the very earth is giving me up to the topside world of daylight. I find I'm hanging onto the rope very tightly and staring up at the light. I have this sense of great expectation.

I understand why they have Jesus at the mine portal. I have a sense of what I'll experience if the rope snaps or the donkey loses its footing: suddenly falling back down the shaft and looking up at the light only to see it blotched out by the falling shape of a donkey. Oh man, and this wasn't even on my list of the top five worst things that can happen in a mine . . . being crushed by an ass in a hole in the ground.

Well, I made it out. And I patted Jesus on the head and kissed my ass goodbye.

The Roller Coaster Gains Speed
(1988)

So, I'm working for a big Australian-based global corporation looking for minerals. And every year the human resources department, aka HR, would send out a skills form to fill out.

So I get this call from an HR guy one afternoon.

"May I speak with Dr. Kuhns?" said the Australian-accented HR guy, who was sitting in his office in the company headquarters in Melbourne, Australia.

"This is he, the doctor is in. Call me Roger," I said. "What can I do for you?" Yada, yada, yada.

"Okay. Nice to meet you, Roger. My name is Colin, and I wanted to run something by you. Roger, you realize that we in human resources take our business very seriously. It's all about people, mate!"

"Yes, I know you do." I was a bit nervous. Anytime HR calls it is because I'm getting promoted or fired or have done something counter to policy, usually a policy of which I was unaware. I listen.

"Well, I was examining your annual review and your skills set," said HR Colin. "As you know you are being considered for a new assignment. But I noticed you put down you speak seven languages."

"I am?" I said.

"You didn't know?" asked HR Colin.

"Nope!" I said.

"OOOOPS!" said HR Colin. "Holy dooley, pretend I didn't spill the beans."

"They're spilled," I said.

"Well, pick them up and put them back in the can. Anyway, you put down you speak seven languages," HR Colin said. "That's a lot of languages, mate."

"Did I?" I said. I actually couldn't recall, and I know I don't speak seven languages.

"Yes, you did, and you list them," said HR Colin. "Well, Roger, we here in HR take these things very seriously. I can tell you speak English, and you've written French and Spanish. But I must say that the other languages really don't count. You've written American, Canadian, Australian, British, and New Zealandican! Roger, I don't think that last one is even a real word. You can see, Roger, that we need you to be serious about these HR reviews."

Oh please . . .

Well, Hugo Dummett gave me the promotion, and I went to live in South Africa. I told him I was *gobsmacked* at the news!

241

The Rosetta Stone Part II: The Styles of Management (1994)

Remember the Rosetta Stone, that ancient book on translating the language of management? Well, another paragraph was reinterpreted from the chiseled letters of the stone tablet. This revealed a great understanding of types of managers. Remember the three languages on the Rosetta stone?

1. Demotic for the legal, human resource, and adminis-trative functions.
2. Hieroglyphics for CEOs and presidents.
3. Greek for the common man, the worker, the artist and scientist and philosopher.

So it is the Greeks who really were able to communicate.

Epicurus said, "We live happiest when we are free from the pains of life, and a virtuous life is the best way to obtain this goal."

Hippocrates turns out to be the Greek philosopher of choice for understanding personality types. Did you ever hear of these personality tests? A really well-known one is Myers-Briggs, known as the MBTI or Myers-Briggs Type Indicator. The MBTI dichotomies include:

Extroversion (E)	Introversion (I)
Sensing (S)	Intuition (N)
Thinking (T)	Feeling (F)
Judgment (J)	Perception (P)

So, it works like this. You have people, and some people are managers, and some managers are good managers and some managers are bad managers. It all started with Hippocrates figuring this out in about 400 BC, with insights from Plato at about the same time, then a host of philosophers and psychologists from Carl Jung in 1921 to David Keirsey to Isabel Briggs Myers and her mother Katharine Cook Briggs, and a dozen variations on a theme. You might even find your astrological characterization in there somewhere.

A manager might be a Prometheus-like, rational, sensing judging *protector* (SJ). This type includes John D. Rockefeller, Sally Field, Jack Benny, Warren Buffett, Mother Teresa, and the Dalai Lama.

Some managers may be more of an Epimetheus-like guardian, sensing perception types known as *creators* (SP). These include Jack Nicholson, Madonna, Eddie Murphy, Lucille Ball, Donald Trump, Clint Eastwood, Barbra Streisand, and Steven Spielberg.

And there are the personality types that are more Apollo-like idealists, intuitive thinking people who fall into the class of *intellectuals* (NT). These include Franklin D. Roosevelt, Whoopi Goldberg, Steve Martin, Al Gore, Katie Couric, and Albert Einstein.

And finally the personality type of Dionysus-like artisans, intuitive feeling, called *visionaries* (NF). These include Margaret Mead, Mark Twain, Bob Dylan, Bill Cosby, and John F. Kennedy.

Well, this is all a lot to absorb. But it boils down to what natural tendencies people will use to manage or lead people. Whether they are bull-headed or compassionate, controlling or team-oriented; more on this a little later.

The New Wild West: La Salvacion, Venezuela
(1992)

At night the jets come into Caracas airport like cars through a tollbooth during rush hour. Venezuela is a hub of activity because of its natural resources: oil, gold, diamonds, agriculture, and low-cost human resources. I'm here for the gold and diamonds.

From the Caracas airport my team and I board two Cessna 208s. The team is small. It includes, among the half dozen people, a Fort Lauderdale high-risk-taking business man with a Cayman Islands account named Robert Cooper, a good field geologist from Arizona named John Hoyt, and me.

Cooper bought the two Cessnas so he can fly when and where he wants. They're stocked with beer and sandwiches. As we taxi to the runway I can see row after row of private planes. I notice an incredible mix of foreigners here, most furtively moving from aircraft to private limo, most wearing sunglasses to shield their eyes and identities, most with brief cases and bodyguards.

We fly south out of Caracas to Caicara, past the coastal mountains, and over the flat mid-interior terrain. We fly above the meandering Orinoco River. The flat terrain becomes hilly and hummocky.

Upon landing in Caicara, we book rooms at Hotel Miami for the night. Dinner is local river fish, *pabon*, with yucca tuber and Venezuelan Polar beer. One of Bob Cooper's geologists joins us and drops two small leather pouches on the table in front of me. No words are spoken. I open the first bag and carefully spread the contents out on a saucer. There are 120 carats of diamonds. I open the second bag and do the same. Out onto the saucer roll 150 grains of gold.

"These are from the Guaniamo placers," Bob says. "I want to take you there."

In the morning we fly farther south. This time the terrain is much more hilly and changes into true rain forest habitat. The land is a hummocky green surface interspersed by rounded mountains. And then flat-topped tepuis appear on the horizon: these are ecological lost worlds, plateaus that rise thousands of feet above the jungle. Fantastic waterfalls grace their cliff sides. They are made of the Roraima quartz arenite sandstone, from which gold and diamonds are being weathered into the modern rivers.

We find the Guaniamo River and continue south above its light brown water, deeper into the jungle. Under this blanket of green and holding up the tepuis is 2.6 billion-year-old granite that has been injected by 1.7 billion-year-old kimberlite intrusions. These kimberlite rocks brought diamonds up from 150 miles underground to daylight on the surface of the ancient earth, erupting as volcanoes.

In time they weathered, releasing their stash of diamonds into ancient rivers. A billion years ago the gravel from those rivers became the Roraima quartz arenite sandstone.

The banks of the Guaniamo are pocked with alluvial mining pits. The rain forest has been dug up looking for gold and diamonds in the underlying gravels. This is an ecological disaster.

Soon we see the town of Milagro, and we spot the only landing strip. As we come in, we have to drop fast because of the close, steep tepui cliff faces. As we reduce altitude I can see bits and pieces of other aircraft in the surrounding jungle, those that failed to successfully complete their flight plan, falling short of the runway! The dirt runway rises up fast, and we are catapulted into our shoulder harnesses as the plane brakes.

The town is called Milagro for a reason; it means "the Miracle," and it is indeed a miracle we landed safely!

The mining towns established along the river include Milagro and La Salvacion, meaning "Salvation," and Coracolita. These towns are cluttered, poor, hungry places with ad hoc tin shacks made from flattened-out 55 gallon fuel drums. The atmosphere is humid and vibrating with Latin music. The main street is potholed and crowded with open-air bars, dirty cafes, mining supplies shops, grocery stores, beauty salons, and gold and diamond buyers. Every fifth building has a sign: "Compra Oro e Diamantes." Posters depicting Jesus are tacked to walls against which are leaning scantily clad and woeful prostitutes. Telephone wires and power lines form a montage that seems to connect the buildings. The town itself is held together with mud; it is everywhere. In the town's central square is a statue of Simón Bolívar: the hero! Milagro is a frontier boomtown in the absolute sense.

Bob Cooper says, "Every woman you see from now on is a hooker! And every man a pirate!"

I say, "Hmm—does that include you, Bob?"

Bob laughs, and says, "Oh I hope so, because all the pirates are rich as kings!"

The next few days are spent along the gold and diamond workings in and along the Guaniamo River.

The operations are thus: first a pump is set up and water is drawn from the river and blasted out a fire hose onto the gravel. This washes and moves the gravel. Slowly a hole, then a crater is excavated by the high-pressure water. The washed sediment is then pumped out of the slurry-filled hole, and then the material is put through a jig. The jig is simply a set of steel screens that catch the coarse sand and fine gravel, and hopefully diamond crystals and gold nuggets, but let the larger rocks roll off and the clay and silt wash through to the river. This is why the river is mud-choked.

The diamonds and gold slowly accumulate on the jig screens. Toward the end of the day they clean the jig. I watched this many times. Carefully one of the miners pulls out the coarse screen that has captured the right size fraction to find gold and diamonds. Then he first sifts through the gravel with his fingers looking for big stones and nuggets. The big stones are easy to spot: brilliant white crystals that outshine any other mineral grain in the river. Quartz is dull in comparison.

John and I wander along the Milagro trail and come across more workings. We come upon a huge pile of excavated gravel and a half dozen muddy and muscled Venezuelans who are working with two men from India and three men from China. We strike up a conversation. The Venezuelan, whose name is Jesus, can speak passable English. But John is fluent in Spanish.

It seems they have discovered a buried gravel layer that is particularly rich in diamonds and have decided to follow this as an underground mine. The "mine" is only about twenty feet down into the gravel. They have one shaft, about four feet square. There is a wooden hoist arrangement above the hole and a heavy rope dangling in the darkness of the shaft.

Déjà vu!

I take a look down the hole and can see a mud-caked face looking up at me, smiling broadly. Jesus says, "You want to go down and have a look?"

John says, "That's nuts, Roger, that's just gravel, and it could cave in by just looking at it."

John is right, but I figure, well, maybe if I just slip down and have a quick look I'll beat the odds. I look at the hoist, geared to the back wheel of a truck on blocks. You bring people up by shifting into first gear, and you lower people down by putting it in reverse.

So I tell Jesus yes and wrap the rope around my waist. They hand me a hard hat, which has a carbide lamp burning away on it, and I step out over the shaft.

I look at John and say, "John, if I get in trouble, ask Jesus to save my ass!"

John just shakes his head and smiles broadly. He says, "No tan inteligente!"

Jesus signals to a guy in the truck cab to put it in reverse, and I am lowered at about a half mile an hour into the gravel shaft. I am now thinking I agree with John . . . *No tan inteligente!*

These guys are working in a coffin. The narrow, low tunnel is just staying open by the good graces of God. Yes, this is a fitting mine for the town of La Salvacion and Milagro—the *salvation* and the *miracle!* And with a foreman named Jesus.

I squeeze into one of the low tunnels. I can feel the coarse gravel cobbles on my back and bits of sand sprinkling onto my hard hat. I aim the carbide light on the gravel walls and can see black seams of heavy minerals. It is within these thin layers that gold and diamonds occur. I belly crawl forward a bit to take in more of the geology. But the space is tight, and the air is not so good. I meet a miner hauling another bag out to the shaft area. He hands it to me, and I back out pulling the heavy bag. That one goes up, too. I squeeze back into the gravelly grotto and take a few samples and snap a couple photographs. By then another heavy bag of gravel is handed to me. I repeat the process backing out, but then follow the rope up and out of the pit.

I was pretty happy to be hauled back up in first gear to the daylight. I like the sun!

On the walk out we run into a miner also hiking out to town. He is dressed in worn and torn shorts, muddy and frayed tennis shores. He has a pouch strung to the one remaining belt loop on his shorts.

John and I look at each other, and I hold up my hand to the man and smile. He stops and greets us.

John says in Spanish, "Have you had luck with gold or diamonds?"

The miner smiled and nodded. "Are you buyers? American?" he asks.

John and I nod. I ask, "What do you have? Any stones for sale?"

The miner nods again, and says, "Yes, cash only." We nod, and he reaches for his pouch and pours out a half dozen nice diamonds. They range from about a quarter carat to nearly two carats.

With the stones in his palm, I roll them over with my finger and then roll two of them away from the others. These I look at with my ten-power loupe. Under this magnification, the standard used for grading diamonds, I can see slight flaws, such as minute mineral inclusions. The color, when held up to daylight, is also striking—these stones are nearly perfect, nearly colorless. I nod and tell the miner I would like to buy the two stones I've selected.

The miner looks at them and says, "Muy agradable!" Then he pulls out a cell phone from the pouch and punches a number. Holding it to his ear he tells his contact that he has a buyer for two diamonds, one is a three-quarter carat white VS1—meaning perfect color but a barely discernible inclusion under the ten-power loupe. The other is a one and a half carat slightly yellow VS2—a touch of yellow in the color and a slightly more visible inclusion under the same magnification. John looks at me and raises his eyebrows as we listen to this boomtown prospector in the middle of the jungle getting well-informed instructions from someone on the other end of the phone.

The miner says, "Sí señor, el precio es sesenta dólares y quilate."

I look at John, who clarifies the translation as US$60 per carat.

"This is good," I say. "I will buy these two stones for US$60 per carat. I think the total is 2.25 carats for the two stones, and that is $135."

John confirms this with the miner, who nods and smiles his agreement. I reach into my wallet and pull out $75 cash. John has another $40 in cash. We only have $115 in US dollars on us.

The miner notices the British pounds in my wallet and points to them. He says, "Que va a hacer." And John confirms that we can pay the rest in British pounds. I can't remember the exact conversion; it's around US$1.70 to the pound. Suddenly the miner is on his cell phone and asks his contact for the day's conversion rate.

"He says it is £1 equals US$1.7566." John laughs and then says, "I think that's close enough for a jungle transaction."

I hand the miner a £10 and a £5 note; I have nothing smaller. He accepts the payment and hands me the two diamonds. The deal is completed. The miner puts the cell phone back in his pouch and walks on down the trail.

"That was a pretty good deal," I say to John.

"Well, yeah. But you paid three pounds too much!"

Over the next week we conclude our visit and meetings. We also visit the diamond and gold buyers in town. The daily harvest from the placer mines remains impressive in terms of ounces, carats, and quality. But safety and average hourly wages don't register on any progressive scale, to be sure. Nevertheless, we have collected a mountain of data from these placer deposits, mining operations, and diamond and gold markets. These types of deposits are better suited for smaller high-risk companies rather than large conservative mining corporations. The prize can be huge, but it is hard won.

After wrapping things up, John and I return to the airport and board the Cessna 208 to Caicara. We have to stop there and pick up a package that Bob Cooper has agreed to transport to Caracas.

In Caicara we learn that the "package" is the local commandant's wife. Cooper has agreed to let her fly with us to Caracas, where she wants to go shopping. The commandant runs the show here and is part of the kickback scheme that allows the diamond underground to function at a profit. Everyone is paid off: pirates, soldiers, police, politicians, and wives who want to go shopping; the miners are of course the least paid.

John and I see this pile of luggage and a round, plump, buxom, wide and heavy woman who is all dolled up to go on her shopping trip. We learn she does not like to fly; she fidgets nervously. And she has a lot of baggage. The commandant approaches us. The pilot looks at the already-packed plane and shakes his head.

The commandant looks past the pilot into the plane and says, "There is room for everything; put the two men in the very back!"

John and I look at each other. "Oh, this is going to be good," John says. "Have you made out your will?" He pauses, then says, "No tan inteligente!"

"You seem to be saying that a lot: not so intelligent!" I say.

There is a frenzied hour of stowing and arguing between the pilot and the commandant. Soon the plane is absolutely packed. John and I are instructed to crawl over and between boxes, suitcases, shopping bags, and a crate holding who knows what. I ask, "Has this woman already gone shopping?"

The commandant says, "No, no, she needs this to go shopping!"

John looks at the commandant and then at his wife and whispers to me, "For him to agree to this, well, the sex must be incredible!"

We also start thinking that maybe the commandant has hidden a stash of cash or gold or diamonds in the mess. He's part of the underground economy here, and right now we are all in!

We start to taxi out onto the runway. We can tell the plane is too heavy. The pilot guns the engine, and the plane lurches forward. We are far beyond our weight limits for this aircraft!

I yell out to John, "LEAN FORWARD!"

The runway is eaten up by the increasing speed of the plane. Soon the dirt gives way to weeds and bumps and garbage, and we're still not in the air. The pilot is gritting his teeth. The fat commandant's wife is screaming and crossing herself; her enormous boobs are flopping up and down as we go over the crude runway. John sees this, shakes his head, and focuses on looking straight ahead. We are both willing the plane to become airborne.

We're up an inch, then two, then six. Vegetation is shredded by the landing gear, and we climb a few feet. The runway is behind us; the overrun field is about to give way to a steep drop-off. Inch by inch we gain altitude. And then we're over the valley, and the plane slowly sinks toward the lower landscape, but the pilot is stubborn and is pulling back on the yoke. The trees seem to rise up to grab at us. We level off just above the thick, dark green jungle canopy, the same one in which we had seen the remnants of crashed planes when we first arrived.

The pilot looks back at me with this expression of amazement and fear. "We are never doing that again!"

The fat commandant's wife continues to shriek and scream and hits the pilot in the shoulder with a shaking manicured hand. She then throws up all over the instruments.

We are on our way home.

Nelson Mandela Stops By to Chat
(25 March 1999)

He is a man of peace and forgiveness but with strength and charisma like none I have ever seen. He is known to say, "In my country you first go to prison and then become president." Nelson Mandela headed an underground movement even from prison. When he was free, the flood gates were open, and the sun shown in on the soul of South Africa.

I wonder what it would be like to work with him?

Nelson Mandela is at a brief informal gathering in Cape Town. I am here because of my involvement with Southern Africa economic summits, and I've helped advise a committee regarding mining and environmental policies. There is the need to make environmental policies more strict and mining regulations more universal. I am, at the time, the general manager for Africa and the Mediterranean regions for one of the world's largest mining companies.

But upon meeting President Mandela, I realize that the roads I have traveled, the ordeals I have faced, are but dust under his boots. I am humbled and filled with hope by his charisma and wisdom.

The president is in Cape Town preparing to speak the next day to the South African parliament. I heard he was at an informal gathering, so I impulsively drove over to the hotel. This impromptu meeting, in March 1999, was just a couple months before the end of his presidency.

Because Mandela was about to retire as president he had joked at the World Economic Forum earlier in the year that "if anyone should see an old man by the road carrying a placard saying, 'No job, no money, new wife, big family,' please spare a thought!"

The scale of President Mandela's tasks and accomplishments boggles the mind. Pulling a country into democracy from the horrors of apartheid. When he came into office 30 percent of the population, some twelve million people, did not have clean drinking water. He gave water to two million people. When he was elected 63 percent of the people lacked electricity in their homes, and now that number is down to 36 percent. Mandela ushered in the African Renaissance.

Our small impromptu group of fans, I would say, is standing next to President Mandela. He says in his deeply resonant voice, "The sadness, and our greatest challenge, is the distance we need to go to equalize education. Our people have the talent, they have the strength, but they hadn't the chance. We are fixing this. This must be part of our gaining respect and defeating fear. We'll never have our equality, neither will we have peace without these things."

In our very brief chat, President Mandela asked where I felt the mining companies should stand with regard to people. I said that from my perspective, mining companies should be all about people, about their communities. I said that it is incumbent on the mining companies to behave as responsible citizens. The mining companies must practice compassion and humility. Their efforts must be genuine. I am such the dreamer!

Nelson Mandela said, "This journey to equality is a never-ending road. We will never be done with this pursuit."

And then he had to go.

The president's very fiber instills within the global community lessons in humanity and people-centric leadership. It's all about people.

ACT 2

Derailed
Hartley: Metal, Music, and Money Revisited
(1990)

I can hear drumming—it is a rapid rhythm, wooden percussive tone—and the joyous chanting of many voices. I'm taking a few days off to visit an archaeological wonder in the heart of Zimbabwe. The place is called Great Zimbabwe, and it is here that the national symbol, a great bird, was found as an artifact carved from soapstone.

But work calls, and I drive back to Harare. I am working with a lanky, loud, and perhaps brilliant British mining engineer who lives in Johannesburg, South Africa, and works in Zimbabwe. His name is Steve Godden. I am also working with an introverted, sardonic, introspective Canadian geologist named Wayne Hewgill. We are here assessing a platinum and palladium deposit within a geologic domain known as the Great Dyke of Rhodesia.

Rhodesia was named for the aggressive king's agent Cecil Rhodes, who claimed this land by standing on a high rock and uttering: "I claim all that I can see from horizon to horizon for his Majesty, the King of England!" He did so regardless of the dreams and wishes of the land's existing occupants. Cecil Rhodes's management type was that of a field marshal. With the very onset of such repression, an underground movement for liberation begins to form.

Wayne, Steve, and I are renting a farmhouse from a family with Portuguese colonial roots. Andy Ferreira is the farmer's name. He grows one of the country's most lucrative crops: tobacco. The house is located a ways from Zimbabwe's capital city of Harare, outside of the small town of Selous. Andy is a hulking, solid man with rounded shoulders from hard work and a welcoming smile to those he likes. His farm has a hundred native Zimbabweans living and working here. He pays them, but it is minimal; it's survival. It is just such an arrangement that will ultimately enrage the country's president, Robert Mugabe.

Andy's wife, Beth, told me one day, "We didn't have apartheid here; at least we never called it that. But we didn't leave like so many others did. We are here and will work with the change. We love our country."

Our project manager is a long way away in San Francisco. He's an old Rhodesian, and he is on a power trip. He has his own stack of human resource challenges that revolve around gender and race, command and control, fame and responsibility avoidance. He practices management in the fashion of the Myers-Briggs field marshal personality type, oddly enough just like Cecil Rhodes. He is a challenge! Steve Godden, my team engineer, when a bit testy about the boss, calls him "our own little Napoleon"!

During the days we work on the rocks and slowly figure out the trend and size and grade and minability of the platinum reef. Our own little Napoleon has a way of commanding us to get things done. He'll say, "Roger, I need this done quickly, quickly!"

Oliver Warin is vice president of exploration; his executive assistant, Georgette Cobbs, a black woman from Oakland working in the San Francisco headquarters office, calls me and says, "Oh, Roger, *Quickly-quickly* just told me to tell you that he wants you to call him quickly. I told him I'd do it 'just now'!" She laughs loudly about this.

Georgette has learned the South African phrase "just now," which means we'll get to it whenever we damn well feel like it. Georgette says, "When I told Quickly-quickly we'd do it 'just now,' he told me to do it 'just now now' and 'quickly, quickly'!"

I call the boss. He tells me to prepare for a meeting in San Francisco in the next month or so to present our findings. He said to prepare a report and presentation material "quickly, quickly" so we can layout the underground development plan and start blasting rock and moving ore.

A couple weeks go by. The work continues, and the findings are pointing more and more to the difficulty of the project in terms of human lives. We have also determined that a mine training program will have to be an expanded, ongoing effort, because we could possibly lose a high percentage of employees to AIDS every year.

Meanwhile, Mugabe rules Zimbabwe as an autocrat, as a dictator. He spouts rhetoric about the good of the people but suppresses the press, steals money from hard-won resources, and brutalizes any political opponent who dares to challenge his reign, and is dismantling the farming communities. He basically is managing his country like some of the South African businessmen manage their mining companies. People learn by example! When greed rules, people take a backseat.

A good bit of time has passed, and we've prepared the requested documentation for the project. I fly to San Francisco to present our findings to the vice president of exploration, Oliver Warin, his team leader, Hugo Dummett, and our own little Napoleon, Mr. Quickly-quickly, the project manager. In the long run, when Oliver retires, Hugo will step up to fill his shoes. But that was still years away.

The first part of the meeting goes well, as I review the geology and engineering of the platinum reef. By my team's determinations, the rock above the platinum reef is very unstable. The rock mechanics and engineering Steve, Wayne, and I have done show that if we don't support the roof it will cave in on our heads. Little Napoleon, Mr. Quickly-quickly, knows that some supports are needed, but he doesn't want to hear about the greater number that we are suggesting.

Remember my list of the worst things that can go wrong in an underground mine? The fear of a cave-in is number one!

But I press the point. I put it to Quickly-quickly this way: it comes down to two ethical choices. One: move ahead with the mine and know that such a decision will cost lives; we already know this situation exists in the South African mines. Two: stop the project and find a safer ore deposit to mine. Mining a dangerous deposit costs not only irreplaceable lives, but also a lot more money to keep it open. The ore is also more difficult to follow and recover than in the South African mines of this type. Everything is more expensive, and then there is President Robert Mugabe. There have been rumors of nationalizing the mines. The risk is very high on this one. I recommend we stop the project. I know that this second choice opens a new can of worms and risks the huge investment. But are we about people, or is it just business?

Little Napoleon turns as red as a tomato and beads of sweat form on his forehead. He's staring at his hands, which are laying flat on the table in front of him. He has pushed this project for years. It is his career builder. He tightens his lips and frowns.

Oliver says, "Roger has a point. If we know our work will kill people, we shouldn't do it!" Hugo agrees.

Little Napoleon looks up. He's got the ear of people higher up the food chain than Hugo or Oliver. Quickly-quickly says, in a very controlled and logical sounding voice, "No. I think we must move forward with the mine. I think Roger and his team's assessment is too critical, too conservative. I think the rock conditions are better than they report. This will be a safe mine."

The room is silent. I start to speak, but Little Napoleon holds up a hand and says, "Roger, thank you for your work, but this is the decision."

I flew back to Harare, and Wayne picked me up at the airport. I explained what had been decided. Wayne just looked forward as he drove in silence. Then he said, "I knew he'd put money before people."

Well, another year went by. I was pulled from the project because, as Little Napoleon said, "If you can't fully support it, then you must not be part of it." But in time the underground workings were developed, and I flew to the site by invitation from Little Napoleon to see how safe the platinum reef mine would be.

So here I am, staring at the underground workings. The platinum reef is a black ore zone in a black host rock. I tip my head and look up at the roof. The slabs and cracks and "widow makers," as we call big loose rocks, are peering out between the supports. I can see that a decision has been made to space them farther apart than my team had recommended.

Two days later a three-ton slab of rock falls from the roof onto one of the local miners. He was young, and he had a wife and a new baby. This job was going to help him achieve a future never dreamed of in the otherwise struggling economy. He dies instantly. I feel like we killed him.

The main concern Wayne, Steve, and I had come true.

Within a year the increasingly obdurate Zimbabwean president, Robert Mugabe, endorsed the withdrawal of the company from the Hartley mine. The way this works is that the company sells its share for a paltry $3 million to its Zimbabwe partner, which will result in a total $657 million asset write-down by the company.

In May of 1998 I was at the World Economic Forum in Windhoek, Namibia. Before the session started I was sitting at one of the round tables. A number of men came into the room and sat at the empty seats. I looked up. Across from me was President Robert Mugabe. His lined dark face was moist with sweat from the warmth of the day. He was wearing a traditional patterned robe and pillbox hat. He looked at me and then at my name tag. He saw the company name.

President Mugabe said, "Ah, I know your company. Yes, it is a very good decision of your company to consider to leave the mine. Maybe the people will take back what is the peoples, what is ours, what is not yours. The days of foreign control of our resources are coming to an end in my country."

I introduce myself, and said, "But, even if it were safe, the mine will close. So then who gains?"

Mugabe said, "It is better to keep it from your company than to share it with your company."

"Well, it isn't a safe mine, anyway," I said.

"We have many miners," Mugabe said. He leaves it at that.

It's just business; it's not personal.

The Dalai Lama Comes to Jo'burg
(1996)

It is the morning of August 24, 1996; I am in a modest room in the Carlton Hotel in downtown Jo'burg. Seated before me is Tenzin Gyatso, who is better known as the Dalai Lama. We are meditating, about fifteen of us.

The night before he had spoken to a large group in an auditorium, and after just about everyone had gone, he looked at the few of us left and invited us to this meditation.

When we make eye contact, he smiles. His face illuminates with kindness and charisma. "I feel Buddhism," he says, "holds the answer for myself. It is a personal journey of discovery."

Everything is personal with this guy. The Dalai Lama's management and leadership style is that of the protector, that of a sensing introvert. As I look into his eyes I see history and human compassion. I see cleverness and kindness. I see a sense of humor.

He then closes his eyes and falls into meditation. He's in his personal space. We in the room do the same. Time slips by; now and then I take a peek at the Dalai Lama to see if he's looking at us. I've never meditated like this.

The Dalai Lama is the fourteenth in the line of a reincarnated life force. This man of many lives sits before us dressed in a deep saffron robe with maroon edging. He is the religious leader of the Gelug or Yellow Hat branch of Tibetan Buddhism. He has close-cropped hair, glasses, and an infectious easy smile. But his eyes are windows to the universe.

This guy is going up against China! He's doing it above ground and underground.

He has said elsewhere that he believes the purpose of life is to be happy.

Isn't this kind of what the Greek philosopher Epicurus said? He said, "We live happiest when we are free from the pains of life."

I think the Dalai Lama has been reading the Rosetta Stone!

The Dalai Lama looks up and says, "We must be tolerant of all languages and religions. One should never change religions because the old one made you angry. You should study Buddhism, and if it makes sense, then research it some more before acceptance. The acceptance of Buddhism is very involved. It is metaphysical and difficult. It only seems simple on the surface."

He then closes his eyes again. We meditate. I find myself focusing on how I deal with anger. What am I angry about? It's more a frustration with poor *managers*: the sub-genre. I am intolerant of managers who treat people like commodities, like a resource, like a human resource. Caution here, I find myself thinking, isn't this how hate in corporations is propagated? Isn't this exactly what Oliver Warin has talked about? I look up at the Dalai Lama.

The Dalai Lama is looking at me, and then to all of us says, "I strive to find out the 'why' of the 'what.' It is very messy! The cause creates effect, but the effect influences the cause." He looks at all of us, strong eye contact, and says, "People want happiness, they do not want suffering."

He then closes his eyes again. We meditate.

I'm frustrated with business people who say, "It's just business, nothing personal!" I think about how I manage. I've been told that I spend too much time on people and not enough time on the hard business decisions, like *optimizing people* . . . I am told I'm too quick to give people second chances.

The Dalai Lama likes to fix watches. He's a natural engineer.

The Dalai Lama looks up, and says, "We cannot achieve our self-enlightenment without overcoming this enemy within, this anger." He looks right at me again. How does he do that? How does he know?

He then closes his eyes again. We meditate.

How does he know? Oh, wait he's the spiritual ocean. He's the manifestation of Avalokiteśvara . . . the bodhisattva of compassion. He is the reincarnation of this line of so named *tulkus* . . . the spiritual leaders. He is not a god; he is a reincarnated man. This is something that many scientists just can't accept, the reincarnation thing. I've heard said: *where's the data?*

I am just some guy.

And I am thinking: Why aren't more people like the Dalai Lama and Nelson Mandela and Oliver Warin in leadership roles and as managers? The lessons from these men are that it is people first, and it is never just business.

The Dalai Lama looks up and says, "Life would be so much simpler if there weren't any people in the world. But then we wouldn't know, would we?"

The Tech Help Desk
(2007)

Bub: "Hello, this is the company technical help desk. My name is *Bub*. Do you have a problem?"

I smile inwardly. The gentleman's thick accent is that of a technical support guy probably living in Mumbai.

Roger: "Hi, yes, my computer isn't working. I called in a repair number."

Bub: "And you are?"

Roger: "I'm Roger in the Philadelphia office, my computer number is 235678-BAW-25H-3339672-TVMX- 3-27."

Bub: "Thanking you. Please reboot your computer. That should help the problem."

Roger: "Ok. And I am speaking Bob?"

Bub: "Oh yes, I am introducing myself again. I am *Bub*. My name is *Bub*. Yes."

And I am thinking of the big picture: the global scene, nay a global community. We outsource jobs to the far corners of the planet. I worked in India for a while, and remember there is a province called Gondwana.

Roger: "Bob? Okay, hi Bob."

Bub: "Yes, very pleased. I am helping you now, and it is time to reboot your computer."

Roger: "I haven't told you the problem. My screen's freaking out and my programs crash."

Bub: "Thank you. Yes, rebooting your computer should help."
Roger: "I did that."
Bub: "Thank you; please do a reboot again."
Roger: "I did that four times."
Bub: "Thank you, and did that fix the problem?"
Roger: "No, not at all."
Bub: "Oh my, my, my. Maybe it is a virus. Go into your applications and see what your virus status is."

Bub's voice is singsong, one that is just a little mesmerizing, and would be fun to listen to if I didn't have a mountain of work with deadlines totally reliant on a working computer.

Roger: "I did that. No viruses that are being detected."
Bub: "Thank you. Hmmm. Maybe reboot?"
Roger: "What office are you in Bob?"
Bub: "I am in the Kansas City office technical help desk."
Roger: "So you're in Kansas City?"

I don't think *Bub* is in Kansas City. This is worth exploring. But I think about Gondwana; I'm distracted by the geologic possibilities of a physiographically linked global community. Gondwana was, before being a province in India, the southern super continent (Gondwanaland). It was a marriage of India, Australia, Antarctica, South America and Africa. North of that was the super continent of Laurasia, a marvelous mosaic of North America, Europe, Siberia and Western Asia. That was all 330 million years ago in the Mississippian Period of geologic time. Then these two super continents bumped into each other forming Pangea, a super duper continent. That happened in the Permian Period, about 260 million years ago. Think of it, if our landmasses looked like that today we would truly be a globally connected – physically connected – community. Maybe the Gondwana Province in India is a reminder of that global connection and now…outsourcing potential. Bub is confirming that he is in Kansas City.

Bub: "Thank you, yes. Kansas City. It is very nice place."
Roger: "It's pretty nice up here in Philly, how is it in KC?"
Bub: "KC?"
Roger: "Yes, KC—Kansas City."

Bub: "Ahhh, yes, KC Kansas City. Thank you, yes, it is sunny and nice also."

Roger: "It's sunny in KC?"

I know that it is raining there right now, even experiencing some tornado warnings. I'd been on the phone with a colleague not but an hour ago and she said that her morning was already interrupted once by that disquieting urgency of tornado sirens.

Bub: "Oh yes, very nicely much so, I am telling you. Our weather is very nice."

Roger: "Huh, that's funny, I was just looking at the Weather Channel, and there are tornado warnings."

Bub: [*a long pause*]

Roger: "Bob?"

Bub: [*a long pause*] "Yes, Mr. Roger, I can see right now this very moment tremendous rains are descending upon Kansas City; it is very surprising!"

Roger: "And you're in the head office tech station? And it's *tornadoey* out there?"

Bub: [*a long pause*] "Oh my, yes, and here they come now, the tornadoes."

Roger: "Well you'd better take care."

Bub: "Yes, I am liking it very much, and taking care. Thank you."

Roger: "So how do I fix my computer? Should I bring it in?"

Bub: "Oh no, I've taken control of your computer and am troubleshooting the systems. Everything seems okay. You can now reboot now?"

Roger: [*I reboot.*] "No change, still glitching."

Bub: "It should be working just fine now, thank you."

Roger: "It's not—it's still glitching."

Bub: "Yes, thank you. Has this help desk been satisfactory to you?"

Roger: "Not really, Bob."

Bub: "Thank you. I hope you will use our service again."

Jack, one of the veterans in the company, came into my office and said, "Look, if your computer is not working, the best thing to do is stand on your desk and hold your computer over your head, and then drop it. You'll get a new one. It'll work for a while. When that one breaks, repeat this maintenance process."

ACT 3

Daylight

We all get this memo from human resources because now the company is reorganizing . . . and that means people will lose jobs. These came from Melbourne:

> **MEMORANDUM**
> TO: Transitioning Managers
> FROM: N. C.
> SUBJECT: We're FBC with the GTF strategy
>
> With this latest round of transitions, our new goal is to multitask our human resources—you. HR is in SSD now. We are FBC using the BMPs with the new GTF strategies, and assisted by ISAP to help you help us help you. We are procedurally rationalizing the organization, all subject to a provisional review, of course! We're on it. Please send me your ideas and revisions ASAP!!!
> *Drive Our Vision Forward*

Again, the translation:

With this latest round of transitions, our new goal is to multitask our human resources—you. Human resources is in the shared services department now. We are faster better cheaper using the best management practices with the new get there first strategies, and assisted by improved standard accounting procedures to help you help us help you. We are procedurally rationalizing the organization, all subject to a provisional review, of course! We're on it. Please send me your ideas and revisions as soon as possible.

So, I grab my Rosetta Stone so I can translate this. Everyone is saying "multitasking" for everyone. We all now have 10 percent of the help, and 1,000 percent of the job and responsibility.
And then this comes in . . .

MEMORANDUM
TO: Potential PLT Direct Reports
FROM: Stephen Glich, HR Department
SUBJECT: Reorganization
DATE: 7 December 1999

I want to inform all of you that a new message has been conveyed from corporate: Big Quick Growth. Because we need to follow this new strategy of BQG, we will be reorganizing the managers and offices again, but this time into PLTs [*portfolio leadership teams*]. I realize this reorganization is happening before we could get the other reorganization into place, but we must follow the BQG strategy. The new PLTs will be headed up by the COO [*chief operating officer*], CSO [*chief strategy officer*], CAO [*chief administration officer*], and CDO [*chief development officer*].
You will report to one of the PLTs in terms of BL [*business leadership*], SALDS [*strategic advisory leadership discovery services*], and PTS [*payroll transactional services*], as we discussed earlier.
The PLT feeds into Assets, which we're calling the Asset Football. Keep your eyes on the ball. This is a RELATIONAL MODEL not a REPORTING MODEL. It is a departure from the old command and control style of the company. We are pushing a strategy triangle with the three corners identified as PEOPLE, PROCESS, and SYSTEMS with *tollgating*

between PROCESS and STRUCTURE. This will help with pivotal and enabling roles and plays into our new organizational structure from the PSM [*process system measure*]. Remember to keep the three I's in mind as we move forward [*Implementation, Integrity, Institutionalization*] Thank you, and strive to put this new practice in place before we change it again.

Drive Our Vision Forward

The company drove its mission forward by cutting five hundred people in our group alone, 75 percent of our staff, and we'll cut half the offices and reduce the countries we work in from thirty to twelve.

After the decisions of which staff members get laid off and which offices will be closed were made, Hugo just wandered off by himself. None of the managers felt they wanted to be around anyone else. We all split up; no common dinner, no circling of the wagons, all of us just going away. The team had fragmented, and the leadership had failed. I walked through San Francisco alone. We are only steps from being homeless.

The Rosetta Stone Part III: Gangs of Management (2010)

The personality types of managers can be typed by using the Myers-Briggs method, as I mentioned above. Sometimes this identifies groupings of similar people and helps understand what drives them to act or make their decisions and choices. This can be stretched to identify what I'll call "gangs" of manager types. So I drew up this diagram to see if I could make sense of managers.

One gang is, I think, a good gang and clusters in the upper right of the diagram. It consists of a bunch of introvert-intuitive people. Nelson Mandela, Pixar's John Lassiter, Oliver Warin, the Greek god Apollo, and I'm surprised to say . . . me. I fell right in there with Oliver.

Another gang that clusters in the lower left of the diagram includes extrovert-sensing people. This, interestingly, includes the human resource people encountered on this particular journey, as well as the La Salvacion pirate prospectors and the consultant the company brought in to advise us on reprioritizing in the company. Pirates!

And finally, another key gang of managers clusters in the lower right of the diagram. These are the field marshals and, interestingly, turn out to be the mine managers in southern Africa. Really good people reside here too, like Hugo. It is all about the quality of the people, not the box they fall in. It is how we treat each other. Telling!

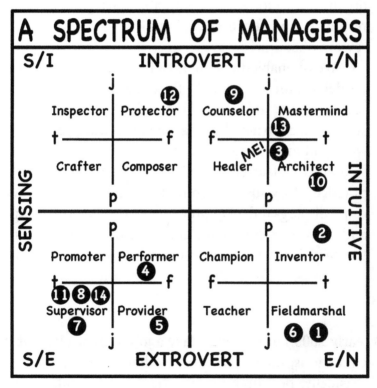

A SPECTRUM OF MANAGERS

S/I — INTROVERT — I/N

Inspector | Protector | Counselor | Mastermind

Crafter | Composer | Healer | Architect

SENSING

Promoter | Performer | Champion | Inventor

Supervisor | Provider | Teacher | Fieldmarshal

INTUITIVE

S/E — EXTROVERT — E/N

ME!

1. RSA mine manager
2. Hugo
3. Oliver
4. miner
5. Mexican family miner
6. Little Napoleon
7. La Salvacion pirates
8. Mr. Pechi
9. Nelson Mandela
10. Apollo
11. HR guy
12. Dalai Lama
13. Creative manager
14. The Consultant

This is another one of the HR memo that came in during big transitions with one of my employers . . .

MEMORANDUM
TO: Transitional Managers
FROM: Stephen Glich, HR Department
SUBJECT: Team Rationalizing
DATE: 28 March 2000

This is to inform all of you that HR is now part of shared services and we are rationalizing the organization to ensure equitable charge-ins, rapid response, and flexibility, all subject to a provisional review, of course!

We've enabled a system to improve our portfolio model leading to global efficiency at economies of scales that are re-engineered, optimized and standardized to new, long-lasting procedures, although we're still in transitional management.

To ensure clear communications we are engaging a practice of exclusive terminology (ET), one that we can call plug-and-play procedures similar to the dig-and-deliver or command-and-control terminology of the past. This will enable more clear communications.

Drive Our Vision Forward

By early 2000 I am asked to take a job in Australia, but it would be in acquisitions, the acquisition of other mining companies. This would basically be climbing on the backs of other successful exploration groups, buying the fruits of their efforts, and then laying them off. It's not what I want to do. In 1998 I traveled to fifteen countries, and I saw my kids only 20 percent of the time. In 1999 I traveled to twenty countries and only saw my kids 15 percent of the time. It was time to go home. So I take a severance package and return home to America.

What If Humanity Got a Pink Slip from God?
(Dec 31, 1999)

There's a New Year's Eve party going on: The master of ceremonies is interrupted by God, who has an important message.

MC: "Well, it's only a few minutes to the new millennium . . . how exciting!"

God: "Ah, pardon me."

MC: "Yeah, uh, we're busy here."

God: "Well, yes, but I've been watching things and been noticing that there has been a lot of corporate downsizing, and I think it's time to look at the human race, you know, a kind of efficiency thing."

MC: "What exactly are you saying?"

God: "I'm saying your budget has been cut."

MC: "What budget?"

God: "Humanity's budget. That's it. *Terminado.* Finished. *Wán. Fini. Afgewerkt. Fertig.* Yada yada yada. The human race is laid off, retrenched, downsized, right-sized, optimized, reprioritized, mismatch realigned, success-failure ratio rebalanced, the big shakeup, voluntary pursuits of other opportunities, out of loop closure, workplace reengineered, . . . whatever you want to call it."

MC: "But, can't we get an extension?"

God: "No can do, buckaroo! It's a corporate thing. It's business, not personal. Too much protein - not enough fiber. I know you'll understand and agree. I've conducted the Egon Zehnder 360 reviews. Humanity doesn't pass muster. I got the angel investors together and the Cloud Board. We got our devils and demons to deal with. Gotta go with the majority on this one...which makes humanity the minority. It's not personal, it's just business."

MC: "Certainly you'll need consultants. I can be your consultant, you know, organize stuff, do things; I've got career value, intellectual capital, hands-on experience, people skills. God knows I put in my time!"

God: "I've hired Armageddon Consulting – they are the last word in management reorganization. Got plenty of angels up here sitting around on their wings watching the Nature Channel. Too many consultants – don't need more . . . besides, they cost!"

MC: "But this isn't fair. We've worked so hard!"

God: "Deal with it; write a self-help book!"

MC: "But why is this happening?"

God: "One word . . . market. Show me the money. You've seen it in the movies. You folks don't produce."

MC: "But God you keep changing the rules!"

God: "The rule is that the rules change. You just reproduce and consume and throw stuff away. Look at the mess you've made of the planet's climate. Getting by is not sustainable. Not the same thing. You consume instead of generate profits and revenue. The rich get richer, the poor get poorer, and it's time for the big layoff. Savvy? Hey, we're nearly bankrupt here. And who the hell is going to bail us out? Expenses have gone through the heavens. Time for minimization."

MC: "Well, we get a good package, don't we. I mean for the layoff. Don't we get a retrenchment package?"

God: "Nope. Not in the plan, not in the budget. Had to use the pension fund to balance the books. Besides, once I lay you off, there are no more jobs, there's no more nothing, and you're on your own. *Own it!* Oh, and one more thing: *Drive Our Vision Forward.*"

MC: "I hate it when you go all Old Testament on us. I thought we were in that Newer version."

Pink slips start raining from the heavens.

I wonder where God would plot on the Myers-Briggs diagram? He'd probably be all over the place.

The Phoenix Rises: Lucky Boy Underground
(2010)

So my SmallCo, which I call SustainAudit LLC, took off a little bit, in a small way.

A couple of clients signed on. Sometimes I notice that without the big business banner behind me people like to think I'll work for free.

But one client is a startup mining company. I said I'd sign on if we practice sustainability in all that we do. Now a mine will never be sustainable because the natural resource is a limited asset. But you can work toward a zero net impact to the environment while improving the community and doing so economically. That's sustainability, not of the resource, but of the process of managing the resource.

They said yes.

One of my first tasks was to map a gold-copper property in Nevada. It is appropriately called the Lucky Boy. There are some underground workings I had to map. These were dug by unrealistically optimistic, headstrong, safety-unaware, extrovert sensing people who are also known as wild-assed prospectors.

They fall into the "Pirate" category on my personality types chart.

So, I'm underground again. My two companions, Lee Saunders and Skip Yates, are staying up-top should something go wrong. The small workings are a tight fit; and of course on me there a little more around the waist and a little less of the no guts, no glory attitude. I rig up a climbing rope and rappel down into the rocky maw of a blasted and hand-dug shaft. I hit bottom at forty feet. I can see pretty good gold ore scattered around.

I work along the various tunnels and shafts the prospectors have put into the earth. I can tell these guys are greedy-hungry for gold. They haven't put any safety practices in place. It's like the small mining operations in Mexico or Venezuela or some of the countries in Africa. I work my way down deeper, climbing down rickety wooden ladders and crawling along narrow tunnels to sample the quartz-gold veins. The roof of the tunnels is manky, just lousy and ready to fall. I move on carefully and turn on my video camera to record what I'm seeing. The gold grades look good, but the rock conditions are bad.

Finally, I am at the very bottom of the workings: dark, dusty, tight, and not well oxygenated. I look down on the ground before me. My mine light settles on a prospector's joke. I just gotta smile.

There, one of the prospectors has placed a $1 poker chip from the Monte Carlo Resort & Casino in Las Vegas.

Yes. When pirates and field marshals are involved, it's all just one big crapshoot working underground.

I climbed back out of the myriad of tight adits and shafts, and looked up into the snowy day. Fresh air is good. It clears the mind.

It's nice to be up here in the daylight.

Finally.

fin

Afterward

These stories are true to the best of my recollection and the notes in my journals. As a storyteller I have left some events out to allow my on-stage story telling in a reasonable amount of time. I have intentionally not included one or two people who wished not to be mentioned.

The songs appearing in the text of this book are available in recorded form online and as CDs.

Contact information and bookings:
rogerjameskuhns@gmail.com
www.rogerjameskuhns.com

Acknowledgments

Thank you to my daughter, Madeleine, and son, Matthew, with whom I continue to explore the world and the art of being a parent and friend. Special thanks to my wife, Anne Schmidt, for all her love and support for the telling of stories. For the *urging-ons* and many laughs, so much thanks to my family. Thank you to Ronn Toebaas for stage direction and inspiration in my monologue performances. Thank you to Judy Drew, who—when director of the Third Avenue Playhouse—booked my shows year after year. Thank you to my brother Dave Kuhns for urging me into fringe festivals, and Mark Moede for insights into all things theater. Thank you, Siobhan Drummond, for excellent editing and insights. Special thanks for all you wonderful friends and acquaintances reading my stories and coming to my shows and joining me on field trips around Door County Wisconsin and places beyond. My thanks to the many people who have enriched my life and are in my stories. Some I have only met once, others remain friends for life, and some have passed on, especially Oliver Warin and Hugo Dummett, both of whom urged me to write about our adventures. Special thanks to Audace Ntungicimpaye and his wife Beatrice, who sang the Swahili parts on our South African recording of my song "Jesus in Sumbawanga." And to Madani Diallo and Serge Nikiema, who taught me about West Africa.

Mystic, Connecticut
April 2014

About The Author

Roger Kuhns holds a PhD in geology. He has worked for 35 years around the world in over 80 countries and in the South Atlantic. He has taught at City College, New York, and University of Wisconsin Field Station. Roger teaches geology and writing classes at The Clearing in Ellison Bay, Wisconsin. He writes and performs monologues about his life. He lives in Mystic, Connecticut, with his wife, Anne, and their two cats.

You can follow Roger at:
www.rogerjameskuhns.com
He invites readers to e-mail him at:
rogerjameskuhns@gmail.com